BIBLICAL INTERPRETATION

Society of Biblical Literature

Symposium Series

Christopher R. Matthews, Editor

Number 26

BIBLICAL INTERPRETATION
History, Context, and Reality

edited by Christine Helmer
with the assistance of Taylor G. Petrey

BIBLICAL INTERPRETATION
History, Context, and Reality

edited by
Christine Helmer
with the assistance of Taylor G. Petrey

Society of Biblical Literature
Atlanta

BIBLICAL INTERPRETATION

History, Context, and Reality

Copyright © 2005 by the Society of Biblical Literature

All rights reserved. No part of this work may be reproduced or transmitted in any form or by any means, electronic or mechanical, including photocopying and recording, or by means of any information storage or retrieval system, except as may be expressly permitted by the 1976 Copyright Act or in writing from the publisher. Requests for permission should be addressed in writing to the Rights and Permissions Office, Society of Biblical Literature, 825 Houston Mill Road, Atlanta, GA 30333-0399, USA.

Cover photo of Pesher Habakkuk, Qumran, courtesy of the D. Samuel and Jeane H. Gottesman Center for Biblical Manuscripts, The Israel Museum, Jerusalem.

Library of Congress Cataloging-in-Publication Data

Biblical interpretation : history, context, and reality / edited by Christine Helmer with Taylor G. Petrey.
    p. cm. — (Society of Biblical Literature symposium series ; no. 26)
Includes index.
ISBN 1-58983-089-X (paper binding : alk. paper)
    1. Bible—Criticism, interpretation, etc.—History—Congresses. 2. Bible—Philosophy—History—Congresses. I. Helmer, Christine. II. Petrey, Taylor G. III. Series: Symposium series (Society of Biblical Literature) ; no. 26.

BS500.B5495 2005
220.6'09—dc22
                                                    2004030351

12 11 10 09 08 07 06 05   5 4 3 2 1
Printed in the United States of America on acid-free, recycled paper
conforming to ANSI/NISO Z39.48-1992 (R1997) and ISO 9706:1994
standards for paper permanence.

Table of Contents

Acknowledgments vii

Contributors ix

Source Abbreviations xi

Introduction
   Biblical Theology: Reality and Interpretation
   across Disciplines
   Christine Helmer 1

Part 1: Historical and Theological Interpretation

Biblische Theologie heute: Formale und materiale Aspekte
   Bernd Janowski 17

New Garments for Biblical Joseph
   Maren R. Niehoff 33

Heracleon and John: Reassessment of an Early Christian
Hermeneutical Debate
   Harold W. Attridge 57

The Enscripturation of Philosophy: The Incorporeality of God
in Origen's Exegesis
   Karen Jo Torjesen 73

Part 2: Philosophical Interpretation

The Democratization of Messianism in Modern Jewish Thought
   Marvin A. Sweeney 87

Verkündigung in Übereinstimmung mit der Vernunft:
Fichtes Auslegung des Johannesevangeliums
Stephan Grätzel 103

The Consummation of Reality: Soteriological Metaphysics
in Schleiermacher's Interpretation of Colossians 1:15–20
Christine Helmer 113

Die Dialektik von Freiheit und Sünde: Hegels Interpretation
von Genesis 3
Joachim Ringleben 133

Anerkannte Kontingenz: Schellings existentiale Interpretation
des Johannesprologs in der *Philosophie der Offenbarung*
Wilhelm Gräb 141

Feuerbach and the Hermeneutics of Imagination
Garrett Green 155

Select Bibliography 165

Index of Biblical Passages 169

Index of Names 173

Index of Subjects 177

Acknowledgments

Biblical theology was conceived at its origins by Johann Philipp Gabler as a bridge discipline between historical-critical and conceptual-theological approaches to scripture. This collection of essays furthers Gabler's intention by staging a dialogue between scholars of scripture, theology, and philosophy. I thank the authors for their contributions to this volume, their creativity in molding their own work to address the biblical-theological questions motivating this study, and their stunning willingness to engage history in the pursuit of answers to those philosophical questions driving the human heart.

The production of this book was wonderfully facilitated by the kind participation of colleagues as well as by the support of several institutions. I thank Taylor G. Petrey for his editorial assistance. Taylor's thoughtful attention to detail, his never-failing enthusiasm for work on the texts, and the wisdom he provided from his own field of New Testament and Early Christianity sustained the editorial process from its early efforts to its final submission. I am most appreciative to Armin Lange, dear friend and colleague, for translating the pertinent English abstracts into German. Harvard Divinity School provided support of Taylor as my research assistant during the fall of 2003. The final preparation of this manuscript for publication was made possible by a research leave granted during the spring 2004 by the Claremont School of Theology and by generous funding from the Alexander von Humboldt-Stiftung for my stay as a Humboldt Research Fellow at the Eberhard Karls Universität Tübingen. I thank these three institutions for their financial assistance of this project.

The biblical-theological dialogue documented in this volume initially took place as a seminar of the Biblical Theology Group during the Society of Biblical Literature's International Meeting in Berlin (July 20, 2002). I thank Christof Landmesser for his contribution to the concept and his participation in the discussion leading up to the Berlin session. I also thank the SBL's organization, particularly Kristin De Troyer and Matthew Collins, for making room for the group on the Berlin program.

The editor of the SBL Press's Symposium Series, Christopher Matthews, kindly consented to publish this volume in the series, and the editorial directors of SBL Press, Rex Matthews, Frank Ritchel Ames, and Bob Buller, lent the generous type of moral support that eased me of any burdens associated with the book's production. I thank them for their enthusiastic commitment to the interdisciplinary content and the bilingual form of this book as well as for their concrete encouragement of future directions in biblical theology.

A note must be made concerning this volume's bilingual structure. The collection includes essays in either English or German. For each essay, an abstract in the "other" language is provided.

My own understanding of the mutual cooperation, harmony, and complementarity between historical and conceptual descriptions of reality was inspired by Robert A. Orsi, who moved me to think and live in ways attentive to those aspects of reality that convey the deepest truths of life.

Contributors

Harold W. Attridge is Dean of Yale Divinity School and Lillian Claus Professor of New Testament, Yale Divinity School (New Haven, Conn., USA).

Wilhelm Gräb is Professor of Practical Theology in the Theology Faculty at Humboldt-Universität zu Berlin (Berlin, Germany).

Stephan Grätzel is Professor of Philosophy in the Philosophy Department at Johannes Gutenberg-Universität Mainz (Mainz, Germany).

Garrett Green is Class of 1943 Professor of Religious Studies in the Department of Religious Studies at Connecticut College (New London, Conn., USA).

Christine Helmer is Associate Professor of Theology at Claremont School of Theology and Associate Professor of Religion at Claremont Graduate University (Claremont, Calif., USA).

Bernd Janowski is Professor of Old Testament in the Protestant Theology Faculty at Eberhard Karls Universität Tübingen (Tübingen, Germany) and a member of the Heidelberger Akademie der Wissenschaften.

Maren R. Niehoff is Senior Lecturer in the Department of Jewish Thought at Hebrew University (Jerusalem).

Taylor G. Petrey is a Th.D. candidate in New Testament and Early Christian Studies at Harvard Divinity School (Cambridge, Mass., USA).

Joachim Ringleben is Professor of Systematic Theology in the Theology Faculty at Georg-August-Universität in Göttingen (Göttingen, Germany).

Marvin A. Sweeney is Professor of Hebrew Bible at Claremont School of Theology and Professor of Religion at Claremont Graduate University (Claremont, Calif., USA).

Karen Jo Torjesen is Dean of the School of Religion and the Margo L. Goldsmith Professor of Women's Studies in Religion at Claremont Graduate University (Claremont, Calif., USA).

Source Abbreviations

AB	Anchor Bible
ABD	*Anchor Bible Dictionary*, 6 vols.
ANF	*Ante-Nicene Fathers*
ANRW	*Aufstieg und Niedergang der römischen Welt: Geschichte und Kultur Roms im Spiegel der neueren Forschung*
BETL	Bibliotheca ephemeridum theologicarum lovaniensium
BEvTh	Beiträge zur evangelischen Theologie
BG	Irenaeus' *Apocryphon of John* ms: Berlin Gnostic Papyrus 8502,2
BibInt	*Biblical Interpretation*
BJS	Brown Judaic Studies
BThZ	*Berliner Theologische Zeitschrift*
BZ	*Biblische Zeitschrift*
BZAW	Beihefte zur Zeitschrift für die alttestamentliche Wissenschaft
BZNW	Beihefte zur Zeitschrift für die neutestamentliche Wissenschaft
CBQMS	Catholic Biblical Quarterly Monograph Series
CCARJ	*Central Conference of American Rabbis Journal*
CJ	*Classical Journal*
CurBS	*Currents in Research: Biblical Studies*
EdF	Erträge der Forschung
EKL	*Evangelisches Kirchenlexikon*, 3rd ed., 4 vols.
EncJud	*Encyclopaedia Judaica*, 16 vols.
EvTh	*Evangelische Theologie*
ExpTim	*Expository Times*
FOTL	Forms of the Old Testament Literature
GAT	Grundrisse zum Alten Testament
HBT	*Horizons in Biblical Theology*
HTR	*Harvard Theological Review*
JAAR	*Journal of the American Academy of Religion*
JEA	*Journal of Egyptian Archaeology*
JJS	*Journal of Jewish Studies*
JQR	*Jewish Quarterly Review*
JRS	*Journal of Roman Studies*

JSJ	*Journal for the Study of Judaism in the Persian, Hellenistic, and Roman Periods*
JSPSup	Journal for the Study of the Pseudepigrapha: Supplement Series
JSS	*Journal of Semitic Studies*
KuD	Kerygma und Dogma
LNPF	Latin Nicene and Post-Nicene Fathers
LThK	*Lexikon für Theologie und Kirche*
NHC	Nag Hammadi Codices
NovT	*Novum Testamentum*
NTS	New Testament Studies
OTL	Old Testament Library
PG	Patrologia graeca, 162 vols.
PhB	Philosophische Bibliothek
QD	Quaestiones disputatae
RE	*Realencyklopädie für protestantische Theologie und Kirche*
RevExp	Review and Expositor
RGG	Religion in Geschichte und Gegenwart, 7 vols., 3rd ed., or 8 vols., 4th ed.
SBLSymS	Society of Biblical Literature Symposium Series
SC	Sources chrétiennes
SNTSMS	Society for New Testament Studies Monograph Series
SPhilo	*Studia philonica*
StPB	Studia post-biblica
STW	Suhrkamp Taschenbuch Wissenschaft
SVTP	Studia in Veteris Testamenti pseudepigraphica
ThLZ	*Theologische Literaturzeitung*
ThPQ	*Theologisch-praktische Quartalschrift*
ThRev	*Theologische Revue*
TRE	Theologische Realenzyklopädie
TSAJ	Texte und Studien zum antiken Judentum
VuF	*Verkündigung und Forschung*
WUNT	Wissenschaftliche Untersuchungen zum Neuen Testament
ZNW	*Zeitschrift für die neutestamentliche Wissenschaft und die Kunde der älteren Kirche*
ZRGG	*Zeitschrift für Religions- und Geistesgeschichte*
ZThK	*Zeitschrift für Theologie und Kirche*

Introduction
Biblical Theology: Reality and Interpretation across Disciplines

Christine Helmer

1. Biblical Theology and Reality

The history of biblical interpretation has long been a branch of biblical theology that bypasses those biblical scholars and their achievements rendered obsolete by new developments in the technology of biblical research. More recent critical approaches to the Bible usually consign to mausoleums of the past what once broke new exegetical ground. In this regard, the theme of the history of biblical interpretation as a key issue in biblical theology might arouse quaint curiosity at best, mere indifference at worst. Others might argue with scholarly seriousness that the history of biblical interpretation serves as a prelude to the more important task of constructing a biblical theology for the contemporary context. History is significant only to the extent that it marks exegetical paths exhausted by those who have traversed them.

It is precisely the relation of the history of biblical interpretation to the question of reality that is the particular focus of this volume. Access to history is guided by questions posed in and quite possibly for the present, and this hermeneutical assumption already implies the philosophical question of reality to be decisive for the interpretation of history. Any serious encounter between present and past, any wrestling with transhistorical items of interest, presupposes a common reality to be investigated. Without consensus regarding the one world that is experienced and known in different ways and articulated in diverse culturally located expressions, the attempt to know for oneself would be hermetically sealed off from the intersubjective inquiry into truth and knowledge. Transhistorical dialogue assumes a common interest in the world, and in the case of religious dialogue, a common interest in the relation of the world to a power that creates and sustains it. With agreement in place, the methodologically controlled, hermeneutical practice of dialogue with the past can begin. Access to the past by a critical and sympathetic apparatus is the method established by historiographical consensus in order to understand it in terms that the past can claim as a true description. The determination of what kind of world is given to be known is inherently a metaphysical question with hermeneutical implications.

The historiographical task of extracting the past in its individual uniqueness and of distinguishing it from the present, requires the disentanglement of past construals of reality from present ones. One way to be attentive to historical distance is to describe conceptual differences between present and past conceptions of reality. The question of change in time was the question that Aristotelian physics wisely linked to metaphysics; relations of change require reasons that are, more often than not, built into the very description of these changes. Where the phenomenon of aging is observed, for example, an Aristotelian potency-act metaphysic might be helpful in describing both that aspect of identity that changes through time and the other aspect that remains self-identical. Each historical epoch has its own categories for describing the relations of motion. Yet each presupposes the reality of motion, the flow from past to present that establishes continuity while highlighting difference, and the interpretative encounter between present and past that gives life to the past while making the present more rich.

These are deeply metaphysical questions. The relation of change to self-identity, particular to universal, and appearance to reality are age-old philosophical questions. The question of reality has remained a stable object of human curiosity, at least in Western philosophy. Philosophers, since Plato, have marveled at the world of taste and sound, and have sought to determine stable reality behind Protean appearance. Where the phenomenon reveals itself in all its mystery, there it is to be related to enduring substance. If the world is characterized by appearance, then where is its ground, its stability, its promise that it will not revert back to the nothing from which it came? With a passion for the philosophical argumentative finesse characteristic of the medievals, the debates concerning universals have witnessed to the human soul's longing for metaphysical clarity.

Access to appearance and reality is not unbroken. Where the phenomenon appears to conceal while revealing, there the metaphysical question is intimately concerned with the methodological one. What instruments are applied rightly to perceive appearances? What tools are used to correct misperceptions, and by what means are diverse phenomena classified and divided? The question of reason, its limits and its capacity to categorize data intuited, perceived, and felt, exposes the complexity of encounters with reality itself. Perception and judgment are embodied together in the complex interweave of spirit and nature. The Enlightenment contributed to the carving-out of a realm of *Geist* in order to determine the spiritual and epistemological factors in getting at causal, narrative, or logical relations in reality. Kant's transcendental analysis exemplified the modern turn to the subject. And the post-Kantian turn to reason's incarnation in language, culture, and history placed the metaphysical question in full view of the historicity of all reality as schematized by that most historical of beings, the human itself.

It was Heidegger's early work on being and time that consolidated the claim for twentieth-century philosophy that the question of being (*Sein*) is really the question posed by that being (*Dasein*) capable of asking this question: the human being. The mere articulation of this question reveals the transparency of human being to being itself and the constitutive characteristic of being, its historicity. There is no other reality except the one constituted by the historicity of human existence, and there is no other reality except one that humans produce through action and reflection. History is what humans do because of who they are.

If the question of reality is the question of reality's historicity, then the determination of metaphysical constituents is itself a historical-philosophical theme. Metaphysics, at least in the Western philosophical tradition, has studied the constants of self, world, and God in relation to each other. Since Kant's Copernican revolution, those same metaphysical constants have been filtered through the requirements of critical philosophy. The three transcendental ideas of reason—self, world, and God—were, for Kant, the unifying functions of reason (*Vernunft*) that grounded the phenomenal objects of experience in a supra-phenomenal or noumenal unity. Kant's ideas of the self, the world, and God that replaced the rational psychology, rational cosmology, and rational theology of the preceding Leibnizian-Wolffian school, became paradigmatic for post-Kantian metaphysics. Whether in its Absolute Idealist form, as is the case with Fichte or Hegel, or in its realist form, as is the case with Schleiermacher, post-Kantian metaphysics wrestled with the inherently historical and hermeneutical ways of framing the metaphysical question. The historical dimension to metaphysics was opened up by posing the question regarding the world's historical development in relation to its ground in the Absolute as that relation could be known by the human self. The hermeneutical dimension to metaphysics took seriously the linguistic expression of all claims to knowledge and the intersubjective nexus in which those claims were made.

History as constitutive of reality and the self/world/God relation as constitutive of metaphysics are academic issues intimately related to the Enlightenment and the post-Enlightenment study of religion. At least in one of its modern forms from the nineteenth century, the study of religion determines a theory of religion according to the self/world/God constellation, and then applies this theory to the comparison of particular historical religions. This form of the study of religion has, with good reason, been maligned for privileging Christianity (usually Protestant Christianity) in the typology developed from the application of theory to practice. Although this model is no longer tenable in the contemporary study of religion, it does provide one significant bone to chew on if religion is not to lose its necessary relation to the metaphysical dimension posed inherently by historical religion. Such a model offers a powerful description of religious reality according to a philosophy of religion's construal of metaphysical constants in order to give conceptual constancy, making comparative work at all possible. By defining the nature of religion in the terms of a self/world/God relation, metaphysics stipulates a minimum of conceptual requirements that can be used when interpreting past records of religion. The hermeneutical task of determining manifestations of religion in the past require such metaphysical markers. Although this volume does not advocate a retrieval of a nineteenth-century form of the study of religion, it does argue for a serious turn to metaphysical questions in order to understand the history of religion.

This particularly nineteenth-century Western understanding concerning the reciprocal relation between historical-religious and metaphysical subject matter need not result in stiff competition between two antagonists. The Western tradition has admittedly, at times, supported a supersessionist relation between the two, yet at other times has acknowledged their productive complementarity. Some of the Absolute Idealists under consideration in this volume, for example Hegel, conceptualize the expressions of religion and philosophy in a relation of sublation. Although the content of religion is the same as the content of speculative philosophy, its narrative form does not bring the content to truthful unity with its more adequate speculative form in the concept. It is perhaps this model, in which philosophy is seen as a corrective from "on high" to religion, that is the foil of contemporary religious studies. Nevertheless, another model, one provided by Schleiermacher for example, distances the two discourses from each other. Philosophy is dialectics, the study of the production of knowledge under the conditions of intersubjective rationality, and the study of religion is the historical investigation of lived forms of faith. According to Schleiermacher, dialectics only inform religion in the extreme formal sense of prescribing rules for the intersubjective pursuit of making claims of religious and theological knowledge. Schleiermacher's model, even if not deemed a viable solution to the ills of contemporary religious studies, does offer a way of conceiving the relation between the empirical study of religion and the inherent rationality of its claims on philosophical grounds. Philosophy does not bring conceptual specification to religious narrative elements, but treats religion as an inherently historical expression of human nature; its forms are the historically situated forms at its disposal, and its symbols, the products of art and culture (*Bildung*). It is this model of complementarity that, at the very least, argues for a bridge between those two aspects of knowledge that biblical theology has traditionally tried to span. If the empirical and conceptual sciences are brought into a productive and nonpolemical relation with each other, then the historical study of religion can be opened for philosophical and theological study as well.

In whatever way the relation between philosophy and the study of religion is conceived, both disciplines require concrete manifestations of religion in order to proceed. The privileged sources for religious descriptions of reality are those accounts that have been established as transhistorically powerful to shape the history of their interpretation. The scriptures of a historical religion are very viable candidates for this purpose. In the Jewish and Christian religions, the scriptures are the anchor to specific narratives of religious reality. Individual and communal expressions of religious experience are recorded in these key texts that have shaped centuries of religious life and thought. It is in these texts that the foundational claims of a self/world/God relation are documented, although such a stable worldview shows remarkable flexibility throughout a history of variation. The adaptability of a particular religious perspective to new historical contexts can be demonstrated both intratextually and extrabiblically. For example, texts like Job and Ecclesiastes continue to exert their interpretative power in new generations longing to explain the coexistence of good and evil to the satisfaction of a theodicy. Biblical texts are persuasive in their descriptions of reality from a religious perspective because they have the capacity to absorb manifold disparate phenomena and yet remain foundational in such a way as to invite their reconceptualization and recontextualization in light of philosophically distinct epochs.

2. Biblical Theology and Interpretation

The relation between religious reality and its articulation in various expressions, including linguistic forms, is both a philosophical and biblical subject of inquiry. How does the experience of reality find its expression in language? From a philosophical perspective, this question explores the onto-anthropological relation between experience and expression, the nature of reality in relation to its individual and communal schematization, and the mechanisms by which expressions are produced and tested for their truth value. From a biblical perspective, this same question covers the historical analysis of the move from oral source to written form, the history of text production that includes the social-cultural context of production as well as reception, and a description of the precise reality expressed in those texts. The overlap in subject matter, historically situated experience as it is expressed in language, permits both conceptual and empirical research access. A mutually informing inquiry between philosophical and biblical study can take place when the philosophical questions concerning language, truth, and reality are brought into relation to biblical questions concerning text, referentiality, and context. History is the medium of both perspectives of inquiry; their common focus is tuned to that which constitutes the human and its experience in the first place.

If the historical subject matter is expressed in language, then its study must take into account its linguistic incarnation. It is hermeneutics, the modern science paradigmatically associated with the name of Friedrich Schleiermacher, that has taken its place as queen of contemporary arts and sciences. The modern commitment to the linguistic expression of knowledge acknowledges hermeneutics to be the discipline informing all areas of academic investigation. The "art of conducting conversation" was Schleiermacher's own conviction against the Absolute Idealists that every pursuit of thinking (that leads to knowledge) is conducted in an intersubjective milieu.[1] That milieu discloses reason's own capacities for the logical and metaphysical dimensions

---

1. Schleiermacher's own dialectic, his theory of the production of knowledge, is attuned to the linguistic form of the type of thinking required for the pursuit of knowing (pure thought) and to the intersubjective milieu in which all linguistic expressions are articulated. See Friedrich Schleiermacher,

of the search for knowledge; only in intersubjective argument are the presuppositions, aims, and procedures of dialogue unveiled. Modern philosophy is characterized precisely by its attentiveness to the linguistic incarnation of reason. From a Wittgensteinian approach to the investigation of meaning in contextual use to recent developments in critical theory that stipulate the responsibility of disclosing the biases of scientific perspective, modern research tools have deepened this insight into the discursive inevitability of all discussions of subject matter. History and interpretation are inextricably linked.

The idea that reality is linguistically constituted in some way is a philosophical assumption of modern academic study. This assumption, however, does not preclude paying attention to the nondiscursive, emotional, and attitudinal involvement with reality. In fact, as Schleiermacher and Heidegger have argued, mood (*Befindlichkeit*) is perhaps constitutive, in the deepest way, of all ways of being in the world. And in current research, criticism has been raised against the excessive fixation of some research programs on texts. Nevertheless, in view of records of human experience from the past, texts are the privileged bearers of revelation. Texts are representative in revealing individual and communal categorizations of reality in their linguistic expressions of it. They are transhistorical documents that give interpretative access to the ways in which reality has been interpreted in the past. In virtue of precisely their referential capacity, texts from the past are relevant for subsequent generations. They give in language something of the world to be known. With this claim, texts enter into the intersubjective and transhistorical discussion concerning the multitude of ways in which the predicates of the world are schematized. Reality can never be exhausted by discrete encapsulations in language, and conversely, texts perpetually open up domains of experience in the history of their reception for experience, testing, and comparison. Reality and interpretation are intimately conjoined in a relationship of surplus; reality perpetually supercedes its interpretation and interpretation continues to betray infinite variety in historically located experience. The power of texts rests precisely in their transhistorical potential to speak to subsequent readers about the reality articulated in them.

Language has the capacity to open up as well as to occlude reality. Interpretation carves out a piece of reality and casts it in finite light. Where one dimension of reality is disclosed by language, another might be concealed, to use Heidegger's insight borrowed from Nietzsche. From both a subjective and an objective perspective, interpretation and language give finite contours to reality and experience. If the question of knowing the individual is problematized in modernity by Leibniz, Kant, and Schleiermacher, then the question of individual perspective is made the methodological requirement of critical theory. In epistemological terms, on the one hand, categorial knowledge is essential in determining the predicates of a particular

---

Kritische Gesamtausgabe, vols. II.10/1–2, *Vorlesungen über die Dialektik* (ed. Andreas Arndt; 2 vols.; Berlin: de Gruyter, 2003).

object; the individual is known in comparison with empirical knowledge of individuals of its same species and in light of speculative knowledge concerning its genus, as the classic definition of the definition stipulates. Yet Kant, who knew no concepts of singulars, could not determine an individual qua individual,[2] and left to posterity the question of access to the individual through categorial knowledge, the analogy, and a variety of hermeneutical strategies. In methodological terms, on the other hand, the notion of individual perspective has greatly affected the contemporary determination of method. Each method applied to the subject matter is shaped by subjective perspective. Although the study of method has raised consciousness about different ways of interpreting reality and has contributed to the scientific control of subjective factors, method itself is determined culturally; it imposes a subjective standpoint onto inquiry. Neither epistemology nor individual perspective shields against the "surplus of subjectivity." Yet it remains the critical standpoint of intersubjectivity to investigate where subjectivity occludes aspects of reality that must necessarily be part of its description. The trustworthiness of any discrete interpretation of reality is itself established in the context of intersubjectivity.

It is this problem of the imposition of a subjective standpoint that has plagued both the historical and the theological disciplines. On the one hand, historical objectivity has resulted in, at least at one level, an antipathy toward the speculative disciplines that are alleged to impose their speculative fictions onto the subject matter. On the other hand, theological doctrines tend to abstract their conceptual normativity from any intimate association with lived religious practice. This inevitable abstraction has tended to result in charges of imposing subjective norms onto material that, when investigated with historical-critical tools, reveals another reality. For example, the seventeenth-century doctrine of a complete canon inspired by the spirit does not hold in light of historical study of the growth, development, and shaping of the canon in the early stages of the Christian church. Nevertheless, the standoff between history and theology is untenable on hermeneutical grounds. Historical description is inevitably shaped by subjective mood and location. Theological description inevitably uncovers the ways in which individuals and communities from the past determine the self/world/God relation; the history of theology offers powerful explanations for human motivation in thought and action that cannot be dismissed by the historical allegiance to "objectivity."

If history and theology are close allies in conceiving the relation between subjective engagement and objective reality, then their proximate tasks would together help shape new ways of relating biblical and theological studies. A close look at the history of biblical interpretation from the perspective of their cooperation in view of the determination of reality represents this volume's biblical-theological theme. In

---

2. See Manfred Frank, *"Unendliche Annäherung": Die Anfänge der philosophischen Frühromantik* (6th ed.; STW 1328; Frankfurt: Suhrkamp, 1998), 83–84; also more recently, idem, *Selbstgefühl: Eine historisch-systematische Erkundung* (STW 1611; Frankfurt: Suhrkamp, 2002), 44–51.

fact, Marvin A. Sweeney's essay, "The Democratization of Messianism in Modern Jewish Thought," is representative in pointing out the limits of historical-critical questions and in highlighting the theological and philosophical issues at stake when biblical passages are actualized in new contexts. By integrating conceptual concerns with historical study, this volume is critical of the usual, and often superficial, charge of "dogmatic imposition" onto historical description. This charge assumes a dualism between description and prescription that is untenable on epistemological grounds, and confuses hermeneutical prejudgment, interpretive sympathy, and subjective location with subjective imposition. The contributions in this book, each in its respective way, argue for the legitimacy of conceptual questions on hermeneutical, methodological, and historical grounds. Subjective engagement is not only admitted but is in fact condoned, as it succeeds in opening up dimensions of the subject matter that might be concealed by alleged descriptive objectivity. A dialogical encounter between present and past presupposes some sympathy with the past on the transhistorical ground of subject matter. Biblical theology cannot avoid assuming or arguing for specific constructions of reality, the reality of biblical "authors," their tradents, and their interpreters. In fact, hermeneutical honesty permits a probing of philosophical issues embedded in any expressions of experience.

Perhaps the philosophical-hermeneutical issues at stake in biblical theology are best attested by what some might consider to be the extreme speculative case of nineteenth-century German philosophical interpretation of scripture. Some might balk at the legitimacy of speculative questions and ridicule the answers allegedly yielded from the Bible. What a study of these philosophers, Hegel and Schelling, for example, shows, is the conviction that the Bible does answer questions of metaphysical truth in relation to historical contingency. The biblical interpretation of these philosophers discloses the questions driving their own epoch: questions concerning the relation between reality and the ways by which reality can be known and the structures of the world that reveal their relation to a ground that sustains their freedom and dependence. A view of biblical interpretation from its nineteenth-century "Berlin" perspective shows that interpretation is moved by those important questions arising from human experience. The Bible is a common dialogical point precisely because it offers both answers to those questions and a language for conceptualizing the answers.

3. Biblical Theology across Disciplines

The interdisciplinary nature of biblical theology is shown in this volume by the dialogue it stages among historians, biblical theologians, systematic theologians, practical theologians, and philosophers. The common field of vision of different perspectives is the one question regarding the hermeneutical encounter between different conceptions of reality as presented in the history of biblical interpretation. The first aspect to the central question in this volume's dialogue concerns the historical issues at stake in various hermeneutical proposals regarding reality. An answer is offered by a detailed look at renowned figures in the history of biblical interpretation who have significantly shaped their contemporary perceptions of reality by transformative encounters with biblical texts. Such an encounter might yield the inscription of biblical stories into contemporary reality (to use Maren R. Niehoff's phrase), or the enscripturation of philosophical concepts in biblical terms (to use Karen Jo Torjesen's term), or result in hermeneutical novelty when the reception of biblical texts is concretized in distinct historical and cultural situations. The first section, "Historical and Theological Interpretation," promises such a look at notables from the past: Josephus, Philo, Origen, and Heracleon, and studies them with an eye to the fact that biblical interpretation has the power to shape the future of biblical reception.

The second section, "Philosophical Interpretation," might on the surface appear to be an esoteric addition to the volume. When philosophers such as Mendelssohn, Fichte, Schleiermacher, Hegel, Schelling, and Feuerbach are brought as relevant experts to the topic of biblical exegesis, then the results, as is no surprise, are often shocking. What does Athens have to do with Jerusalem? Yet the inclusion of these philosophical notables, who concentrated their work in eighteenth- and nineteenth-century Berlin, is more than the accident caused by celebrating Berlin, the site of the Society of Biblical Literature's International Meeting in July 2002. The central question tying together all the contributions in this section is the question concerning the relationship between philosophy and biblical interpretation. The details of this relation are worked out in view of epistemological questions, such as the grounding of reason in the Absolute, and metaphysical questions, such as the constitution of reality according to an appearance/power metaphysic. Even at their speculative best, the philosophers under investigation engage the biblical texts in such ways as to tease out insights crucial to their own understanding. The relevance of biblical texts to philosophical questions is the plot of this section. Its yield is the demonstration of scripture's power to challenge, inspire, and articulate distinct religious views that are worked out in philosophical terms.

The first section ("Historical and Theological Interpretation") begins with Bernd Janowski's essay, which sets the conceptual and historical parameters for this volume's biblical-theological theme. In his chapter, "Biblische Theologie heute: Formale und materiale Aspekte," Janowski provides a brief history of biblical theology and discusses the twofold meaning of the term "biblical theology" in order to identify the discipline's contemporary task as one tailored to both historical reality and normative expression. Janowski argues that the descriptive aspect, focused on the canon's formation and the diversity of its textual material, accesses historical reality by both presupposing the conceptual distinction between text and subject matter and assuming that biblical discourses articulate experiences of the transcendent. The reality accounted for in the text is also the subject of theological inquiry. Diversity at the descriptive level is correlated to its unity, a common subject matter funding the complex interrelations between the parts (*Sachzusammenhang*). The fit, for example, between a history of religions approach to the Bible and a theology of the Hebrew Bible or the Old Testament is a natural consequence of locating the subject of inquiry in history.

Maren R. Niehoff's chapter, "New Garments for Biblical Joseph," addresses the interpretations of the biblical Joseph story in the works of Flavius Josephus and Philo of Alexandria. The study of each and the comparison between the two biblical interpreters reveals the significant point that biblical interpretation does not only reflect contemporary views of reality, but that it can be used to shape that reality as well. According to Niehoff, Philo depicts the Joseph story in his own Egyptian context in order to shape Jewish identity in that land. Philo contrasts Jewish values with those of the Egyptians and aligns them with the Roman elite living in Egypt. Joseph serves as the model on which Philo hangs the garments of Jewish religion and culture (to continue Niehoff's metaphor). One generation later, Josephus appeals to the Joseph story in order to tailor this exemplary figure to his own circumstances. For his particular Roman context, Joseph embodies the image of a peace-loving person who was victimized by his brothers. This image resurfaces in Josephus's autobiography and may have served as a model for the historian's justification of his own relationship with fellow leaders in the early stages of the great revolt.

Harold W. Attridge takes up the issue of differing philosophical conceptualities in relation to exegetical differences in his essay, "Heracleon and John: Reassessment of an Early Christian Hermeneutical Debate." Attridge places Heracleon's commentary on John's Gospel in light of new research on Heracleon's fragments, thereby counteracting the predominant evaluation, set primarily by Origen's synopsis of Heracleon's position, that the "heretic" is to be interpreted in continuity with Valentinian Gnosticism. By demonstrating Heracleon's own careful exegetical work, Attridge argues that both Origen and Heracleon were deeply concerned with preserving a high view of the Logos and a participative view of humans in the soteriological process. Yet it is primarily a metaphysics of motion, borrowed from Aristotle's potency-act distinction, that philosophically shapes Heracleon's exegesis. Heracleon determines a conceptual alignment between God and the world through the action of spirit that preserves, on the one hand, the feature of finitude as subject to change, and affirms, on the other hand, participation in a divine nature. Hence a metaphysical conception of the relation between being and becoming shapes the theological results gleaned from the Johannine material.

Karen Jo Torjesen's chapter, "The Enscripturation of Philosophy: The Incorporeality of God in Origen's Exegesis" poses a key question about the relation between the philosophical conception of reality and biblical interpretation. The question Torjesen asks concerns the apparent "collision" between Origen's appeal to scriptural language in articulating his philosophical-theological understanding of divine incorporeality and the fact that biblical-anthropomorphic descriptions of God seem to preclude such a philosophical claim. If incorporeality is absent from biblical depiction, then why does Origen clothe his philosophical doctrine in its language? Torjesen answers this question by showing how Origen "enscripturates" his philosophy by virtue of scripture's own capacity for rendering multiple meaning. Through the application of allegory, Origen can plumb scripture for its philosophical meaning; when anthropomorphic language is read, incorporeality is heard.

The second section ("Philosophical Interpretation") begins with Marvin A. Sweeney's essay, "The Democratization of Messianism in Modern Jewish Thought." Sweeney asks the question of reality in this chapter from the perspective of the contextualization of messianic motifs by three Jewish thinkers. By appealing to the contextualization category, Sweeney argues for the necessity of extending the subject matter of Jewish biblical theology beyond the study of the Bible to the tradition of Judaism. This move is crucial for the posing and answering of theological questions regarding biblical interpretation in the contexts of Jewish exile, the Diaspora, and the Shoah. Sweeney's argument turns on the interpretation of the messianic theme of the Davidic covenant in Isa 55:3 in view of Jewish self-understanding in bringing about the *Tikkun Olam*, the "Repair of the World." This Kabbalistic idea, rather than marginal, is central to modern Jewish thought. It was first articulated by Isaac Luria in the sixteenth century, then developed by Moses Mendelssohn in his conceptualization of Judaism in the Enlightenment philosophical terms of eighteenth-century Berlin, and finally appropriated by Asher Ginzberg (Ahad Ha-'Am) in laying the theoretical foundations of modern Zionism in a nineteenth-century German context. All three thinkers interpret a "democratized messianism" in their respective contexts as the nonpersonalist reality of an inner spiritual essence of Judaism that is externalized by modern forms of Judaism in working out, together with the world, the sanctification of the world.

Another example of contextualizing a distinct biblical passage in the post-Kantian philosophical discussion is provided by Stephan Grätzel in his essay on Fichte, "Verkündigung in Übereinstimmung mit der Vernunft: Fichtes Auslegung des Johannesevangeliums." In this chapter, Grätzel shows how Fichte reads two verses in John's Prologue (verses 1 and 14) as the fact of religious revelation that the philosopher then uses to investigate the metaphysical question concerning the transition from being (*Sein*) to existence (*Dasein*). This transition is revealed paradigmatically in the historical fact of Jesus of Nazareth as a transition to life in the flesh as one constituted by love. Furthermore, this transition reveals the reason for existence in the imperative: "be" (*soll*). Revelation is reason's point of departure for providing a philosophical determination of existence as an interconnected whole that is grounded in a hidden unity. In Fichte's case, religious revelation in the Bible is integrally linked to the operation of philosophical reason in pursuing the metaphysical truth about the reality of and the reason for the relation of existence to its ground.

Christine Helmer's essay, "The Consummation of Reality: Soteriological Metaphysics in Schleiermacher's Interpretation of Colossians 1:15–20," takes up the standard criticism against Schleiermacher's alleged imposition of dogmatic categories onto his interpretation of the New Testament. In his defense, Helmer argues that the criticism cannot be sustained in the face of Schleiermacher's philological and hermeneutical sensitivity to the New Testament texts: his discovery of the literary parallel in Col 1:15–20 is one example. Rather, the charge must be reinterpreted in terms of the metaphysic that Schleiermacher uses to conceptualize the relation between Christ's work in creation and redemption. Schleiermacher determines a soteriological metaphysic according to the power/appearance dynamic of the inner power of redemption in Christ that permeates reality in extending into the world. Schleiermacher's metaphysical claim, however, overdetermines the Colossians' passage. It seems that the answer to the question of reality hermeneutically privileges Schleiermacher's own position and shapes his interpretation of the text. Whether correct on historical-critical grounds or not, this interpretation serves to argue for the importance of considering metaphysical issues in making judgments upon hermeneutical results.

In his essay, "Die Dialektik von Freiheit und Sünde: Hegels Interpretation von Genesis 3," Joachim Ringleben investigates the way in which Hegel interprets the fall in Gen 3 according to his concept of subjectivity. As is the case with Schelling, Hegel situates his interpretation in the transcendental Idealist philosophical discussion concerning the relation of the subject to its ground. In contrast with Schelling, Hegel offers a rational metaphysical explanation for this relation: the natural genesis of subjectivity toward freedom requires an emancipation from its ground. Necessary disunity, although a transitional state of consciousness, implies the inevitable production of sin and evil. This example of Hegel's biblical interpretation demonstrates both Hegel's method of sublating myth into the philosophical concept in order to tease out its speculative truth and his understanding of the speculative reality intended by the biblical text. Hegel knows that the reality articulated in Gen 3 is neither a historical nor a transhistorical reality, but a speculative one capable of full philosophical determination.

Wilhelm Gräb takes up the nineteenth-century transcendental Idealist question concerning the relation between reason and its ground in being by concentrating on a representative interpretation of John's Prologue. It is the later Schelling's controversial lectures of 1841–1842, the *Philosophy of Revelation*, that serve as the representative text for Gräb's study of a philosophical interpretation of the Bible in the chapter, "Anerkannte Kontingenz: Schellings existentiale Interpretation des Johannesprologs in der *Philosophie der Offenbarung*." According to Gräb, Schelling's philosophical access to John's Prologue provides him with answers to both the speculative and historical questions of existence. The speculative metaphysical question of being is posed when reason asks the question concerning the transcendental condition for the possibility of knowing; the metaphysical answer grounds reason in being that precedes it, never to be exhausted by rational determination. The historical question concerning the contingent relation of individuality to the ground of being is answered by its historical revelation in the person of Jesus of Nazareth. The reality of historical revelation is transparent to metaphysical reality; contingency witnesses to its ground in God.

Garrett Green discusses the famous projection theory of Ludwig Feuerbach in his essay, "Feuerbach and the Hermeneutics of Imagination," in the context of Feuerbach's theory of religion and its implications for biblical hermeneutics. According to Green, the imagination plays a key role in Feuerbach's construction of religion. It represents one answer to the nineteenth-century question concerning the human capacity for religion that challenges the restriction of this capacity to a rational mechanism. Feuerbach appeals decisively to the imagination in his own philosophy of religion and uses it to explain the metaphysical status assigned to the content of projection. Appealing to the model of objective self-consciousness, Feuerbach shows that the imagination is involved in its own deception. When this theory is extrapolated into the study of the Bible, it explains the imagination's self-deception concerning the literal sense of this written form of revelation. Feuerbach thus uses a philosophical argument to fund a biblical hermeneutic of suspicion that has had a significant impact on both critical theories of religion and biblical scholarship.

The intention of this volume is to provide "local" studies in the history of biblical interpretation with the precise question concerning reality at the forefront of investigation. Whether that reality is conceived historically, contextually, or metaphysically, it is used to inform the approach to a biblical theology that takes seriously the power of biblical texts to address human questions regarding religion, experiences in religion, and the transhistorical relevance of religion.

PART 1

Historical and Theological Interpretation

BIBLISCHE THEOLOGIE HEUTE:
FORMALE UND MATERIALE ASPEKTE

Bernd Janowski

Mit den folgenden Überlegungen soll ein Überblick über einige Grundprobleme der Biblischen Theologie gegeben werden, wie sie sich seit den Anfängen biblisch-theologischer Arbeit im 17. Jahrhundert entwickelt haben und gegenwärtig darstellen. Dabei kommt es im Sinn einer Problemskizze weniger auf die Diskussion der Einzelheiten als auf die großen Linien und Zusammenhänge an. Nach einer Definition des Begriffs "Biblische Theologie" (I) und einer kurzen Darstellung der Forschungsgeschichte (II) folgt eine Skizze derjenigen Probleme, die gegenwärtig am intensivsten diskutiert werden (III). Gemäß den Arbeitsschwerpunkten des Verfassers steht dabei das Alte Testament und seine Bedeutung für eine gesamtbiblische Theologie im Vordergrund.

1. Zum Begriff "Biblische Theologie"

"Biblische Theologie" ist kein eindeutiger Begriff. Er meint entweder *die schriftgemäße Theologie* oder *die in der Bibel enthaltene Theologie*. Im ersten Fall ist "Biblische Theologie" ein normativer, im zweiten Fall ein historischer Begriff:

> Das eine Mal bezeichnet "Biblische Theologie" die rechte Art von Theologie überhaupt, das andere Mal eine bestimmte geschichtliche Ausprägung von Theologie. Das eine Mal betrifft der Begriff "Biblische Theologie" die Theologie in ihrem Wesen, das andere Mal nur partiell einen Aufgabenbereich der Theologie, eine bestimmte theologische Disziplin. Das eine Mal geht "biblische Theologie" die Dogmatiker, das andere Mal die Historiker unter den Theologen an. Auch wenn wir diese Gegenüberstellungen als eine nur vorläufige Charakteristik nehmen, so ist doch klar, daß wir uns bei der bloßen Unterscheidung der beiden Bedeutungen von "biblischer Theologie" nicht beruhigen können.[1]

Die Frage ist, wie beide Formen von Biblischer Theologie zusammenhängen und

---

1. Gerhard Ebeling, "Was heißt 'Biblische Theologie'?" (1955), in *Wort und Glaube*, Bd. 1 (3e Aufl.; Tübingen: Mohr Siebeck, 1967), 70.

welche Wechselbeziehung zwischen ihnen besteht. Je nachdem, wie hier die Akzente gesetzt werden, ergibt sich eine etwas andere Konturierung des Begriffs[2]

—Liegt die Betonung auf "biblisch"—im Gegensatz zu "dogmatisch"—, dann ist Biblische Theologie deskriptiv und historisch, nicht aber normativ verstanden;

—liegt die Betonung auf "Theologie"—im Gegensatz zu "Religionsgeschichte"—, dann wird die Bibel nicht nur (religions-)geschichtlich, d. h. als ein Dokument der Religionsgeschichte Israels/des Urchristentums gelesen, sondern auf ihren theologischen Gehalt hin, d. h. als Zeugnis vom Reden Gottes, untersucht;

—wird die Differenz der Bibel zu ihrer Umwelt—Mesopotamien, Ägypten, Kleinasien, Altsyrien, Persien, griechisch-römische Welt u. a.—betont, dann arbeitet Biblische Theologie die Eigenart (das sog. Proprium) des biblischen Zeugnisses trotz der Ähnlichkeit mit seiner jeweiligen Umwelt heraus;

—wird schließlich der innere Zusammenhang der Bibel—die "Einheit der Schrift"—im Gegensatz zur Vielfalt ihrer Überlieferungen hervorgehoben, dann steht Biblische Theologie im Kontrast zu den Theologien des Alten und des Neuen Testaments bzw. zur Theologie einzelner biblischer Schriften bzw. Überlieferungen (prophetische, apokalyptische, paulinische, johanneische Theologie).[3]

Abgesehen von der Klärung des Nebeneinanders eines historischen und eines dogmatischen Umgangs mit der Schrift gehört die Verhältnisbestimmung von *Genese* (Entstehung der Überlieferungsvielfalt) und *Geltung* (Verbindlichkeit der Schrift) zu den Hauptaufgaben einer Biblischen Theologie. Sie hat demnach Rechenschaft zu geben über das "Verständnis der Bibel im ganzen, d. h. vor allem über die theologischen Probleme, die dadurch entstehen, daß die Mannigfaltigkeit des alt- bzw. neutestamentlichen Zeugnisses auf ihren Zusammenhang hin befragt wird."[4] Die Suche nach einer Antwort auf die Frage, wie dieser Zusammenhang zu begründen ist und ob die Biblische Theologie dabei als Teildisziplin theologischer Fächer, als interdisziplinäres theologisches Programm oder als regulative Leitidee einer der Bibel gemäßen Theologie fungiert, gehört zu den Zukunftsaufgaben der Theologie.[5]

---

2. Vgl. James Barr, "Biblische Theologie 1," *EKL* (3e Aufl.; 1986), 1:488–89.

3. S. dazu von neutestamentlicher Seite zuletzt Ferdinand Hahn, "Vielfalt und Einheit des Neuen Testaments," *BZ* 38 (1994): 161–73 und Peter Stuhlmacher, "Wie treibt man Biblische Theologie?," (Biblisch-theologische Studien 24; Neukirchen-Vluyn: Neukirchener, 1995), ferner John Reumann, "Profiles, Problems, and Possibilities in Biblical Theology Today I-II," *KuD* 44 (1998): 145–69.

4. Ebeling, "Was heißt 'Biblische Theologie'?," 88.

5. S. dazu Michael Welker, "Biblische Theologie II," *RGG* (4e Aufl.; 1998), 1:1549–53 und im folgenden.

2. Aspekte der Forschungsgeschichte

Der *terminus a quo* für das Aufkommen des Begriffs "Biblische Theologie" ist das neuzeitliche, mit dem Zeitalter des Rationalismus beginnende Auseinandertreten von historischer und systematischer Theologie. Die Wortprägung "Biblische Theologie," die—weil die Heilige Schrift nach reformatorischem Verständnis Quelle und Richtschnur für die Lehre (*doctrina*) ist—zwar reformatorisch klingt, von den Reformatoren aber noch nicht gebraucht wurde, ist zum Zeitpunkt ihrer Entstehung (1. Hälfte des 17. Jahrhunderts)[6] die Lösung für ein theologisches Reformprogramm, das weder am Inhalt der orthodoxen Dogmatik noch an der Gestalt als systematischer Theologie an sich, sondern nur an gewissen Auswüchsen wie der Überfremdung der "einfältigen" biblischen Aussagen durch "fürwitzige Subtilitäten"[7] der Dogmatik Kritik übte. Aber die unter der Bezeichnung "Biblische Theologie" vorgebrachte *formale Kritik* an der Spannung zwischen der Bibel einerseits und der herrschenden Gestalt der Theologie und ihrem Inspirationsdogma andererseits zog das *hermeneutische Problem* nach sich, die Spannung von Text und Auslegung grundsätzlich zu bedenken und eine Rückbindung der Theologie an die Schrift zu propagieren. In diesem Zusammenhang stehen Bemühungen, zu den einzelnen dogmatischen Loci *dicta probantia* aus der Schrift—und im katholischen Bereich auch aus Kirchenvätertexten[8]—zusammenzustellen,[9] um die Theologie an ihr Schriftfundament zurückzubinden.

Die Konsequenzen dieses Verfahrens, das die Biblische Theologie noch nicht über den Status einer Hilfsdisziplin der Dogmatik hinaushob, wurden erst im 18. Jahrhundert sichtbar, als sich protestantische Theologen der Aufklärung der Aufgabe einer Biblischen Theologie annahmen und diese schrittweise zu einer Konkurrentin der Dogmatik entwickelten. Der entscheidende Durchbruch zu einer selbständigen, historisch-kritisch verfahrenden Disziplin neben der Dogmatik ist mit dem Namen Johann Philipp Gabler verbunden, der in seiner Altdorfer Antrittsvorlesung *De iusto discrimine theologiae biblicae et dogmaticae regundisque recte utriusque finibus* ("Von der richtigen Unterscheidung der biblischen und der dogmatischen Theologie und der rechten Unterscheidung ihrer beiden Ziele") vom 30. März 1787[10] programmatisch zwischen der Biblischen Theologie als einer historischen Disziplin und der

---

6. Vgl. Ebeling, "Was heißt 'Biblische Theologie'?," 75, Anm. 8.
7. So Philipp Jakob Spener, *Pia Desideria (1675)*, s. dazu die Nachweise bei Ebeling, "Was heißt 'Biblische Theologie'?," 74–76.
8. S. dazu Peter Walter, "Biblische Theologie I," *LThK* (3e Aufl.; 1994), 2:426 mit entsprechenden Nachweisen.
9. Vgl. S. Schmidt, *Collegium biblicum in quo dicta Veteris et Novi Testamenti iuxta seriem locorum communium theologicorum explicandur* (Argentorati, 1671; 2e Aufl., 1676).
10. Deutsche Übersetzung bei Otto Merk, *Biblische Theologie des Neuen Testaments in ihrer Anfangszeit: Ihre methodischen Probleme bei Johann Philipp Gabler und Georg Lorenz Bauer und deren Nachwirkungen* (Marburger theologische Studien 9; Marburg: Elwert, 1972), 273–84.

dogmatischen Theologie als einer didaktischen Disziplin unterschied. Die Brücke zur Dogmatik wird dabei von der die biblischen Grundideen herausarbeitenden "reinen Biblischen Theologie" geschlagen:

> Die Biblische Theologie besitzt historischen Charakter, überliefernd, was die heiligen Schriftsteller über die göttlichen Dinge gedacht haben; die Dogmatische Theologie dagegen besitzt didaktischen Charakter, lehrend, was jeder Theologe kraft seiner Fähigkeit oder gemäß dem Zeitumstand, dem Zeitalter, dem Orte, der Sekte, der Schule und anderen ähnlichen Dingen dieser Art über die göttlichen Dinge philosophierte. Jene, da sie historisch argumentiert, ist, für sich betrachtet, sich immer gleich (obwohl sie selbst, ja nach dem Lehrsystem, nach dem sie ausgearbeitet wurde, von den einen so, von den anderen anders dargestellt wird): Diese jedoch ist zusammen mit den übrigen menschlichen Disziplinen vielfältigen Veränderungen unterworfen: Was ständige und fortlaufende Beobachtung so vieler Jahrhunderte übergenug beweist ... Das freilich soll von mir nicht so gemeint sein, daß alles in der Theologie für unsicher und zweifelhaft gehalten werden soll; sondern nur so viel möchten diese Worte ausrichten, daß wir das Göttliche vom Menschlichen sorgfältig unterscheiden, daß wir eine gewisse Unterscheidung der Biblischen und der Dogmatischen Theologie festsetzen und nach Ausscheidung von dem, was in den heiligen Schriften allernächst an jene Zeiten und jene Menschen gerichtet ist, nur diese reinen Vorstellungen unserer philosophischen Betrachtung über die Religion zugrundelegen, welche die göttliche Vorsehung an allen Orten und Zeiten gelten lassen wollte, und so die Bereiche der göttlichen und menschlichen Weisheit sorgfältiger bezeichnen. So endlich wird unsere Theologie sicherer und fester, und so wird sie selbst vom heftigsten Angriff der Feinde nichts weiter zu fürchten haben.[11]

War die Idee einer Biblischen Theologie ursprünglich nur als Reform der systematischen Theologie gedacht, so mußte sie jetzt durch die Emanzipation von der Dogmatik und die Behauptung ihrer methodischen und materialen Eigenständigkeit um so größere Rückwirkungen auf die Dogmatik haben. Andererseits lag es in der Konzeption der Biblischen Theologie als historischer Disziplin, daß sich diese Neubesinnung auf ihr Fundament sowohl in allgemeinen Erwägungen über das Wesen der Geschichte bzw. des historischen Erkennens als auch in der Quelleninterpretation niederschlug. Die in der Folgezeit an diesen Prämissen orientierten Entwürfe einer Biblischen Theologie sind z. T. durch gegenläufige Tendenzen bestimmt, die im folgenden kurz skizziert werden sollen.

2.1. BIBLISCHE THEOLOGIE UND HISTORISCHE KRITIK

Aus der historisch-kritischen Ausrichtung der Biblischen Theologie wird zunächst die Konsequenz einer getrennten Darstellung der Theologie des Alten Te-

---

11. Gabler, "Von der rechten Unterscheidung" (zitiert nach Merk, *Biblische Theologie des Neuen Testaments*, 275–76).

staments und der Theologie des Neuen Testaments gezogen (Georg Lorenz Bauer) und darüber hinaus das methodische Instrumentarium Gablers weiterentwickelt (Wilhelm Martin Leberecht de Wette, Ferdinand Christian Baur, Daniel Georg Conrad von Cölln u. a.).[12] In Ferdinand Christian Baurs *Vorlesungen über neutestamentliche Theologie (1864)*[13] sind Gablers und Baurs programmatische Gesichtspunkte—das Ineinander von historischer Rekonstruktion und theologischer Interpretation—auf den damaligen Höhepunkt kritischer Forschung geführt. Damit werden Perspektiven sichtbar, die weit bis in die nachbaur'sche Ära reichen, aber bis zum Ende des 19. Jahrhunderts zu den ungelösten Fragen einer Biblischen Theologie des Neuen Testaments zählen.[14]

2.2. Religionsgeschichte vs. (Biblische) Theologie

Die Konzeption der Biblischen Theologie als historische Disziplin vollzog sich zwar im Kontext des aufkommenden historischen Bewußtseins, gleichzeitig aber im Wissen um die Relevanz der Heiligen Schrift für den christlichen Glauben. Die Folge war die doppelte Einsicht, daß Biblische Theologie als historische Disziplin nicht nur an den geschichtlichen Standort des erkennenden Subjekts, sondern auch an die Auffassung gebunden ist, die dieses vom christlichen Glauben hat. Entsprechend der Gewichtung des einen oder des anderen Aspekts gibt es dabei ein weites Spektrum von Variationsmöglichkeiten. Folgenreich wurde in diesem Zusammenhang die Position der Religionsgeschichtlichen Schule, die die Wahrnehmung der historischen Distanz zum Erkenntnisprinzip erhob und etwa in William Wredes Programmschrift *Über Aufgabe und Methode der sog. Neutestamentlichen Theologie (1897)* zum Tragen kam:

> Der Name "Biblische Theologie" bedeutet ursprünglich nicht eine Theologie, welche die Bibel hat, sondern die Theologie, welche biblischen Charakter hat, aus der Bibel geschöpft ist. Das kann uns gleichgültig sein.[15]

Konsequenterweise nahm die Biblische Theologie des Alten bzw. des Neuen Testaments immer mehr den Charakter einer Religionsgeschichte Israels bzw. des Urchristentums an.[16]

---

12. S. dazu Otto Merk, "Biblische Theologie II," *TRE* (1980), 6:455–77.

13. Ferdinand Christian Baur, *Vorlesungen über neutestamentliche Theologie (1863)* (hrsg. von Ferdinand Friedrich Baur; Leipzig: Fues, 1864).

14. S. dazu zusammenfassend Heinrich Julius Holtzmann, *Lehrbuch der neutestamentlichen Theologie* (Bde. 1–2; 2e Aufl.; hrsg. von Adolf Jülicher und Walter Baur; Tübingen: Mohr Siebeck, 1911); vgl. Merk, "Biblische Theologie II," 459–61.

15. William Wrede, *Über Aufgabe und Methode der sogenannten Neutestamentlichen Theologie (1897)* (Göttingen: Vandenhoeck & Ruprecht, 1897), 79; s. dazu aber Ebeling, "Was heißt 'Biblische Theologie'?," 69–70.

16. Hermann Gunkel hat sich 1927 zu diesem Problem sehr programmatisch geäußert: "Blickt man nun tiefer und versucht, die letzten Gründe dieser Unzulänglichkeiten der Biblischen Theologie zu erken-

2.3. (Biblische) Theologie vs. Religionsgeschichte

Parallel zum Aufkommen der Dialektischen Theologie machten sich in den 20er und 30er Jahren des 20. Jahrhunderts allerdings Widerstände gegen die Ergebnisse der historisch-kritischen Bibelwissenschaft bemerkbar, die in dem Vorwurf der *analytischen Überschärfe*, des *historischen Relativismus* und der *mangelnden theologischen Interpretation* gipfelten.[17] In Reaktion darauf wurden Theologien des Alten Testaments und des Neuen Testaments geschrieben, die die bisherigen Darstellungen einer "Religionsgeschichte des Urchristentums" durch die Herausarbeitung der *Gemeinsamkeiten* zwischen den Überlieferungsgeschichten der christlichen Bibel wie die *Differenzen* zu ihrer Umwelt zu korrigieren suchten. Tendenziell war dabei die strukturelle Einheit der alttestamentlichen Glaubenswelt und ihr Zusammenhang mit dem Neuen Testament im Blick (Walther Eichrodt, Ludwig Köhler).[18] Daneben gab es bei einigen Forschern den Kompromißversuch, eine "Religionsgeschichte Israels" neben einer "Theologie des Alten Testaments" zu verfassen (Eduard König, Ernst Sellin, auch Georg Fohrer).[19] Die gegenwärtige Diskussion ist (wieder) von der Alternative "Religionsgeschichte Israels" vs. "Theologie des Alten Testaments" und dem "Plädoyer für eine forschungsgeschichtliche Umorientierung" (Rainer Albertz) geprägt.[20] Daß diese Alternative aber keine sachgemäße Antwort auf die anstehen-

---

nen, so bemerkt man, daß diese von der altkirchlichen Inspirationslehre beherrscht wird; daher muß sie den gesamten biblischen Stoff wie auf einer Fläche dehnen und kann die Gedankeneinheit, die sie in der Bibel zu besitzen glaubt, nach einheitlicher Disposition systematisch anordnen. Wird aber dieser Anordnung gegenwärtig widersprochen, so bedeutet das im letzten Grunde, daß der Geist geschichtlicher Forschung in dieser Wissenschaft eingezogen ist. Die Erscheinung, die unser Geschlecht erlebt hat, wonach die Biblische Theologie durch die 'Religionsgeschichte Israels' ersetzt wird, erklärt sich also daraus, daß an Stelle der Inspirationslehre jetzt der Geist der Geschichtsforschung zu treten beginnt" (Hermann Gunkel, "Biblische Theologie und biblische Religionsgeschichte," *RGG* (2e Aufl.; 1927), 1:1090 [Hervorhebung im Original]), zur gegenwärtigen Diskussion des Verhältnisses Religionsgeschichte Israels und/oder Theologie des Alten Testaments s. die Hinweise unten Anm. 21.

17. S. dazu bereits Martin Kähler, "Bibel," *RE* (3e Aufl.; 1897), 2:691: "Die geschichtliche Forschung strebt danach, die vergangene Wirklichkeit festzustellen und aus ihrer Entwicklung heraus zu verstehen; deshalb löst sich ihr die Einheit der Bibel auf, und die Bibel gilt ihr lediglich als Sammlung abzuwertender Berichte und Urkunden. Die meisten Bibelleser suchen dagegen in jedem ihrer kleinsten Teile ein Gotteswort, das sich auf jeden in seinen Lebensumständen anwenden lasse. Über beide Einseitigkeiten, die in scheinbar unauflöslichem Widerstreit leben, kann die besonnene Erwägung der Tatsachen hinausheben, daß jene vielen einzelnen Schriftstücke durch ihre Zusammenfassung zur Bibel einen neuen Wert über ihre ursprüngliche Bedeutung hinaus gewonnen haben, und daß diese Bibel in ihrer Wirkung durch die Jahrhunderte hin eine unvergängliche Gegenwart hat, statt nur das Denkmal einer großen Vergangenheit zu sein," vgl. ders., "Biblische Theologie," *RE* (3e Aufl.; 1897), 3:195.

18. Zur neutestamentlichen Problematik s. Karl Kertelge, "Biblische Theologie IIB," *LThK* (3e Aufl.; 1994), 2:430–1.

19. S. dazu Rainer Albertz, *Religionsgeschichte Israels in alttestamentlicher Zeit* (GAT 8/1–2; Göttingen: Vandenhoeck & Ruprecht, 1992), 20–24.

20. S. dazu die Beiträge in Bernd Janowski und Norbert Lohfink (Hrsg.), *Religionsgeschichte Israels oder Theologie des Alten Testaments?* (Jahrbuch für biblische Theologie 10; Neukirchen-Vluyn: Neukirchener, 1995; 2e Aufl. 2001).

den Grundfragen ist, zeigen die jüngsten Äußerungen zum Thema, die stattdessen Argumente für eine integrative Perspektive, d. h. den Sachzusammenhang von Religionsgeschichte *und* Theologie beizubringen suchen.[21]

Eine zukünftige Biblische Theologie wird dabei weder von der Literatur- noch von der Religionsgeschichte Israels/des Urchristentums absehen können, da es immer auch um die konkrete Geschichtserfahrung geht. In der Einbeziehung der Religionsgeschichte meldet sich die alte Frage nach der Relation von *Genese* und *Geltung* zurück: Wie kann von der Einheit des Alten und Neuen Testament bzw. der christlichen Bibel gesprochen werden, wenn gleichzeitig der *Vielfalt* ihrer religiösen Überlieferungen Rechnung getragen wird? Und: Schließt die Erhebung des (sozial-)geschichtlichen Lebenshintergrunds religiöser Aussagen und theologischer Konzepte des Alten und Neuen Testaments die Frage nach der Einzigartigkeit des JHWH-Glaubens grundsätzlich aus oder sind nicht beide Aspekte im Rahmen eines integrativen Modells notwendig aufeinander bezogen? Wie ein solches Modell aussehen könnte, wird in der gegenwärtigen Forschung kontrovers diskutiert.[22]

2.4. Biblische Theologie und Canonical Approach

Eine Neuorientierung der Disziplin wurde erst von Gerhard von Rad initiiert, der in seinem epochalen Entwurf die Theologie des Alten Testaments als Exegese der alttestamentlichen Texte in ihrem traditionsgeschichtlichen Zusammenhang konzipierte und die Frage nach der Korrelation von Offenbarung und Geschichte zu ihrem hermeneutischen Prinzip erhob.[23] Ausgehend von diesem Ansatz wurde teils die *Geschehenstruktur des JHWH-Glaubens* (Claus Westermann, Horst Dietrich

---

21. S. dazu Matthias Köckert, "Von einem zum einzigen Gott: Zur Diskussion der Religionsgeschichte Israels," *BThZ* 15 (1998): 135–75; Hans-Jürgen Hermisson, *Alttestamentliche Theologie und Religionsgeschichte Israels* (Forum Theologische Literaturzeitung 3; Leipzig: Evangelische Verlagsanstalt, 2000); Othmar Keel, "Religionsgeschichte Israels oder Theologie des Alten Testaments?," *Wieviel Systematik erlaubt die Schrift? Auf der Suche nach einer gesamtbiblischen Theologie* (hrsg. von Frank-Lothar Hossfeld; QD 185; Freiburg: Herder, 2001), 88–109; Bernd Janowski, "Theologie des Alten Testaments: Plädoyer für eine integrative Perspektive," in *Der Gott des Lebens: Beiträge zur Theologie des Alten Testaments*, Bd. 3 (Neukirchen-Vluyn: Neukirchener, 2003), 329–50; Joachim Jeremias, "Neuere Entwürfe zu einer 'Theologie des Alten Testaments'," *VuF* 48 (2003): 54–58. Auch in der neutestamentlichen Wissenschaft bahnt sich eine ähnliche Diskussionslage an, s. dazu den Bericht von Reinhard von Bendemann, "'Theologie des Neuen Testaments' oder 'Religionsgeschichte des Frühchristentums?'," *VuF* 48 (2003): 23–28.

22. S. dazu mit unterschiedlichen Optionen Welker, "Biblische Theologie II," 1549–53 und Eilert Herms, "Was haben wir an der Bibel? Versuch einer Theologie des christlichen Kanons," in *Biblische Hermeneutik* (hrsg. von Ingo Baldermann u.a.; Jahrbuch für biblische Theologie 12; Neukirchen-Vluyn: Neukirchener, 1997), 99–152, ferner Gerhard Barth, "Biblische Theologie: Versuch einer vorläufigen Bilanz," *EvTh* 58 (1998): 398–99; Hans Hübner, "Fundamentaltheologie und biblische Theologie," *ThLZ* 123 (1998): 443–58 und die Kritik von Michael Welker, "Sozio-metaphysische Theologie und Biblische Theologie: Zu E. Herms 'Was haben wir an der Bibel?'" in *Die Macht der Bilder* (Jahrbuch für biblische Theologie 13; Neukirchen-Vluyn: Neukirchener, 1998): 309–22 am Entwurf von Eilert Herms.

23. S. dazu Manfred Oeming, *Das Alte Testament als Teil des christlichen Kanons? Studien zu gesamtbiblischen Theologien der Gegenwart* (Zürich: Pano, 2001), 51–62 und 71–125.

Preuß), teils unter dem Begriff der "Selbigkeit JHWHs" die *Mitte des Alten Testaments* (Walther Zimmerli) hervorgehoben.[24] Im angelsächsischen Raum setzte nach der Phase des "Biblical Theology Movement"[25] die Suche nach einer "neuen Biblischen Theologie" ein, für die Brevard S. Childs mit seiner "Biblical Theology of the Old and New Testaments" (1992)[26] einen bedeutenden, kanonisch orientierten Ansatz vorgelegt hat. Der kanonische Ansatz einer Theologie des Alten Testaments, wie ihn in Deutschland vor allem Rolf Rendtorff vertritt,[27] legt nicht nur die kanonische Anlage der Hebräischen Bibel zugrunde, sondern macht auch "die Texte selbst in ihrer vorliegenden 'kanonischen' Gestalt zum Ausgangspunkt der Darstellung."[28] Allerdings ist sie ebenso wie die von ihr kritisierte historische Kritik auf—z. T. weitreichende—Hypothesen angewiesen.[29]

3. GEGENWÄRTIGE PROBLEME

Der kurze Abriß der Forschungsgeschichte hat die Problematik des Begriffs "Biblische Theologie" deutlich gemacht, insofern die theologische Einheit nicht nur der Bibel, sondern auch diejenige des Alten und des Neuen Testaments fraglich geworden ist.[30] Seit dem vielzitierten Schlußpassus im zweiten Band der "Theologie des Alten Testaments" Gerhard von Rads ist diese Problematik immer wieder beschworen und gleichzeitig der Versuch zu ihrer Lösung unternommen worden.[31] Nach von Rad zeichnet sich

> ein noch ferneres Ziel unseres Bemühens ab, nämlich das einer "Biblischen Theologie", in der der Dualismus je einer sich eigensinnig abgrenzenden Theologie des Alten und des Neuen Testaments überwunden wäre. Wie sich eine solche biblische

---

24. Bernd Janowski, "Der eine Gott der beiden Testamente: Grundfragen einer Biblischen Theologie" (1998), in *Die rettende Gerechtigkeit: Beiträge zur Theologie des Alten Testaments*, Bd. 2 (Neukirchen-Vluyn: Neukirchener, 1999), 249–84, hier: 273–81.
25. Vgl. Merk, "Biblische Theologie II," 468–69.
26. In deutscher Übersetzung als Brevard S. Childs, *Die Biblische Theologie der einen Bibel*, Bd.1, *Grundstrukturen* (übers. von Christiane Oeming; Freiburg: Herder, 1994); Bd. 2, *Hauptthemen* (übers. von Christiane Oeming; Freiburg: Herder, 1996); s. dazu Rolf Rendtorff, "Rezension B. S. Childs, Biblical Theology of the Old and New Testaments," in *Sünde und Gericht* (hrsg. von Ingo Baldermann u.a.; Jahrbuch für biblische Theologie 9; Neukirchen-Vluyn: Neukirchener, 1994): 359–69; ferner Barth, "Biblische Theologie: Versuch einer vorläufigen Bilanz," 392–99.
27. S. dazu Rolf Rendtorff, *Theologie des Alten Testaments: Ein kanonischer Entwurf*, Bd. 1, *Kanonische Grundlegung* (Neukirchen-Vluyn: Neukirchener, 1999), 1–9, vgl. bereits ders., "Theologie des Alten Testaments: Überlegungen zu einem Neuansatz," in *Kanon und Theologie: Vorarbeiten zu einer Theologie des Alten Testaments* (Neukirchen-Vluyn: Neukirchener, 1991), 1–14.
28. Rendtorff, *Theologie des Alten Testaments*, Bd. I, 1.
29. S. dazu Jeremias, "Neuere Entwürfe zu einer 'Theologie des Alten Testaments'," 40–42.
30. Vgl. Ebeling, "Was heißt 'Biblische Theologie'?," 82–87.
31. Vgl. Barth, "Biblische Theologie: Versuch einer vorläufigen Bilanz," 384 mit Anm. 4.

Theologie dann darzustellen hätte, ist noch schwer vorstellbar. Es ist aber ermutigend, daß sie heute immer lauter gefordert wird.[32]

Das war vor über vierzig Jahren. Im Blick auf die bleibende Aufgabe einer Biblischen Theologie, die *Mannigfaltigkeit* der biblischen Überlieferungen auf ihren *Zusammenhang* hin zu befragen, um so ein "Verständnis der Bibel im ganzen"[33] zu fördern, sind heute vor allem vier Problemaspekte zu berücksichtigen und im folgenden zu skizzieren: die Frage nach der "Mitte" der Schrift, die Frage nach dem Kontinuum der Offenbarung, der Sachverhalt der zweigeteilten christlichen Schrift und die Bedeutung des biblischen Kanons.

3.1. DIE "MITTE" DER SCHRIFT

Die Suche nach einer "Mitte" der Schrift ist neuerdings (wieder) in Mißkredit geraten, weil sie angeblich der apologetischen Nötigung folgt, sich eine übergreifende Einheit zurechtzulegen, die die Vielfalt der biblischen Überlieferungen aufhebt und ihre Widersprüchlichkeiten einebnet.[34] Die Schwierigkeit, von einem partikularen Begriff wie "Bund," "Gerechtigkeit" oder "Gottesherrschaft" her die Mitte des Alten Testaments zu bestimmen,[35] besteht in der Tat. Ihr kann aber mit dem Hinweis auf die Differenz zwischen Text und Gegenstand begegnet werden: Nicht die begrifflich fixierbare Mitte einer pluriformen *Textsammlung* (Altes Testament), sondern die Sachmitte eines *Geschehens* (JHWH-Israel-Verhältnis) ist als Mitte des Alten Testaments anzusprechen. Diese kann mit Hilfe der sog. Bundesformel—der *locus classicus* ist Dtn 26,17–19 (JHWH der Gott Israels—Israel das Volk Gottes)[36]—oder mit Hilfe des Toraverständnisses[37] expliziert werden. Sie ist,

---

32. Gerhard von Rad, *Theologie des Alten Testaments*, Bd. 2, *Die Theologie der prophetischen Überlieferungen Israels* (10e Aufl.; München: Chr. Kaiser, 1993), 447.

33. A.a.O., 88, vgl. Christoph Dohmen, "Probleme und Chancen Biblischer Theologie aus alttestamentlicher Sicht," in *Eine Bibel—zwei Testamente: Positionen Biblischer Theologie* (hrsg. von Christoph Dohmen und Thomas Söding; Uni-Taschenbücher 1893; Paderborn: Schöningh, 1995), 9–16.

34. S. dazu Janowski, "Der eine Gott der beiden Testamente," 251–55 und 273–81.

35. Diese Schwierigkeit hat in der diesbezüglichen Kontroverse zwischen Gerhard von Rad und Walther Zimmerli eine zentrale Rolle gespielt, s. dazu Henning Graf Reventlow, *Hauptprobleme der alttestamentlichen Theologie im 20. Jahrhundert* (EdF 173; Darmstadt: Wissenschaftliche Buchgesellschaft, 1982), 138–47; Horst Dietrich Preuß, *Theologie des Alten Testaments*, Bd. 1, *JHWHs erwählendes und verpflichtendes Handeln* (Stuttgart: Kohlhammer, 1991), 25–27 u. a. Kritische Anfragen bei Jon D. Levenson, "Warum Juden sich nicht für Biblische Theologie interessieren," *EvTh* 51 (1991): 402–30; Rainer Albertz, "Religionsgeschichte Israels statt Theologie des Alten Testament! Plädoyer für eine forschungsgeschichtliche Umorientierung," 11–12 u. a., s. dazu Janowski, "Der eine Gott der beiden Testamente," 249–84.

36. So Rudolf Smend, "Die Mitte des Alten Testaments" (1970), in *Die Mitte des Alten Testaments: Gesammelte Studien*, Bd. 1 (BEvTh 99; München: Chr. Kaiser, 1986), 73–82. Zur Rezeption dieser Bestimmung in der alttestamentlichen Wissenschaft s. Janowski, "Der eine Gott der beiden Testamente," 278, Anm. 135.

37. So Otto Kaiser, *Der Gott des Alten Testaments: Theologie des Alten Testaments*, Bd. 1, *Grundlegung* (Uni-Taschenbücher 1747; Göttingen: Vandenhoeck & Ruprecht, 1993), 329–53, s. dazu Hermann

trotz des spannungsvollen Verhältnisses zwischen Altem und Neuem Testament überdies neutestamentlich anschlußfähig und zwar so, daß "Jahwe der Gott Israels, Israel das Volk Jahwes" die interne und "Jesus Christus" die externe Mitte des Alten Testaments ist, wobei "die externe Mitte von der internen nicht zu trennen ist, weil 'Jesus Christus' in seiner Bedeutung nicht ohne jenen Bezug zu 'Jahwe und Israel' zur Sprache kommen kann."[38] Damit stellt sich erneut die Frage nach dem Sachzusammenhang von Altem und Neuem Testament.

3.2. Das Kontinuum der Offenbarung

Die Frage, wie das Kontinuum des in der kanonischen Einheit von Altem und Neuem Testament bezeugten Offenbarungsgeschehens zu präzisieren ist, ist in neuerer Zeit *traditions-* bzw. *offenbarungsgeschichtlich* (Hartmut Gese, Peter Stuhlmacher) oder *kanongeschichtlich* (Brevard S. Childs) beantwortet worden. Das Verhältnis beider Testamente, die durch das Zeugnis von dem einen Gott und seinem Rettungshandeln an Israel und der Welt verbunden sind, stellt sich nicht in Gestalt einer ungebrochenen, die geschichtlichen und theologischen Spannungen überspringenden Kontinuität, sondern als "kontrastive Einheit"[39] dar. Im Horizont einer gesamtbiblischen Theologie hat dieses Geschehen, das in der Selbstmitteilung Gottes in Jesus Christus seine volle Verwirklichung findet, den Charakter einer *eschatologisch* ausgerichteten und in ihrer Dynamik wesenhaft *offenen Heilsgeschichte*.[40] Die Einheit der Offenbarung Gottes, die in Jesus Christus ihre eschatologische Deutlichkeit gewinnt, umschließt daher die Vielfalt der zuvor "zu den Vätern durch die Propheten" ergangenen Worte (Hebr 1,1–2) und integriert diese in die Erwartung eines kommenden, Israel und die Welt richtenden und rettenden Gotteshandelns.

3.3. Die christliche Bibel als zweigeteilte Schrift

Der Entwurf einer Biblischen Theologie hat folglich von der Existenz und der Anerkennung eines aus den beiden Testamenten bestehenden christlich-biblischen Kanons auszugehen. Inwiefern für eine gesamtbiblische Theologie das Faktum des Kanons relevant ist, ergibt sich aus der Tatsache, daß ein theologisch bestimmtes Verhältnis beider Testamente zueinander schon für die Entstehung des christlichen

---

Spieckermann, "Die Verbindlichkeit des Alten Testaments: Unzeitgemäße Betrachtungen zu einem ungeliebten Thema," in *Biblische Hermeneutik* (hrsg. von Ingo Baldermann u.a.; Jahrbuch für biblische Theologie 12; Neukirchen-Vluyn: Neukirchener, 1997), 43–46.

38. Hans-Jürgen Hermisson, "Jesus Christus als externe Mitte des Alten Testaments," in *Jesus Christus als die Mitte der Schrift: Studien zur Hermeneutik des Evangeliums: Festschrift für Otfried Hofius* (hrsg. von Christof Landmesser u. a.; BZNW 86; Berlin: de Gruyter, 1997), 232, anders etwa Merk, "Biblische Theologie II," 471–72.

39. Vgl. Erich Zenger, "Heilige Schrift der Juden und der Christen," in *Einleitung in das Alte Testament* (5e Aufl.; Kohlhammer-Studienbücher Theologie 1,1; Stuttgart: Kohlhammer, 2004), 11–33.

40. Vgl. Ernst Haag, "Biblische Theologie IIA," *LThK* (3e Aufl.; 1994), 2:428–29; Hermisson, "Jesus Christus als externe Mitte des Alten Testaments," 227–33 und Kertelge, "Biblische Theologie IIB," 433.

Kanons vorauszusetzen ist. Mit dem Rückgriff auf die im Werden begriffene Bibel Israels (Tanach/Altes Testament), durch die Gestalt der christlichen Bibel begründet wurde, geht es den neuttestamentlichen Autoren um ein Verständnis des Christusereignisses als einer "endgültig entscheidenden Heilssetzung Gottes 'von der Schrift her',"[41] also darum, daß der Gott Israels sich in Jesus Christus neu offenbart hat und gerade darin seiner Verheißung treu blieb. Die urchristliche Hermeneutik des Alten Testaments gehört deshalb an den Ursprung christlicher Theologie und ist ihr nicht nachträglich aufgepfropft worden.[42] In diesem Vorgang wird deutlich, daß das Neue Testament sich von seiner eigenen Schrifthermeneutik her gar nicht als von der Lektüre des Alten Testaments unabhängiger Kanon, der additiv neben das bereits abgeschlossene Alte Testament gestellt wurde, versteht, sondern zusammen mit jenem ersten Teil—dem später und aufgrund dieses Vorgangs so genannten "Alten Testament"—die eine zweigeteilte christliche Bibel sein will.

3.4. Die Bedeutung des Kanons

Entscheidend für das Werden des christlich-biblischen Kanons ist schließlich der Sachverhalt, daß die alttestamentlichen Texte der vielstimmige Niederschlag von Gotteserfahrungen sind, die zunächst in schwach ausgebildeter Form in das kommunikative Gedächtnis Israels und Judas eingingen (*Mündlichkeit*), ehe sie sich im Rahmen komplexer Entscheidungs- und Selektionsprozesse als institutionalisierte Formen der Mnemotechnik verfestigten (*Schriftlichkeit*) und schließlich als fixierte Bestandteile die Identität des biblischen und nachbiblischen JHWH-Glaubens konstituierten (*Kanonbildung*).[43] Zu den für die Entstehung des Alten Testaments als Kanon relevanten Aspekten gehören dabei der Diskurscharakter der Überlieferung, die Synthese des Gewordenen und die Kohärenz des Kanons.

3.4.1. Der Diskurscharakter der Überlieferung

Im Alten Testament gestaltet sich das Werden der Überlieferung als *Explikation des Redens von Gott*, die eine wesentliche Funktion von Theologie ist. Diese Explikation des Redens von Gott ist Rechenschaft über den Glauben, die seit dem Deuteronomium (7. Jahrhundert vor Christus) zunehmend in diskursiver Form auftritt, also Begriffe benutzt, lehrhafte Sätze bildet, Argumentationen pflegt und schriftgelehrte Interpretationen übt.[44] Gemäß dieser Definition gehe ich mit Christof Hardmeier vom "Diskurscharakter biblischer Überlieferung",[45] d. h. von dem

---

41. Vgl. Zenger, "Heilige Schrift der Juden und Christen," 14.
42. Textbeispiele bei Kertelge, "Biblische Theologie IIB," 432–33 und Janowski, "Der eine Gott der beiden Testamente," 261–64.
43. Vgl. Ludger Schwienhorst-Schönberger, "Gottesbilder des Alten Testaments," *ThPQ* 148 (2000): 362.
44. S. dazu Janowski, "Theologie des Alten Testaments: Plädoyer für eine integrative Perspektive," 337–40.
45. Christof Hardmeier, "Systematische Elemente einer Theo-logie in der Hebräischen Bibel: Das Loben Gottes—ein Kristallisationsmoment biblischer Theologie," in *Religionsgeschichte Israels oder The-*

Sachverhalt aus, daß die verschiedenen und z. T. widersprüchlichen Aussagen über JHWH und Israel als Aspekte einer "Systematik von Redevollzügen" zu verstehen sind, die "das vielfältige Reden von und zu Gott in den überlieferten Texten selbst und als solches ins Auge faßt und die dieses Reden als symbolisch-interaktives Beziehungsgeschehen durchdenkt."[46]

Ihren Grund hat diese Vielfalt des Redens von Gott in der Struktur der alttestamentlichen Gotteserfahrung und ihres von der Alltagswirklichkeit signifikant unterschiedenen Gehalts. Versteht man unter einem Gottesbild die kulturell geprägte *Explikation von Transzendenzerfahrungen*, dann treten diese Explikationen im Alten Testament in großer Polyphonie und reicher Metaphorik auf: JHWH ist, um nur einige Beispiele zu nennen, der erschaffende, der segnende, der rettende, der gebietende, der richtende, der vergebende oder der allmächtige Gott,[47] und er ist der Hirte, der König, der Vater, die Mutter, der Krieger, der Löwe oder der Arzt. Diese *Polyphonie des alttestamentlichen Redens von Gott* ist ein Spiegel der Einheit Gottes in der Vielfalt seiner Äußerungen—und zwar von Äußerungen, die schon immer kulturell geformt sind. Verstehen der biblischen Offenbarung heißt deshalb immer auch Verstehen eines *kulturell geprägten Formenzusammenhangs*.

3.4.2. Die Synthese des Gewordenen

Entscheidend für den Prozeß der Kanonbildung ist ferner die Beobachtung, daß die biblischen Texte nicht einfach nur gesammelt, sondern ausgewählt, kommentiert und ergänzt wurden. Da dieser *Prozeß der Redaktion* von theologischer Bedeutung für das Werden des Alten Testaments als Schriftsammlung ist, wird man sorgfältig auf jene "Schnittstellen"[48] achten müssen, die—wie das Deuteronomium, das Deuteronomistische Geschichtswerk oder die Priesterschrift—für die Redaktion der alttestamentlichen Texte sowie den Prozeß der Kanonwerdung entscheidend geworden sind.

---

ologie des Alten Testaments? (hrsg. von Bernd Janowski und Norbert Lohfink; Jahrbuch für biblische Theologie 10; Neukirchen-Vluyn: Neukirchener, 1995; 2e Aufl. 2001): 111–27, hier: 113. Zu dieser alttestamentlichen "Diskurshermeneutik" s. auch Erich Zenger, "Exegese des Alten Testaments im Spannungsfeld von Judentum und Christentum," *ThRev* 98 (2002): 363–66.

46. Hardmeier, "Systematische Elemente," 112–13.

47. Vgl. Schwienhorst-Schönberger, "Gottesbilder des Alten Testaments," 366 und Zenger, "Exegese des Alten Testaments im Spannungsfeld von Judentum und Christentum," 363.

48. Zum Ausdruck "Schnittstellen" s. Ernst-Joachim Waschke, "Zur Frage einer alttestamentlichen Theologie im Vergleich zur Religionsgeschichte Israels," in *Der Gesalbte: Studien zur alttestamentlichen Theologie* (BZAW 306; Berlin: de Gruyter, 2001), 257. Die Epoche des 7./6. Jahrhunderts vor Christus dürfte eine solche "Schnittstelle" für das Werden der alttestamentlichen Überlieferungen und damit für die Formierung der alttestamentlichen Theologie im Sinn einer "Theologie im Alten Testament" sein, vgl. zur Sache Rudolf Smend, "Theologie im Alten Testament," in *Die Mitte des Alten Testaments: Gesammelte Studien*, Bd. 1 (BEvTh 99; München: Chr. Kaiser, 1986), 111–15; Janowski, "Theologie des Alten Testaments: Plädoyer für eine integrative Perspektive," 343 und Jeremias, "Neuere Entwürfe zu einer 'Theologie des Alten Testaments'," 30–31.

Dabei meint der zentrale *Begriff der Redaktion* die "Bearbeitung eines vorgegebenen Texts im Rahmen der schriftlichen Überlieferung und dessen Umgestaltung zu einem neuen Ganzen."[49] Im Unterschied zur religions- und traditionsgeschichtlichen *Vorstufenrekonstruktion* führt die Redaktionsgeschichte, die den "Prozeß der Textentstehung in ihrer literarischen und sachlichen Dimension"[50] erhellt, zur *Synthese des Gewordenen*, indem sie die Entstehung eines Textes von seinen Anfängen über sämtliche literarische Stadien bis zu seiner vorliegenden Gestalt (Endgestalt) verfolgt und auf jeder Stufe nach den historischen, religions- und sozialgeschichtlichen Implikationen fragt. Keine dieser möglichen Vorstufen ist unverändert tradiert, alle sind sie aus späterer, meist exilisch-nachexilischer Sicht redigiert worden. Redaktion heißt aber nicht Tilgung älterer Texte oder Konzeptionen, sondern Reformulierung ihres Ursprungssinns unter neuen Verstehensbedingungen.[51]

3.4.3. Die Kohärenz des Kanons

Wenn die Redaktionsgeschichte die *Vielfalt der biblischen Überlieferung* in ihrer literarischen und sachlichen Dimension zum Vorschein bringt, dann wird die Frage unabweisbar, wie sich dies mit der These vom *Kanon als kohärentem Sinngefüge* verträgt: Erzeugt erst der Kanon und er allein diesen Sinn oder stellt er ihn nur dar, indem er vorgegebene und durch die Redaktionsgeschichte freigelegte Sinnanreicherungen und -nuancen sichtbar macht? Diese Frage enthält mehrere Teilaspekte,[52] von denen der—fließende—Übergang von der Kanonwerdung zur Kanonschließung für unsere Fragestellung besonders relevant ist.

Die Kanonschließung ist der Akt, durch den die Texte ihre normative Gestalt und Funktion erhalten und von da ab nicht mehr produktiv "fortgeschrieben," sondern "abgeschrieben" und extern interpretiert werden.[53] Als schriftgewordenes kulturelles Gedächtnis ist der Kanon ein komplexes Gebilde: er *"versiegelt"* den historisch gewachsenen Sinn einer pluriformen Schriftsammlung und *schließt* ihn zugleich *neu auf*; er ist zwar durch Eingrenzung des Ausgewählten und Ausgrenzung des Abgelehnten nach außen abgeschlossen, aufgrund seiner inneren Vielstimmigkeit und der komplexen Architektur seiner Teile aber ist er offen für neue Sinnbildungen. Die älteren Texte/Textschichten fungieren dabei nicht einfach als Verstehensvoraussetzungen für die durch die Redaktion(en) geschaffenen "End-

---

49. Reinhard Gregor Kratz, "Redaktionsgeschichte/Redaktionskritik I," *TRE* (1997), 28:367.
50. Ebd.
51. Vgl. a.a.O., 370.
52. S. dazu Janowski, "Theologie des Alten Testaments: Plädoyer für eine integrative Perspektive," 345–48.
53. S. dazu auch Erich Zenger, "Die Tora/der Pentateuch als Ganzes," in *Einleitung in das Alte Testament* (4e Aufl.; Kohlhammer-Studienbücher Theologie 1,1; Stuttgart: Kohlhammer, 2001), 85–86 im Anschluß an Jan Assmann, *Das kulturelle Gedächtnis: Schrift, Erinnerung und politische Identität in frühen Hochkulturen* (München: Beck, 1992), 93–97.

texte," sondern sie sind selbst von theologischer Bedeutung.[54] Als Sammlung der sinnrelevanten Vergleichstexte bildet der Kanon den "Rahmen, innerhalb dessen die verschiedenen Stimmen laut werden," aber er "tritt nicht an ihre Stelle."[55] Leitend ist aber die Einsicht, daß der Kanon eine komplexe Größe ist, die so etwas wie eine "kontrastive Einheit"[56] darstellt. Darin entspricht er der Polyphonie des alttestamentlichen Redens von Gott, die ein Spiegel der Einheit Gottes in der Vielfalt seiner Äußerungen ist.

Wenn man nach dem biblischen Kanon als einem kohärenten Sinngefüge fragt, dann muß man dieser Vielfalt der Aspekte umsichtig Rechnung tragen—auf der *Ebene der Einzeltexte und Textzusammenhänge* durch die Rekonstruktion ihrer religions-, traditions- und theologiegeschichtlichen Implikationen, auf der *Ebene der Bücher und Kanonteile* durch das Wagnis des "Zusammen-Denkens"[57] und auf der *Ebene des abgeschlossenen Kanons* durch die Erschließung der polyphonen und kontrastiven Rede von Gott, die immer neu zur Anrede Gottes an den Menschen werden will.[58] Und zwar in Situationen, die ihrerseits Ausdruck von Pluralität sind und dementsprechend eine Vielzahl von Interpretationen zulassen oder erfordern. Daß wir Pluralismus dabei nicht von vornherein mit postmoderner Beliebigkeit gleichsetzen, sondern vielmehr als einen *geprägten Formenzusammenhang* verstehen sollten,[59] dazu kann uns der biblische Kanon und die Erschließung seiner inneren Struktur paradigmatisch verhelfen.

4. Schlussbemerkung

Mit der voranstehenden Skizze sind die gegenwärtigen Probleme allerdings noch nicht erschöpfend dargestellt. Denn zu künftigen Aufgaben einer Biblischen Theologie zählt neben der Frage nach dem Verhältnis von Biblischer Theologie und Dogmatik noch die Verhältnisbestimmung von Biblischer Theologie und Jüdischchristlichem Dialog. Das ungeklärte Nebeneinander von (religions-)historischer

---

54. S. dazu auch Walter Groß, "Ist biblisch-theologische Auslegung ein integrierender Methodenschritt?," in *Wieviel Systematik erlaubt die Schrift? Auf der Suche nach einer gesamtbiblischen Theologie* (hrsg. von Frank-Lothar Hossfeld; QD 185; Freiburg: Herder 2001), 139–40 u. ö.

55. A.a.O., 134, vgl. 129–34 und 139–44 und Waschke, "Zur Frage einer alttestamentlichen Theologie," 263–5.

56. Zenger, "Heilige Schrift der Juden und Christen," 19–20.

57. Zum Verfahren dieses "Zusammen-Denkens" s. Magne Saebø, "Vom 'Zusammen-Denken' zum Kanon: Aspekte der traditionsgeschichtlichen Endstadien des Alten Testaments," in *Zum Problem des biblischen Kanons* (hrsg. von Ingo Baldermann u.a.; Jahrbuch für biblische Theologie 3; Neukirchen-Vluyn: Neukirchener, 1988): 121–28, vgl. auch Janowski, "Theologie des Alten Testaments: Plädoyer für eine integrative Perspektive," 344–48.

58. Vgl. Waschke, "Zur Frage einer alttestamentlichen Theologie," 261.

59. S. dazu auch Michael Welker, "Sola Scriptura? The Authority of the Bible in Pluralistic Environments," in *A God So Near: Essays on Old Testament Theology in Honor of Patrick D. Miller* (ed. Brent A. Strawn and Nancy R. Bowen: Winona Lake, Ind.: Eisenbrauns, 2003), 375–91.

Methodik und normativem Anspruch spielt auch im Kontext des jüdisch-christlichen Dialogs eine Rolle, nicht nur weil die Frage nach der "Mitte" des Alten Testaments als eine spezifisch christliche Angelegenheit angesehen wird,[60] sondern weil auch die gesamtbiblische Perspektive den "Keim des Antijudaismus"[61] in sich trage und deshalb für den jüdisch-christlichen Dialog ungeeignet sei. Die Tatsache aber, daß die "Bibel Israels" als Altes Testament die *gemeinsame* Heilige Schrift von Juden und Christen ist, auf die sich beide Glaubensgemeinschaften *unterschiedlich* beziehen, ohne sich gegenseitig zu vereinnahmen, gibt jenseits ideologischer Engführungen hüben wie drüben Anlaß zur Hoffnung.

Trotz dieser offenen Fragen, die sich vermehren ließen, dürfte Einigkeit darüber bestehen, daß, wer sich zu Grundfragen einer Biblischen Theologie äußert, die Absicht verfolgt, zur Identitätsfindung des christlichen Glaubens beizutragen. Die doppelte Aufgabe, unsere Identität als Christen nicht unter Absehung von der Juden und Christen gemeinsamen Bibel Israels (Tanach/Altes Testament) definieren zu können und gleichzeitig die Einheit der Schrift (Altes und Neues Testament) wahren und verantworten zu sollen, gehört zu der zentralen Zukunftsaufgabe aller theologischen Disziplinen. Denn:

> Die mannigfach miteinander verbundenen und zugleich vielfach latent miteinander verflochtenen biblischen Überlieferungen bilden ein Gefüge, das die Wahrnehmung des Wirkens Gottes unter den Menschen, die lebendige Erinnerung daran und die Erwartung dieses Wirkens lenkt und das geschichtliche, kulturelle und kirchliche Lernen und Wachsen in der Erkenntnis ermöglicht.[62]

Darin also, so können wir unsere Skizze beschließen, erweist sich die Selbstreferenz der Schrift als eines lebendigen Ganzen, daß sie in vielperspektivischer Weise auf das göttliche Handeln an und in der Schöpfung verweist, durch das sie selbst zu einer lebendigen Quelle für die Gegenwart wird.

Abstract

This chapter addresses the contemporary task of biblical theology, its challenges and its difficulties, by contextualizing the discussion in both the history of the discipline and its conceptual parameters. The current controversy in determining the discipline's task stems from the twofold meaning of the term "biblical theology." If taken as a description of the theology contained in the Bible (to use Gerhard Ebeling's renowned distinction), then biblical theol-

---

60. S. dazu die Beiträge in Janowski und Lohfink (Hrsg.), *Religionsgeschichte Israels oder Theologie des Alten Testaments?*, ferner Bernd Janowski, "Die 'Kleine Biblia': Zur Bedeutung der Psalmen für eine Theologie des Alten Testaments" (1998), in *Die rettende Gerechtigkeit: Beiträge zur Theologie des Alten Testaments*, Bd. 2 (Neukirchen-Vluyn: Neukirchener, 1999), 141–44.

61. So die Kritik von Levenson, "Warum Juden sich nicht für die Biblische Theologie interessieren," 402–30 u. a., s. dazu Janowski, "Der eine Gott der beiden Testamente," 251–55 und 273–81.

62. Welker, "Biblische Theologie II," 1552.

ogy is deemed a historical discipline; if taken as a construction of a theology that is adequate to the Bible, then biblical theology is considered a normative discipline. Biblical theology's dual descriptive-prescriptive focus is also set by the origins of the discipline. The field took shape in the seventeenth century in order to respond to the growing rift between the emerging historical-critical study of the Bible and dogmatic theology. It was Johann Philipp Gabler who carved a distinct space for biblical theology as the historical study of religious ideas articulated by biblical authors and dogmatic theology as the study of eternal religious truths contained in the Bible.

Subsequent history of the discipline contends with the relation between both poles, either as the relation between the genesis of diverse biblical texts and scripture's normative claims, or as the relation between the plurality of historical expressions and the conceptual unity of the canon. For example, the challenge of the field's contemporary shape is to integrate the history of religions approach with theological inquiry (i.e., the history of Israel with the theology of the Hebrew Bible/Old Testament). Such a fit can be obtained by virtue of the concrete experience of history that provides a common subject matter relating the different parts (*Sachzusammenhang*).

The main problem addressed by the current discussion, from a Christian perspective, concerns the unity of the Christian Bible that is divided into two testaments. Once again, the theological question must be tailored to historical evidence. According to one proposal, the canonical approach (Brevard S. Childs), the historical trajectory of canonization culminates in a normative end-form of the biblical text. Other examples, such as the determination of a "center" (*Mitte*) of scripture or of a tradition history of particular theological concepts, show the relation between experiential diversity and its "contrastive unity." The reality witnessed by different texts can be theologically understood as God's saving activity that, according to Christian self-understanding, is oriented to the eschatological work of God in Christ.

Biblical theology addresses the question concerning reality in view of its historical focus and a presupposed text–subject matter distinction. The diversity of discourses recorded in the biblical texts has intentionality; the texts articulate experiences of the transcendent that are themselves historically and culturally conditioned. Furthermore, the canonical selection of and redacted commentary on texts ensure a canonical coherence based on canonical closure, yet open the canon to new meanings created under new conditions of understanding. For example, Jewish-Christian dialogue on biblical theology has the same text basis in view, yet studies the text from different interpretative conditions. Thus, history, context, and reality are elements molding the form that biblical theology takes today.

New Garments for Biblical Joseph
Maren R. Niehoff

Joseph is dressed and undressed at highly significant points in the biblical story. Each garment conveys a particular view of this opaque character, which the narrator introduces as a new and sometimes rather controversial perspective. In his youth, Joseph is dressed in the famous "colorful coat" that he received from his father as a sign of his special affection.[1] His brothers did not accept this view of him as the preferred son, "stripped him of his coat, the colorful coat which he wore" (Gen 37:23), and sold him into slavery. Next, Potiphar's wife "caught him by his garment" when trying to seduce him, and subsequently showed this same garment, which he had left behind on his flight, to her household as evidence of his attempt to rape her (Gen 39:12–15). Joseph's garment thus plays a crucial role in the complicated question of his guilt and complicity to the lady's plans. Ironically, even when taken off, it hides more than it discloses. More respectful clothes are put on Joseph in Pharaoh's environment. Initially, he "changed his clothes" when called from prison to interpret Pharaoh's dreams (Gen 41:14). This change is obviously made in formal anticipation of Joseph's appearance before Pharaoh. Yet it also indicates a deeper change of perspective: while the chief butler had hitherto forgotten Joseph, he suddenly remembered his oneirocritical services in prison and recommended him as a distinguished dream interpreter to Pharaoh.[2] Finally, Joseph receives "garments of fine linen" as a sign of his new authority over Egypt (Gen 41:42). Once more, these clothes not only suggest status, but also express Pharaoh's view of Joseph as the man "in whom there is the spirit of God" (Gen 41:38).

Ancient interpreters continued to be intrigued by Joseph's character and wove for him ever new garments. Each dress that this biblical figure was made to wear expresses something of the worldview of the interpreter and his cultural background. Joseph thus changed garments in accordance with each new environment in which he made his appearance and quickly established himself. The different midrashim on biblical Joseph provide an excellent opportunity to investigate the long-debated

---

1. Gen 37:3; the masoretic expression כתגת פסים is, of course, rather vague, but I am following here the Septuagintal interpretation (χιτῶνα ποικίλον), on which Philo relied in his allegorical commentary on the story.
2. Gen 40:23; 41:9–14.

question of how exegesis and history are wreathed together. This is especially so, because the Joseph story addresses concrete issues of family life, love, and a career in the Diaspora. Ancient interpreters were thus called to treat issues of intense personal and often political consequence. By examining Joseph's new garments in the midrash, I shall address classic questions that have been raised by generations of scholars: to ask with Joseph Heinemann whether and to what extent exegesis actually reflects contemporary events; to inquire with Abraham Geiger whether current affairs have influenced the exegete to such an extent that he used scripture merely as a pretext to promote his own agenda; and to investigate with Daniel Boyarin which values of the time may inadvertently have shaped the understanding of the text in a particular historical and social setting.[3] Assuming with these scholars as well as with modern theorists of hermeneutics that the process of reading cannot be isolated from the reader's own experience, the crux really is how active and conscious a part each exegete played. Were his views in reality determined by history and his references to specific events nothing but unavoidable signs of his situatedness in a particular historical context? Or rather, did he use scripture to shape the reality of his time and promote his own agenda?

Joseph engaged the imagination of the Jews during the Second Temple period to an unusual extent and inspired a large amount of exegetical treatises. His story was read over and over again, each time interpreted from a different angle. Jews living abroad, especially in Hellenistic Egypt, identified with him and liked to give their sons the name of this biblical hero.[4] For the purposes of this essay, I have chosen to focus on two exegetes, namely Philo and Josephus, the main representatives of Hellenistic Judaism.[5] Their exegetical activities can be placed into a rather well-known historical context. While both lived in world centers of Greco-Roman culture and published their interpretations of scripture in Greek, the lingua franca of their time, they significantly differed from each other in matters of background, style, and motivation.[6] While Philo flourished at the beginning of the first century

---

3. Joseph Heinemann, *Aggadah and Its Development* (Jerusalem: Hebrew University Press, 1979); Abraham Geiger, "Das Verhältnis des natürlichen Schriftsinnes zur thalmudischen Schriftdeutung," *Wissenschaftliche Zeitschrift für Jüdische Theologie* 5 (1844): 53–81; Daniel Boyarin, *Intertextuality and the Reading of Midrash* (Bloomington: Indiana University Press, 1990).

4. Sylvie Honigman, "The Birth of a Diaspora: The Emergence of a Jewish Self-Definition in Ptolemaic Egypt in the Light of Onomastics," in *Diasporas in Antiquity* (ed. Shaye J. D. Cohen and Ernest S. Frerichs; Atlanta: Scholars Press, 1993), 93–127.

5. I do by no means imply that Hellenistic Judaism was a uniform phenomenon, Philo and Josephus representing the essence of that homogenous entity. Instead, the different outlooks and political parties can be identified among Greek-speaking Jews. Philo and Josephus must be considered the main representatives of Hellenistic Judaism in both a qualitative and quantitative sense: their extant work is larger than that of others, even if we take into account the fact that many works have been lost; and, more important, their work was of a particularly high quality and influence.

6. The Roman factor has increasingly been emphasized with regard to both Josephus and Philo. See Martin D. Goodman, "The Roman Identity of Roman Jews," in *The Jews in the Hellenistic-Roman World*:

in Alexandria, the city of his childhood, Josephus composed his works toward the end of that century in Rome, where he had moved in a highly controversial step during the Great Revolt. While both immersed themselves in Hellenistic culture, Philo did so to a considerably greater extent. Greek was his mother tongue, Hebrew a language he hardly knew. He had access to scripture through the Septuagint, which he considered identical to the original.[7] Josephus, by contrast, grew up in Palestine, reading the Bible in the original and adding a Greek education at a somewhat later stage.[8] Josephus was, of course, primarily a historian who celebrated the past of his people, covering within this framework also the biblical period. He himself proudly claimed that he actually "translated" scripture into Greek, "neither adding nor omitting anything."[9] It is no secret that Josephus did not keep his promise and, instead, creatively rewrote the biblical text like many of his contemporaries. Philo, on the other hand, was primarily an interpreter of scripture. Most of his literary efforts were devoted to understanding and explaining this text, which he conceptualized for the first time as an emanation of the divine Logos.[10] He became famous for his allegorical exegesis, which he presented alongside the literal meaning, thus adding a distinctly philosophical dimension to scripture.

Both Philo and Josephus took a special interest in the figure of Joseph, whose life touched issues close to their own heart. Joseph was known for his quarrels with his brothers and his successful career in Egypt. He aroused the interest of Philo, who lived in the same country and was counted among its leading figures, as well as of Josephus, who moved to Rome during the Great Revolt and quickly integrated into the elite, while remaining controversial among many Jews back home. It is now for us to investigate how each of them translated their interest in Joseph's character into innovative midrash of the biblical story and wove a new garment for the hero.

Studies in the Memory of Menahem Stern (ed. Isahia M. Gafni et al.; Jerusalem: Magnes Press, 1996), 85–99; Maren R. Niehoff, *Philo on Jewish Identity and Culture* (TSAJ 86; Tübingen: Mohr Siebeck, 2001).

7. *Mos.* 237–40; see also Jean-George Kahn, "Did Philo Know Hebrew? The Testimony of the Etymologies," *Tarbiz* 34 (1965): 337–45; contra Harry A. Wolfson, *Philo: Foundations of Religious Philosophy in Judaism, Christianity, and Islam* (Cambridge: Harvard University Press, 1947), 1:88–90.

8. At the age of 26 (64 C.E.), Josephus was selected for a political mission to Rome—a fact which testifies not only to his aristocratic family background, but also to his familiarity with Greek language and culture.

9. *A.J.* 1.17; οὐδὲν προσθεὶς οὐδ' αὖ παραλιπών. Josephus compared his effort to that of the LXX (*A.J.* 1.10–13); see also Louis H. Feldman, *Josephus's Interpretation of the Bible* (Hellenistic Culture and Society 27; Berkeley: University of California Press, 1998), 14–23, 37–46.

10. Regarding Philo's notion of scripture and language, see Niehoff, *Philo on Jewish Identity and Culture*, 187–209.

1. Joseph in Philonic Dress

An unusual feature of Philo's interpretation has engaged generations of scholars: Philo praises Joseph in the biography as an ideal statesman, while exposing him to sharp criticism in other, more scattered contexts. Some scholars have simply acknowledged the contradiction, whereas others wished to show that the tension between the two approaches exists only on the surface.[11] Jacques Cazeaux has recently pointed to the different geographical contexts in which Philo's interpretations must be appreciated. Cazeaux argues that Joseph receives positive treatment in *De Iosepho* because he is depicted here in an Egyptian context and favorably compared to the infamously low values of that country. In *De Somniis*, on the other hand, Joseph is measured by the elevated standards of the land of Israel and thus appears far less impressive.[12] Cazeaux's insights are important, especially in our present context, because he has contextualized Philo's interpretation of Joseph, pointing to a tension between Jewish and Egyptian culture as a significant background. This approach is highly promising and deserves further elaboration. I shall indeed suggest that both of Philo's interpretations of Joseph are closely linked to the way he perceived Jewish life in Egypt. Both of Philo's interpretations of Joseph address a Jewish audience and deal with the subject of Jewish acculturation in Egypt.

A key text to Philo's approach in *De Iosepho* is his interpretation of LXX Gen 45:28: "Israel then said: There is great (joy) for me, if Joseph my son is still alive. Going (down to Egypt) I shall see him before I die." This verse depicts Jacob as a warm and loving father, who is concerned about his son's survival despite previous "evidence" to the contrary. Nothing except his great joy is on his mind when anticipating his encounter with Joseph. Not so Philo, who is deeply worried about Joseph's stay in Egypt and attributes the following concerns to Jacob:

> But his joy immediately generated fear in his heart about the prospect (of Joseph) changing his ancestral habits (περὶ τῆς τῶν πατρίων ἐκδιαιτήσεως). For he knew that a youth by nature tends to slip and that living abroad gives license to committing sins, and especially in Egypt, a land blind to the true God, because of her turning generated and mortal things into gods. And besides, he knew the attacks wealth and renown make on minds of small understanding, and moreover left alone, without anyone from his father's house having gone out together with him and chastising him, being alone and bereft of good teachers, he (Joseph) will

---

11. See Erich S. Gruen, *Heritage and Hellenism: The Reinvention of Jewish Tradition* (Hellenistic Culture and Society 30; Berkeley: University of California Press, 1998), 81–87; Jouette Bassler, "Philo on Joseph: The Basic Coherence of *De Jospeho* and *De Somniis* II," *JSJ* 16, no. 2 (1985): 240–55.

12. Jacques Cazeaux, "Nul N'est Prophète en Son Pays: Contribution à l'Étude de Joseph d'Après Philon," in *The School of Moses: Studies in Philo and Hellenistic Religion. In Memory of Horst Moehring* (BJS 304; Atlanta: Scholars Press, 1995), 61–66.

be prepared for a change towards alien customs (ἕτοιμος ἔσται πρὸς τὴν τῶν ὀθνείων μεταβολήν). (*Ios.* 254)[13]

Philo suggests in this passage that Joseph is confronted in Egypt with a culture totally different from his own. Two mutually exclusive worlds clash with each other: on one side of an existential divide are the "ancestral habits" of the Jews and, on the other, the ways of the Egyptians who are blind to the true God and "turn generated and mortal things into gods." Given this dichotomy, the question naturally arises whether Joseph has proven sufficiently strong to withstand the prolonged seduction of the other culture. Did he remain loyal to his upbringing even though he had been isolated in a foreign environment? Philo's Jacob, who recognizes the difficulty, can thus not indulge in pure joy at the prospect of meeting his son. He instead worries that Joseph may have adopted Egyptian customs and died a spiritual death, which would in some sense be equal to his physical decease.

By introducing a deep cultural conflict into the Joseph story, Philo has adapted it to a central theme of his entire work, namely the contrast between the Jews and Mosaic law, on the one hand, and Egypt and her materialism, on the other. Egypt in fact served as Philo's ultimate Other against which he constructed Jewish identity.[14] Philo never grew tired of complaining about Egypt's weaknesses and shortcomings. These, he explained, have derived from the special geographical conditions of Egypt and are thus innate qualities which can hardly be changed. Unlike all other countries, Egypt is famous for being flooded in the summer by the Nile, which rises at a time when every other river dries out. In this way, Egypt is guaranteed exceptional fecundity. In Philo's opinion, this geographical situation, which at first sight appears to be a great blessing, has in reality serious consequences. Since the Egyptians receive their life-giving water not from heaven, as is natural, but from the earth, they are used to looking down at the sources of their sustenance and have become oblivious to its divine origin. Instead of acknowledging the true God as provider of rain and all other water, they worship the earth and fall prey to utter materialism. The natural flooding of the Nile in the heat of the summer moreover exempts the Egyptians from hard agricultural work and enables them to spend their time in pleasure hunting (*Mos.* 2.194–195). The religion of the Egyptians developed accordingly: their materialism has degenerated to such an extent that they worship

---

13. Leopold Cohn and Paul Wendland, eds., *Philonis Alexandrini Opera Quae Supersunt* (7 vols.; Berlin: G. Reimer, 1962), vol. 4. The translations are my own, taking into account both the English translation by Francis H. Colson and G. H. Whitaker, *Philo with an English Translation* (Cambridge: Harvard University Press, 1984), vol. 6, and the Hebrew translation by Suzanne Daniel-Nataf, *Philo of Alexandria: Writings* (4 vols.; Jerusalem: Bialik Institute, 1991), vol. 2.

14. See also Niehoff, *Philo on Jewish Identity and Culture*, 45–74; Sarah Pearce, "Belonging and Not Belonging: Local Perspectives in Philo of Alexandria," in *Jewish Local Patriotism and Self-Identification in the Graeco-Roman Period* (ed. Sian Jones and Sarah Pearce; JSPSup 31; Sheffield: Sheffield Academic Press, 1998), 79–105.

even animals (*Fug.* 180). Philo emphasizes that this worship does not at all conform to the standards of true religion. The Egyptians, rather, engage in the worst and most ridiculous kind of idolatry. On one occasion, Philo enlists support for his disdain of these customs from unexpected quarters:

> What then could be more ridiculous (than this zoolatry)? Indeed strangers upon their first arrival in Egypt, before the blindness of the country has found a lodging in their minds, die of laughter. (*Decal.* 80)

Any civilized tourist to Egypt, Philo asserts, will feel precisely as he does about Egyptian zoolatry. A famous foreigner who had on his first visit to Egypt expressed the kind of scorn Philo expects, was Augustus. According to Dio, Augustus refused to "enter the presence of Apis . . . declaring that he was accustomed to worship gods, not cattle" (Dio, 51.16.5). Augustus uttered this famous statement after his decisive victory over Antony at Actium, which enabled him to conquer Egypt, transform her into a Roman province, and assume nearly unlimited power in Rome. Did Philo in his above polemic against Egyptian zoolatry have this momentous event in mind? Unlikely. He would certainly have been more specific so that his readers could be trusted to recognize the reference. Philo moreover speaks of strangers in the plural and thus clearly thinks of a general attitude found in any civilized person visiting Egypt.

Philo's comment nevertheless points to a significant historical reality. His confidence about contemporary scorn of Egyptian zoolatry is not mistaken. During Philo's lifetime, Egypt did not enjoy a particularly good reputation.[15] This was so because Augustus' rhetoric and politics had been exceptionally successful and had left a lasting impression on Greco-Roman culture. Already during his struggle for supremacy in Rome, Augustus developed a sharp rhetoric against the Egyptians in order to win popular support.[16] He made special efforts to present the civil war as a clash between Rome and Egypt. Official war had not been declared against his rival Antony, but the latter's staunch supporter, the Egyptian queen, Cleopatra.[17] Antony himself was presented as a renegade to the Egyptian side, who "abandoned all his ancestors' habits of life," while "emulating all alien and barbaric customs" (Dio, 50.25.3). Augustus concluded his famous speech against Antony with a fervent appeal to his audience: "therefore let no one count him a Roman but rather an

---

15. See especially John P. V. D. Balsdon, *Romans and Aliens* (Chapel Hill: University of North Carolina Press, 1979), 68–69; Joseph G. Milne, "Greek and Roman Tourists in Ancient Egypt," *JEA* 3 (1916): 76–80; Klaas A. D. Smelik and Emily A. Helerijk, "'Who Knows Not What Monsters Demented Egypt Worships?' Opinions on Egyptian Animal Worship in Antiquity as Part of the Ancient Conception of Egypt," *ANRW* (1984), II 17/4:1938–45.

16. See also Kenneth Scott, "The Political Propaganda of 44–30 B.C.," *Memoirs of the American Academy in Rome* 11 (1933): 35–49.

17. See also Meyer Reinhold, "The Declaration of War against Cleopatra," *CJ* 77 (1981–82): 97–103.

Egyptian" (Dio, 50.27.1). This diametrical opposition between "us" and the Egyptians quickly became part of the discourse in many intellectual circles in Rome. Egyptians and their culture came to be criticized, even though they had thus far enjoyed a rather high prestige. Herodotus, for example, had recognized Egypt as an ancient culture that made a substantial contribution even to Greek civilization.[18] Roman intellectuals, by contrast, tended to vex at Egyptian vice, ridiculing her zoolatry and complaining about the incestuous, unstable, and faithless nature of this country, which was, in their opinion, always bound to revolt against her Roman overlords.[19]

Such views also spread to the province of Egypt and enjoyed institutional reinforcement there. The capital Alexandria, which had since its foundation by Alexander the Great been a center of Greco-Egyptian culture, now became a Greco-Roman city whose inhabitants rather consciously distanced themselves from their Egyptian roots. Alexandria was regarded as distinct to the extent that she was spoken of as being situated "by" rather than "in" Egypt. The dichotomy between the Egyptian countryside and the Hellenistic metropolis was strengthened by the new Roman tax system. Immediately after his conquest of Egypt, Augustus imposed a harsh regime upon the province. While the Ptolemies had tolerated and even encouraged a mixing of cultures and ethnicities, the Romans observed a strict segregation of ethnic groups, with each group belonging to a different social class and being taxed at different rates. Lowest on the Roman scale were the Egyptians, who were charged a heavy poll tax (*laographia*).[20]

Given this historical context, it is not at all surprising that Philo looked down on the Egyptians and viewed Joseph's prolonged sojourn in their country as a cultural challenge. It is indeed striking how much his statements suit the discourse of the contemporary elite. Does this, however, imply that his writings simply reflect the spirit of his time? Was Philo so much a part of his culture and historical setting that he could not avoid vexing at the Egyptians? Philo's interpretation of Joseph in Egypt is certainly highly relevant to his time, yet it seems that Philo was not merely a receptacle of contemporary values. General attitudes did not automatically impose themselves, perhaps even without his conscious acknowledgement. The picture is rather more complex. While Philo was undoubtedly influenced by contemporary stereotypes of the Egyptians, he also used them in a highly creative manner. By inscribing the Joseph story into the larger context of a cultural clash between the

---

18. Francois Hartog, *The Mirror of Herodotus: The Representation of the Other in the Writing of History* (Berkeley: University of California Press, 1988), 212–24; Paul Cartledge, *The Greeks: A Portrait of Self and Others* (Oxford: Oxford University Press, 1993), 38, 58–59.

19. Strabo, *Georg.* 17.801; Cicero, *Tusc.* 5.78; *Nat. deo.* 1.43, 81–82, 101, 3.39; Tacitus, *Hist.* 1.11; Juvenal, *Sat.* 15.44–46; Seneca, *Helv.* 19.6; Cicero, *Rab. Post.* 34–35; see also M. Reinhold, "Roman Attitudes towards the Egyptians," *Ancient World* 3, nos. 3–4 (1980): 97–103.

20. See especially Alan K. Bowman, "Egypt," in *The Augustan Empire, 43 B.C.–A.D. 69* (ed. A. K. Bowman et al.; 2nd ed.; Cambridge Ancient History 10; Cambridge: Cambridge University Press, 1996), 676–702.

primitive and idolatrous Egyptians and the civilized Jews, he in fact pursued important topical aims. He thus constructed an ideal picture of Jewish life in Egypt. The behavior of this Israelite forefather, and especially his segregation from Egyptian culture, was exemplary in Philo's eyes. When visited by his father, Joseph was found to have remained loyal to his ancestral customs. To Jacob's relief, Joseph had not assimilated to the ridiculous ways of the Egyptians, but still preferred genuine riches to the spurious (*Ios.* 258). Philo moreover has Joseph confirm the integrity of his character by saying to his brothers: "I do not change my way of life with the change of times" (*Ios.* 263). By rewriting scripture and thus the Jewish past in Egypt, Philo is making an important statement about Jewish identity in this country. He asserts that "we" have always belonged to the civilized side of an essential divide, which is recognized nowadays by any cultured person. The Jews have from ancient times onward rejected Egyptian values, which are now also despised by the Romans. The antagonism between "us" Jews and the Other Egyptians indeed parallels the dichotomy that Augustus had constructed between authentic Romans like himself and Egyptians like Cleopatra and Antony. In Philo's exegesis, the first Jew, who had come to settle in Egypt, emerges as a defender of the same values as contemporary Romans. This shows not only that Philo necessarily understood Joseph in the terms of his own time, but also that he wished to situate the ancestor of Egyptian Jewry at the top of contemporary values, society, and culture. Jews have, in other words, always belonged to the elite.

Joseph's famous rejection of Potiphar's wife provided Philo with another welcome opportunity to explain his views on the dichotomy between Mosaic and Egyptian values. He was in fact the first interpreter who reconstructed this incident as a paradigmatic refusal of Egyptian culture. Others, such as the author of the *Book of Jubilees*, had identified adultery as the main issue, while the author of the *Testaments of the Twelve Patriarchs* was shocked by the woman's shamelessness and idolatry. Philo's interpretation, by contrast, highlights the confrontation between Egyptian and Jewish values. Potiphar's wife now comes to personify Egyptian licentiousness and vice, while Joseph represents Jewish virtue. Biblical Joseph's concerns for moral and religious righteousness (Gen 39:8–9) are consequently dressed in new garments:

> Yet he proved more powerful than this stroke of bad luck and burst into speech, saying words worthy of free men and his race: What are you forcing me to? We, the descendents of the Hebrews, live under special customs and laws. Among others it is allowed, from the age of fourteen onwards, to be freely intimate with harlots and prostitutes and those who make profit from their bodies, while among us a courtesan is not allowed to live, but the death penalty is appointed for the woman who plies this trade. Before the lawful union we do not know intercourse with other women, but come as chaste men to chaste virgins, seeking as the fulfillment of wedlock not pleasure, but the begetting of lawful children. To this day I have remained pure and shall not begin transgressing against the law by committing adultery, the

greatest of crimes. Even if I had in former times departed from my accustomed manner of life and been drawn by the impulses of youth and had been emulating the softness of this land, I ought nevertheless not make the wedded life of another my prey. (*Ios.* 42–44)

In this passage, Philo attributes to Joseph words "worthy of his race," which highlight his commitment to the special laws of the Hebrews. He dwells here on the severity of Mosaic customs in sexual matters. His Joseph proudly explains to the amorous woman that he did not fall prey to the "luxury of this land," but awaits a lawful union, which will result in lawful offspring. Pleasure is not on his mind, neither in relation to Potiphar's wife nor in relation to other women. Philo apparently took the above-mentioned prohibition of prostitution from the Septuagint, which renders the biblical expression קדשה, temple prostitute, as πόρνη, harlot in general (Deut 23:18). Yet the death penalty which Philo envisioned for this trade is nowhere attested in either biblical or postbiblical Jewish writings.[21] His position was, therefore, exceptionally stringent. It corroborates his general understanding of Mosaic law, which is in his view spiritually so demanding that it has isolated the Jews among the nations (*Spec.* 4.179). Philo indeed believed that *enkrateia* was the essence of Mosaic law, which was, in his opinion, mainly designed to inculcate a particularly high degree of self-restraint. Parallel to many other Hellenistic thinkers, Philo considered *enkrateia* as a broad category relating to sexuality, food, and speech.[22] Jews, he argued, distinguish themselves in all of these fields, being especially modest in matters of sexuality. In contrast to the Egyptians, for example, siblings may not marry each other (*Spec.* 3.23–24).

It is conspicuous that Philo's Joseph has a low opinion of Egyptian morality. He tells Potiphar's wife that even "if I had until now departed from my accustomed manner of life and . . . been emulating the softness of this land, I ought nevertheless not make the wedded life of another my prey" (*Ios.* 44). The softness and ethical laxity of Egypt are once more contrasted with the severity of Mosaic law. By preserving his chastity, Joseph has proven himself to be not only morally superior, but also a stranger to the land of the Nile. He has remained a true Jew, while rejecting Egypt.

Philo's interpretation of Joseph's chastity in an anti-Egyptian vein also seems to be anchored in the circumstances of his life. His notion of Jewish *enkrateia* was somewhat antagonistic to the more permissive environment of daily life in Greco-Roman Egypt. In contrast to classical Athens, women had been given here a more active and visible part in public life. Women were often dominant in the local Isis

---

21. See also Louis M. Epstein, *Sex Laws and Customs in Judaism* (New York: Ktav, 1967), 152–57, 164–67; Samuel Belkin, *Philo and the Oral Law: The Philonic Interpretation of Biblical Law in Relation to the Palestinian Halakah* (Cambridge: Harvard University Press, 1940), 161–256.

22. See especially *Spec.* 2:195; 3:9–10; 1:163; Michel Foucault, *The History of Sexuality*, vol. 2: *The Use of Pleasure* (trans. Robert Hurley; London: Penguin Books, 1985), 63–77.

cult and enjoyed some degree of sexual license during religious festivals.²³ Philo's distance from contemporary culture becomes understandable in light of contemporary Roman attitudes. Many Romans thought of Egypt as dangerously licentious and corrupt. As we saw above, many Romans—whether intellectuals or not—had been horrified by Cleopatra's feminine allurements. Antony's coalition with her had been condemned in the strongest terms as surrender to her sexuality. Egypt as a whole came to be seen as so licentious that Seneca the Younger, when praising his aunt, the wife of a Roman governor in Egypt, insisted that she "had never been seen in public [and] . . . never admitted a native to her house" (*Helv.* 19.6). It is precisely into this Roman discourse of seclusion from licentious Egyptians into which Philo inscribes his hero Joseph. By distancing himself from the sexual laxity of this country, Philo's Joseph strikingly conforms to the ideals of the Roman ruling class in the province of Egypt. This class too is anxious not to be infected with Egyptian daintiness. Philo thus suggests once more a close proximity between Jews and Romans, encouraging his fellow Jews to align themselves with the leaders of the world against barbaric Egypt.

Joseph's career in Egypt is characterized in Philo's biography by both greatest success and personal aloofness from the local culture. It is initially remarkable that Philo does not limit Joseph's promotion to the status of viceroy, but insists that "if the truth be said, [the king] left for himself only the name of rule, while in reality rendering to him the chief command and doing everything else that might give the young man honor" (*Ios.* 119). This embellishment of Gen 41:40, which the Septuagint had still rendered literally, obviously adds power and prestige to Joseph. Philo's ideal statesman has actually reached the very top. God, when addressing Jacob, explicitly says so and simply speaks of Joseph as the χώρας τοσαύτης ἡγεμών (*Ios.* 255). Another Egyptian Jew subsequently highlighted the importance of the biblical Joseph without even showing Philo's initial scruples: the author of the Wisdom of Solomon straightaway claims that Wisdom "brought him the scepter of royalty and the authority over his masters."²⁴ Obviously, both writers as well as another Egyptian Jew, namely Philo the Epic Poet, were extremely proud of their forefather who had reached such an influential position in the land of their own residence.²⁵

If Philo had earlier stressed Joseph's alienation from Egypt, how does he now view his interactions with the Egyptians? As the actual ruler of the country, Joseph could hardly avoid contact with its population and culture. Philo is initially con-

---

23. See Isaak Heinemann, *Philons griechische und jüdische Bildung: Kulturvergleichende Untersuchungen zu Philons Darstellung der jüdischen Gesetze* (Breslau: M. und H. Marcus, 1932), 232–35; Sarah B. Pomeroy, *Women in Hellenistic Egypt: From Alexander to Cleopatra* (New York: Schocken, 1984), 13–28, 60–70; Dominic Montserrat, *Sex and Society in Graeco-Roman Egypt* (London: Kegan Paul International, 1996), 83, 163–79.
24. Wis 10:14: ἤνεγκεν αὐτῷ σκῆπτρα βασιλείας καὶ ἐξουσίαν τυραννούντων αὐτοῦ.
25. See Carl R. Holladay, comp. and trans., *Fragments from Hellenistic Jewish Authors* (4 vols.; Chico, Calif.: Scholars Press, 1989), 2:205–99; Gruen, *Hellenism and Heritage*, 80.

cerned to show that the relations between Joseph and the Egyptians were good, the Egyptians showing respect for Joseph and his family. Philo eagerly asserts that his forefathers had not only been tolerated in the country of his own residence, but had enjoyed high esteem. When Joseph, for example, upon appointment as viceroy visits the different parts of the country, Philo adds to the biblical account (Gen 41:46) that Joseph aroused sympathy among his subordinates because of his personal charm and the benefits he offered them (*Ios.* 157). Toward the end of the biography, Philo stresses in summary fashion that Joseph "was honored by them all" (*Ios.* 267). Pharaoh is moreover said to "honor him as a father" (*Ios.* 242). As a token of Pharaonic sympathy, Joseph's family is given the most fertile part of Egypt to settle in (*Ios.* 251, 257). Equally significant in this respect is Philo's total omission of the biblical reference that the Egyptians could not share bread with the Hebrews "because that is an abomination to the Egyptians."[26] Skipping this information, Philo instead constructs a picture of the Egyptian guests who express respect and gratitude to Joseph. Two Egyptian dignitaries who joined Joseph's welcome party for his brothers praise Joseph for his important contributions to their country:

> It is possible, you know, . . . that the lifestyle of this country was in former times less civilized, and since this man was appointed over state affairs, he introduced good order not only to the important matters, which produce success in peace and war, but in those which are considered less worthy and belong mostly to the lighter side of life. (*Ios.* 204)

Philo's Egyptian dignitaries acknowledge here the importance of Joseph's contribution to the government of their country and its culture. He is said to have introduced "good order" and to have raised the level of civilization. Joseph's office thus emerges as a significant turning point in the history of Egypt. Given the rather general nature of Philo's language, it is intriguing to speculate precisely which achievements his Egyptian dignitaries may have had in mind. The expression "important matters which produce success in peace and war" probably refers to Joseph's management of the famine for which he became famous even beyond the borders of Egypt (*Ios.* 259, 268). The Egyptians moreover praise Joseph for introducing customs belonging to "the lighter side of life." This must be a reference to the festive meal in which they are presently participating. They had already noted with satisfaction that their Hebrew host, like themselves, determines the seating order by the participants' age (*Ios.* 203). During the course of the meal, they, furthermore, become deeply impressed by the meal's modesty. As they put it, Joseph "had turned his back on the odious practice of tasteless display" (*Ios.* 205). Taking into account the prevailing hard conditions of the famine, he had limited expenses

---

26. LXX Gen 43:32: βδέλυγμα γάρ ἐστιν τοῖς Αἰγυπτίοις; Philo's paraphrase of Gen 43:32 without this detail can be found in *Ios.* 201.

and stressed the meal's spiritual aspects. Expressions of kind feeling, toasts, and good wishes thus made up for special culinary delights. Philo now adds a comment of his own, stressing that these were things

> which to liberal and refined minds give more pleasure than the food and drink which those who love to arrange meals and to dine have prepared—those who make a parade of things unworthy of serious attention with a display appropriate to small minds. (*Ios.* 206)

Philo elaborates here upon the Egyptian dignitaries' remark regarding the modesty of the meal. While they had praised Joseph for limiting expenses in times of famine, Philo now generalizes this approach, placing Joseph's modest symposion into the larger context of proper spiritual entertainment. The reader now learns that there are two kinds of meals corresponding to two completely different kinds of people. Liberal and refined minds engage in proper spiritual symposia, while small minds "make a parade of things unworthy of serious attention." This dichotomy characterizes Philo's discussion of the symposion in other places, too. He once harshly criticized the classic Platonic symposion as indulging in licentiousness, ostentation, and pederasty, while the proper symposion is celebrated by the Therapeutae (*Cont.* 58–74). Philo identifies the deteriorated, licentious meal as a characteristic of the Greeks and Greek culture with which he contrasts the superior Jewish customs. It is striking that both his criticism of "the" Greeks and his definition of "Us" correspond in this context closely to the contemporary Roman discourse about *pergraecari*.[27] Many Roman intellectuals were, like Philo, eager to distance themselves from the Greeks and to show that they had not completely succumbed to Greek allurements, but preserved austere dining traditions. The fact that Philo attributes the introduction of the proper symposion to Joseph is thus of great significance. It means that, in his view, an Israelite was responsible for a central aspect of Greco-Roman culture in Egypt. This culture was highly elitist, detached from the local Egyptians and superior to other deteriorated forms of Hellenistic civilization. It is through the figure of Joseph that Philo claims a specific aspect of contemporary life. By tracing the roots of the proper symposion to Joseph, he actually appropriates this cultural icon for his own Jewish heritage. It was in this niche of high Greco-Roman culture in Alexandria where he wanted the Jews, both ancient and contemporary, to feel at home. This was the table at which they should sit down and dine.

These impressions about Philo's midrash are confirmed by the striking fact that Philo does not attribute to Joseph any innovation of specifically Egyptian culture.

---

27. For more details on Roman attitudes to Greeks and Greek culture, see Erich Gruen, *Culture and National Identity in Republican Rome* (Ithaca, N.Y.: Cornell University Press, 1992), ch. 6; Benjamin Isaac, *The Invention of Racism in Classical Antiquity* (Princeton: Princeton University Press, 2004), 381–405.

The Israelite forefather is by no means responsible for the traditional and indigenous aspects of local life, remaining totally aloof from the culture of the Egyptian countryside that had, to some extent, also infiltrated the great metropolis. Philo's approach differs strikingly from that of his predecessor Artapanus, who probably lived in the countryside and enthusiastically supported Jewish-Egyptian symbiosis.[28] In the latter's midrash, Joseph was responsible precisely for classic Egyptian institutions: he divided the land of Egypt into nomes and allotted some arable land to the priests; and he even founded the temple in Athos and Heliopolis (Eusebius, *Praep. ev.* 9.23.2–4).

A totally different picture emerges from Philo's more scattered interpretations of Joseph in other books. Outside the idealizing biography, Joseph is accused of vainglory, opportunism, and licentiousness.[29] He is now said to have succumbed to external influences and to change his mind. He in fact personifies all the vices of a statesman who lacks true inner virtue and easily exchanges principles for personal profit. Perhaps the most striking aspect of these passages is the change of perspective from Joseph's point of view in the biography to the brothers' perspective elsewhere. While Philo in *De Iosepho* treats all events with a very sympathetic eye on Joseph and sees everything through his eyes, in *De Somniis* Philo strikingly identifies with Joseph's brothers. Radically changing the biblical facts, Philo even speaks of their reconciliation with him instead of his reconciliation with them. The reader will immediately ask which sins the brothers forgave Joseph. The biblical story may suggest that they forgave him the provocative behavior of his youth when guarding the flock and announcing his dreams. Not so in Philo's interpretation. Here Joseph's sin is no longer personal arrogance in the family, but assimilation to the ways of Egypt. He is accused of adopting the Egyptian vices of vainglory and licentiousness, thus abandoning his father's customs. The brothers could forgive Joseph only after he had repented and rejected Egypt. Philo explains Joseph's assimilation and subsequent return to Jewish tradition in the following dramatic terms:

> But whenever he changes his life for the better and no longer indulges in visions, nor suffers ill by crawling like a worm after the empty fantasies of vainglory, nor deals with dreams by night and darkness about obscure and unknown deeds; and whenever he remains awake after having risen from deep sleep and accepts brightness before obscurity, truth before false assumption, and day before night, and light before darkness, and when the wife of the Egyptian, namely bodily pleasure, who had summoned him to come in and enjoy intimacy with her, he rejects out of a yearning for continence and an indescribable zeal for piety; when he claims the goods of his kinsmen and father from which he seemed to have been estranged and regards it proper to recover that portion of virtue which falls to himself; when

---

28. See P. M. Fraser, *Ptolemaic Alexandria* (Oxford: Clarendon Press, 1972), 704–6; Holladay, ed., *Fragments from Hellenistic Jewish Authors*, 1:189–90.

29. See especially *Somn.* 1.210–220; 2.10–14; 2.42–47; 2.63–66.

slowly returning from betterment to betterment as though situated on the crowning heights and consummation of his life, utters aloud the lesson which experience has taught him so fully: "I belong to God" (Gen 50:19) and certainly not to anything sense-perceptible of the things which belong to creation, then his brothers will make with him covenants of reconciliation, changing their hatred into friendship, their ill-will to good-will, and I their attendant (ἐγὼ δ' ὁ τούτων ὀπαδὸς), having learnt to trust them as a household slave his masters, shall not fail to be praising him for his repentance (μετανοίας). (*Somn.* 2.105–108)

This is in many ways a remarkable passage. Initially, the extent of Philo's criticism is striking. After reading in the biography about virtuous Joseph, one cannot but be surprised at the venomous descriptions which Philo heaps up here. His former hero is now even said to have been "crawling like a worm after empty fantasies of vainglory." Philo obviously does not judge the character from a rational and balanced point of view, but is carried away by strong feelings. Something more than the character of an ancient figure must be at stake. The deeply emotional and topical nature of this passage further emerges from another striking feature: Philo identifies with Joseph's brothers to such an extent that he openly declares himself to be their "attendant." This highly exceptional statement of personal commitment on Philo's part seems to have been occasioned by the urgency of the matter. It creates a direct link between the biblical Joseph and contemporary Egyptian Jewry. Philo's statement in fact suggests that Joseph is also read as a representative of Egyptian Jews. Philo's Joseph has become something of a caricature of a real figure with real weaknesses. Does his harsh judgment of Joseph not indicate that he is appalled by contemporary features of Jewish assimilation to Egyptian culture?

The notion of Joseph's repentance is equally remarkable. Joseph is no longer the static character he had been in the biography, but rather a person who has fallen deep into the traps of vainglory, but then wakes up from his dreams and manages to recover his ancestral values. The turning point of the story is now Joseph's rejection of Potiphar's wife. The "wife of the Egyptian" personifies bodily pleasure, as Philo does not fail to remind his readers. Whereas in the biography she merely provoked an expected affirmation of Joseph's ethnicity, in the above passage she seems to arouse a more personal transformation. Rejecting her invitation "to come in and enjoy intimacy with her," Joseph becomes more aware of the fundamental dichotomy between Egypt and Mosaic law. His "yearning for continence," the archetypal virtue of the Jews, and his "indescribable zeal for piety" engender in him a process of reclaiming his ancestral heritage "from which he seemed to have been estranged." Philo appears to have entertained hopes that many of his fellow Jews, who had, in his view, gone too far along the road of assimilation to Egypt, would follow Joseph and would return to Mosaic law. Joseph thus became a model for repentance to be emulated in first-century Alexandria. It may have been with a view to these contemporaries that Philo linguistically highlighted the general nature of the Joseph story. He introduced the long chain of subclauses in the above-quoted passage by the conjunction ἐπειδάν (whenever), on which numerous verbs in the subjunctive mood depend. This suggests that the experiences Joseph went through were not unique historical events, but rather more a general pattern. Joseph's repentance indeed occurs "whenever" he wakes up from his illusions. His life story thus becomes a model for any Alexandrian Jew in a similar situation.

These conclusions are confirmed by other passages in *De Migratione*. Joseph is once more accused of vainglory, opportunism, and licentiousness, but praised for his repentance. On one occasion, Philo states his interpretation with particular emphasis:

> Notice that this politician takes his position in the midst between the house of Pharaoh and his father's house, so that he may equally apply himself to matters of the body, which is Egypt, and those of the soul, which are treasured in his father's house. For whenever he says "I belong to God" (Gen 50:19) and other things of this kind, he is faithful to the customs of his father's house. But whenever he mounts "the second chariot" of the mind that fancies itself to be a king, namely Pharaoh (Gen 49:43), he again sets up for himself Egyptian vanity as an idol. (*Migr.* 160)

Philo's exegesis of Gen 50:19 follows here the same pattern as in *De Somniis*: the verse is taken to indicate a return to a self-conscious Jewish identity. Joseph's riding in the second chariot, by contrast, is given as a concrete example of his illusions and mistaken adoption of Egyptian ways. In this passage, Philo moreover states with particular clarity the central theme of his exegesis, namely Joseph's self-chosen position between Egypt and his father's house. It is this ambivalence and lack of commitment to Mosaic law of which Philo strongly disapproves. He seems to have been especially alarmed in light of the repetition of Joseph's mistakes in his own generation.

It thus emerges that the highly critical interpretation of Joseph in Philo's scattered references is complementary to his ideal portrait in the biography. In both frameworks, Philo deals with Joseph in the context of Jewish acculturation in Egypt. While he once draws an exemplary figure that remained loyal to his Jewish identity and introduced congenial aspects of high Greco-Roman culture in Alexandria, he on other occasions also ascribes to Joseph the flaws of contemporary Egyptian Jews who fall short of the ideal and embrace the weaknesses of the land of the Nile. Emulating vainglory and licentiousness, they naturally abandon their Jewish identity to which they must be called back. Joseph ultimately plays a double role in Philo's midrash: he represents the ideal as well as the more frustrating reality of Jewish life in Egypt. Under both hats, however, he conveys the same message, namely that Egyptian Jews must distance themselves from indigenous Egyptian life and instead identify with the Roman elite as well as the Roman interpretation of high Hellenistic culture.

2. Joseph in Flavian Dress

It is immediately obvious that Josephus had completely different interests from those of Philo. No word in his midrash about a deep dichotomy between Egypt and Mosaic law. Living in Rome rather than in Alexandria, Josephus was not interested in the issue of Jewish life and identity in Egypt. His Jacob is thus not concerned with the danger of Joseph's assimilation. Reviving the father's character as depicted in the biblical story, Josephus has him simply rejoice at the prospect of meeting his son whom he had already thought dead (*A.J.* 2.168). Similarly, Potiphar's wife no longer personifies Egyptian vice, but feminine irrationality (*A.J.* 2.41–49). Josephus' attitude to Egypt is indeed so relaxed that he repeats the detail, first mentioned by Artapanus, that Joseph and his family settled not in Goshen, but in Heliopolis, the center of Egyptian sun worship (*A.J.* 2.188). Yet unlike Artapanus, Josephus does not credit Joseph with the introduction of specifically Egyptian institutions. In his midrash, he did not even hold the royal scepter, as Egyptian Jews had proudly insinuated, but was instead concerned to strengthen the loyalty of the Egyptians to their king.[30] Josephus had obviously no desire to inscribe his hero into the history of that country. Egypt was not an issue for Josephus, neither in the positive nor in the negative sense.

What did, however, matter to Josephus was Joseph's individual destiny as prophesied by his dreams. Josephus took an intensely personal interest in Joseph's character and defended him against all possible charges of exaggerated ambition. This idealizing tendency resembles in some respect Philo's midrash in the biography. Josephus indeed begins his paraphrase of the Joseph story along the same lines as his Alexandrian predecessor. Omitting the matter of the "evil report" (Gen 37:2), Josephus highlights Joseph's talents and innocence. As he puts it:[31]

> Jacob, having begotten Joseph from Rachel, loved this son above all others both because of the inborn nobility of his body and the virtue of his soul, for he was distinguished by prudence. Both the father's affection for him and the happiness (εὐδαιμονία), which was announced to him through dreams, which he had seen and told his father and brothers, aroused envy (φθόνον) and hatred among his brothers: so jealous are men of the successes (εὐπραγίας) even of their nearest relatives. (*A.J.* 2.9–10)

Josephus blames Joseph's brothers here for the arising family tension, accusing them of unjustified envy. He generalizes the biblical scene and suggests that success

---

30. *A.J.* 2.193; see also Feldman, *Josephus's Interpretation*, 343–44.
31. Translations are mine; I have consulted the English translation by Henry St. J. Thackeray et al., *Josephus in Nine Volumes* (9 vols.; Cambridge: Harvard University Press, 1966–69), and the Hebrew translation by Abraham Schalit, *Josephus ben Mattitahu: Jewish Antiquities with a Translation from the Greek. Introduction, Commentary, Maps, and Illustrations* (3 vols.; Jerusalem: Bialik Institute, 1944–63), vol. 1.

inevitably stirs up jealousy even among family members. Given Joseph's talents, the tension between the brothers was thus virtually unavoidable. Moreover, Josephus already introduces, at this point, the notion of Joseph's predestined εὐδαιμονία. Even before giving any details about Joseph's dreams and their interpretation, he has, in a characteristic preemptive strike, declared his own view of this complicated matter.[32] The biblical narrator left considerable room for ambiguity concerning the nature of Joseph's dreams. While they ultimately come true and thus prove to have been prophecies, the brothers initially rejected them as self-aggrandizing visions, and even Jacob was worried about the arrogance conveyed by Joseph's dreams. While Philo retained the image of the father angry at his son's exaggerated ambition, Josephus leaves no room for such ambiguity. From the beginning of his midrash, Joseph wears the garment of the distinguished oneirocritic. The motif of Joseph's predicted and thus certain happiness appears now at the very beginning of the story and introduces an overriding exegetical concern of Josephus.

Initially, one may suspect that we are dealing here with nothing but a standard topos, since Josephus also introduces the story of Moses by ominous predictions of his future success (A.J. 2.205–16). Josephus obviously enhanced the importance of the respective character. Both Moses and Joseph were born, he asserts, to serve a great purpose and become heroes of the nation. A closer study of Josephus' Joseph story reveals, however, that the dreams played a very special role. They did not only stress the hero's importance, but also served to explain the complicated fraternal relations.

Josephus takes special care to relate Joseph's dreams and their interpretation. The scene is set by a remarkable opening:

> Having been sent out with his brothers by their father to gather in the crops at midsummer, he saw a vision (ὄψιν) very different from the dreams which regularly visit us during sleep, which after having woken up, he disclosed to his brothers so that they would interpret its significance to him (ἣν περιεγερθεὶς τοῖς ἀδελφοῖς ὡς κρινοῦσιν αὐτῷ τὸ σημαινόμενον ἐξέθετο). (A.J. 2.11)

The reader learns in this passage that Joseph's vision was not a regular dream, but an exceptional vision. It is implied that Joseph's dream did not convey anything trivial or personal. It certainly did not reflect his own aspirations as the brothers suspected in the biblical story. On the contrary, Josephus asserts. His Joseph has not even the slightest idea about the auspicious meaning of his vision and consults his brothers in order to receive an interpretation. Why did Josephus make such exceptional efforts to defend Joseph's innocence? One obvious reason is his wish to highlight the objectivity of the message conveyed in Joseph's dream. In Josephus'

---

32. For other examples of preemptive strikes in Josephus' midrash, see Maren R. Niehoff, "Two Examples of Josephus' Narrative Technique in His 'Rewritten Bible,'" *JSJ* 27 (1996): 31–45.

midrash, the dreamer has become the mere vessel of a prophecy that he himself did not even grasp. It emerges that Joseph has been chosen by the deity for a special role and that his life is guided by divine providence toward a glorious future. Furthermore, Joseph's innocent appeal to his brothers allows Josephus to vilify his brothers to an unprecedented degree. He suggests that they not only rejected the message of Joseph's dream, as they had done in the biblical story, but immediately tried in the most malicious way to prevent its fulfillment:

> But they (the brothers), understanding that the vision announced his power and great deeds and future authority over them, made nothing of these clear to Joseph, as though the dream were not intelligible to them. They uttered curses (ἀράς) that nothing of what they suspected would reach fulfillment and continued to hate him even more. (*A.J.* 2.12)

Josephus raises here the story of the fraternal conflict to a new level. In flat contradiction to the biblical text, he claims that the brothers even refused to give Joseph the solicited interpretation of his dream. They have thus not only violated the most basic oneirocritical norms, but have ruthlessly lied and attempted to obstruct the divine scheme. Hiding the truth from Joseph, they hope to deprive him of his predestined good future. Grasping, however, that Joseph has been chosen by the deity, they invoke curses in order to manipulate the divine realm and change fate—both their own and Joseph's. The reader, who learns about the brothers in Josephus' midrash, will be unable to sympathize with them. While the biblical story left room to identify with their accumulating envy, Josephus arouses nothing but a sense of detestation at their miserable attempts of manipulation.

As if this were not enough, Josephus calls God directly onto the scene. The deity, he explains to his readers, "countered their envy and sent Joseph a second vision far more marvelous than the first" (*A.J.* 2.13). The reader is thus left in no doubt as to the divine providence, which protects Joseph and guides his life. The brothers, who oppose his special position, simply cannot read the signs and remain obdurate. This highly sympathetic view of Joseph, which Josephus has designed for his readers, is now acted out by Jacob. The father, who had in the biblical story chastised Joseph for this second dream, no longer expresses any ambivalence. Like Josephus, he is instead wholly appreciative of Joseph's special destiny and

> was delighted by the dream, grasping in his mind the prediction (it contained) and wisely and carefully guessing its import, he rejoiced at the great things signified, which announced happiness for the child and that, God willing, a time will come when he will be deemed worthy of honor and *proskynesis* by his parents and brothers.... (*A.J.* 2.15)

Jacob emerges here as a very positive figure who is rightly on the side of Joseph and the deity. His reaction is exemplary and represents Josephus' own feelings about the matter. Indeed Jacob's wholehearted approval as well as his renouncement of fatherly pride is the most appropriate behavior. His reaction, as newly reconstructed by Josephus, puts the brothers in an even worse light. In comparison to the father, their resistance appears yet more malicious and petty. Josephus vilifies Joseph's brothers to the extent that he attributes to them murderous intents much before the biblical narrator had done so. In Josephus' midrash, they do not go through a process of ever increasing hatred, which finds a spontaneous outlet when Joseph approaches them guarding the flock away from their father's house. According to Josephus, the brothers instead "were in a rush to slay the lad" even before going out (A.J. 2.18). They leave for Shechem only "after having determined on this plan" (A.J. 2.18). The trip to Shechem now appears as part of their scheme to lure him into a place at which they could easily do away with him. Joseph's brothers have become cold-hearted murderers. Josephus does indeed not miss the opportunity to explain to his readers that the brothers "were delighted" at his approach and treated him as though an "enemy had, by God's will, fallen into their hands" (A.J. 2.20). He moreover repeats that they "were eager to slay him outright and not let slip this opportunity which had offered itself" (A.J. 2.20). Only Reuben understood the true impact of their scheme: he realizes that they are about to profane divine providence and to "rob God of the recipient of His favors" (A.J. 2.28).

What had provoked this intense dislike of Joseph's brothers? Why did Josephus defend the hero of the story to such an extent? A first clue to this enigma is provided by the fact that Josephus actually carries the same name as his hero. Joseph ben Mattitahu could certainly not avoid noticing that he was named after Joseph ben Yaakov. This identity of names may have encouraged Josephus' extreme identification with this biblical hero. More important, some features of Joseph's life must have reminded him of similar situations in his own life. Josephus also claimed to have been blessed by prophetic dreams, in his case indicating that Vespasian would become Roman emperor (B.J. 3.392–402). Josephus, too, entertained a complicated relationship with many of his brothers. The drama of the biblical Joseph story was all too familiar to him. He in fact interpreted the character of Joseph along the same lines as he interpreted his own life. The story which he told about himself fervently appeals to the reader to look with sympathy on events for which Josephus continued to be harshly criticized. These events pertain to his involvement in the Great Revolt against the Romans. Serving at the beginning of the war in the Galilee, Josephus was together with John of Gischala and others responsible for the defense of the country from the north. At a critical point, when hiding with a few remaining men in a cave, he gave himself up to the Romans rather than killing himself as his friends had done (B.J. 3.383–391). He emerged from the cave to become a protégé of the future Roman emperor (B.J. 3.392–408), yet throughout his life this move to prosperity and safety remained highly controversial. The Jews of Jerusalem, for example, when besieged by the Romans at the end of the war, threw a stone at him over the city walls and, when seeing him drop to the ground, gleefully rejoiced at the thought of having killed him (*B.J.* 5.541–543). Josephus' reading of the biblical Joseph story is indeed firmly embedded in his own life, not in the facts as they "really" happened, but as Josephus wished them to have been. In other words, when reading the biblical Joseph story, Josephus faced similar, controversial issues as he did when telling his own life story. Determined to defend both heroes carrying the name Joseph, he suggested similar hermeneutical solutions.

It is striking that Josephus explains his own portentous dreams in exactly the same way as he treated Joseph's dreams. In both cases, Josephus makes special efforts to avoid the impression that the dreams are in fact self-promoting visions. In both cases, he moreover stresses that the dreamer had been chosen by God for a special destiny. The similarity between the two stories is, at this point, so conspicuous that Josephus' account of his own visions could almost be read as the words which he put into the mouth of biblical Joseph. Josephus—or is it Joseph?—says: "I come to you as a messenger of greater destinies" (*B.J.* 3.400). He has been foretold by God in nightly visions of the impending fate of the Romans and Jews (*B.J.* 3.351). It would be a "betrayal of God's commands, if he died before delivering his message" (*B.J.* 3.361). Josephus is extremely eager to convince his readers that he did not go over to the Roman side out of egoistic reasons. Prevailing rumors to the contrary, he insists that he had not aspired to power and prosperity, leaving his less fortunate brethren behind, but altruistically implemented the divine plan (*B.J.* 3.405–406). This is the emphatic message of a special appeal to God that Josephus inserts into the narrative:

> Since it pleases you, who has created the tribe of the Jews, to break your work, fortune having wholly passed to the Romans, and you have selected my soul to say the things which are to happen, I give myself up to the hands of the Romans, willingly and alive, yet I take you as a witness that I go not as a traitor, but as your messenger (μαρτύρομαι δὲ ὡς οὐ προδότης ἀλλὰ σὸς ἄπειμι διάκονος). (*B.J.* 3.354)

Against this background of Josephus' personal life story, it becomes much clearer why he later rewrote the biblical Joseph story with such staunch sympathy for the protagonist. Suspecting that Joseph was exposed to the same kind of criticism as he himself, he defended him as well as he could and, not surprisingly, along the same lines as he had defended himself against charges of self-promoting visions. The answer to envious brothers, both in the Bible and during the Second Temple period, was that Joseph had been selected by God for a special destiny. His rise to prominence was by no means fortuitous, but divinely planned and announced by prophetic dreams. We may now also better understand why Josephus insisted on Joseph's total innocence, suggesting that he neither grasped the significance of his own dreams nor suspected anything bad from his brothers when naively soliciting an interpretation. Dealing with a story of the ancient past, with no eyewitnesses still alive, Josephus could improve the plot of the narrative with considerably more liberty than he could in the case of his own life.

Josephus' vilification of Joseph's brothers now also becomes more transparent. They were in fact made to play the same role as Josephus assigned to his own opponents in his autobiography. We have already seen that Josephus complained about having nearly been stoned to death by the besieged rebels in Jerusalem. He was moreover convinced that he was the man whose "blood they thirsted most," obviously because he had moved over to the Roman side and become a representative of the conquering forces (*B.J.* 5.542). Other rebels disliked him as well and accused him of aspirations to authority over them. Especially the co-leaders of the rebellion in the Galilee made such claims and often threatened him. On several occasions, Josephus complains of having almost lost his life.[33] A particularly strong and outspoken opponent was John of Gischala, who accused Josephus not only of administrative incompetence but, more importantly, of a severe lack of *esprit de corps*. Josephus, like Joseph, was blamed for wanting to rule over his brothers. For him, too, an ambush was prepared, his brothers seeking to kill him. When reading Josephus' account of such an incident, one cannot help recalling Josephus' interpretation of the biblical story:

> I should undoubtedly have been murdered by John, (Jonathan) exclaiming: "Stop this enquiry, men of Tiberias, about twenty pieces of gold. For it is not because of them that Josephus deserves to die, but because he desired to rule over us like a despotic king (τυραννεῖν ἐπεθύμησεν) and, having deceived with words, gained absolute power over the people of the Galilee." (*Vita* 302)

The similarity between the two Josephs is striking. Both are surrounded by envious brothers who seek to obstruct their predestined good fate. In both cases, their jealousy leads them to murderous plans so that they lay an ambush for the innocent protagonist who barely escapes through divine providence. Joseph's brothers have thus become villains in the image of John of Gischala and his gang in Josephus' *Vita*.

One final point in Joseph's life aroused Josephus' special interest and sympathy. This point concerns the brothers' reunification in Egypt. As is well-known, the brothers did not recognize him upon meeting the "ruler of the country" (Gen 42:6), while Joseph postponed the disclosure of his own identity for a very long time. The biblical narrator describes the sequence of events with considerable ambivalence concerning Joseph. Even though he immediately recognized his brothers, he "made himself an alien to them and spoke harshly to them."[34] Moreover, the fact that he remembered the dreams of his youth, which he now saw fulfilled in the brothers' bowing down to him, only strengthened his animosity: he now accuses them of

---

33. See, for example, *Vita* 104, 189–218.
34. Gen 42:7: ויתנכר אליהם וידבר אתם קשות; ἠλλοτριοῦτο ἀπ᾽ αὐτῶν καὶ ἐλάλησεν αὐτοῖς σκληρά.

coming to Egypt for purposes of spying (Gen 42:9). Josephus, it must be remembered, faced similar issues in his own life. He, too, was accused of being vengeful. He also had to defend himself against charges of wishing to punish those who had not been sufficiently loyal to him.[35] Josephus solves this difficulty by insisting on his magnanimity. In *Vita* 353, he fervently asks: "Have you forgotten how, often as I had you in my power, I put none of you to death?!" On another occasion, he stresses that "to Jonathan and his colleagues I promised pardon for the past" (*Vita* 262).

It is precisely along the lines of this rhetoric that Josephus rewrites Joseph's encounter with his brothers in Egypt. His biblical namesake, too, is absolved from any vengeful feelings. Josephus in fact never mentions either that he spoke harshly to his brothers or that he remembered his dreams upon meeting them (Gen 42:7–9). Joseph's refusal to disclose his identity stems, instead, from his desire "to test the feelings" of his brothers (*A.J.* 2.97). He accused them of spying only for good purposes:

> He did so in order to know the circumstances of his father and the things that happened to him after his own departure, wishing also to learn about the circumstances of his brother Benjamin. (*A.J.* 2.99)

Josephus' apologetics for Joseph reach a peak when he transforms the extremely lively scene of Joseph's final disclosure into a moralizing sermon. While the biblical narrator portrays Joseph as overcome by his feelings, weeping, and crying—"I am Joseph, is my father still alive?" (Gen 45:3)—Josephus presents a considerably more composed figure:

> I commend you for your virtue and your goodwill towards your brother and I find you to be better than I expected from your plots against me, for all that I did in order to test your brotherly love. I think that not by your own nature have you done these evil things to me, but by the will of God, working out the happiness that we now enjoy and that shall be ours if He continues to be gracious to us. Having then, beyond all hope, learned that my father is alive and seeing you thus devoted to our brother, I no longer remember those sins against me of which you think yourselves guilty, I shall cease to bear you malice for them as the culprits; and as assistants in bringing God's purpose to the present issue I tender you my thanks. (*A.J.* 2.161)

In comparison to the biblical scene, Joseph's character appears in this passage to be rather flat and even somewhat artificial. Nothing of the strong emotions of the biblical figure has survived. Joseph instead teaches his brothers a moral and religious

---

35. *Vita* 314; see also Shaye J. D. Cohen, *Josephus in Galilee and Rome: His Vita and Development as a Historian* (2nd ed.; Leiden: Brill, 2002), 126–27; Per Bilde, *Flavius Josephus between Jerusalem and Rome: His Life, His Works, and Their Importance* (JSPSup 2; Sheffield: Sheffield Academic Press, 1988), 36–65, 104–13.

lesson. He also forgives them in the same condescending manner as Josephus treated his own former adversaries. It thus emerges that regarding this final point, too, Joseph ben Yaakov and Joseph ben Mattithahu experienced similar difficulties and solved them in the same magnanimous fashion.

3. Whose Garments Are They Anyway?

We started by inquiring into the relationship between exegesis and history. Assuming that the process of reading cannot be isolated from the reader's own experience and situation in the world, we were interested to discover how exactly these two realms interact. Of particular concern was the question of the interpreter's creativity. Our analysis of Philo's and Josephus' midrash on Joseph has yielded interesting results. While both were children of their time, speaking and thinking in contemporary terms, both also showed considerable creativity and transformed the biblical character according to their own specific concerns. Philo did so with a view to Egyptian culture, Josephus with a view to his own apologetics in his *Vita*. Their midrash thus not only reflected the time of the interpreter, but also pointed forward to shape the future. Philo hoped to influence Jews living in Egypt, encouraging them to steer a careful course in the land of their residence. Joseph was to serve as a model of preserving Jewish identity in alien Egypt. Josephus, on the other hand, hoped to convince his readers about the innocence of Joseph's opaque and controversial character. His midrash emerges as a model for the apologetics that he was to apply subsequently to his own person. To speak with our initial metaphor, Joseph's new garments have indeed been carefully prepared. The threads that went into each cloth, while fabricated at a particular time and place, have been woven together with a particular purpose. The weaving itself was done by the interpreter, not by the circumstances of his time.

Zusammenfassung

Dieser Beitrag fragt nach der Auslegung biblischer Texte in der Antike. Es wird untersucht, in wie weit exegetische Fragestellungen ausschließlich durch ihre historischen Kontexte bedingt sind. Weil das Leben Josephs Fragen berührte, die ihnen selbst am Herzen lagen, hatten sowohl Philo von Alexandrien als auch Josephus Flavius ein besonderes Interesse an der Josephserzählung. Joseph war sowohl für seinen Streit mit seinen Brüdern als auch für seine exzeptionelle Karriere in Ägypten bekannt.

Philo verwendet die Josephsfigur, um ein ideales Bild des jüdischen Lebens in Ägypten zu zeichnen. Philo bestärkt die Integrität des Josephcharakters, indem er für Joseph beansprucht, daß er seinen Lebenswandel nicht mit dem Wechsel der Zeiten änderte (*De Iosepho* 263). Josephs berühmte Ablehnung der Madame Potiphar gibt Philo die Gelegenheit, seine Ideen zu dem Gegensatz von mosaischen und ägyptischen Werten zu erörtern: Madame Potiphar verkörpert ägyptische Zügellosigkeit und Laster, während Joseph jüdische Tugenden repräsentiert. Philos antiägyptische Deutung von Josephs Keuschheit scheint ebenfalls in Philos persönlichen Lebensumständen verankert zu sein. Philos Josephsauslegung ist im Kontext der griechisch-römischen Ablehnung von ägyptischer Zügellosigkeit zu verstehen. Indem Philo sich von der sexuellen Freizügigkeit seines Landes distanziert, entspricht Philos Josephsfigur auffallend den Idealen der römischen Oberschicht in der Provinz Ägypten. Josephs Karriere ist bei Philo sowohl von großem Erfolg als auch von persönlicher Distanziertheit von der örtlichen Kultur geprägt. Philos Josephsgeschichte macht deutlich, daß die Juden nicht nur schon immer am Lebensstil der griechisch-römischen Eliten seiner Zeit partizipierten, sondern ihn sogar zu teilen kreiert hatten—ein Lebensstil mit dem Philo sich selbst identifizierte.

Obwohl Josephus die Josephsgeschichte in ähnlichen Bahnen wie sein Alexandrinischer Vorgänger versteht, schlägt seine Deutung der Josephsfigur eine ganz andere Richtung ein. Im Gegensatz zu Philo ist Josephus weder an Josephs Leben in Ägypten noch an kultureller Assimilation der Juden interessiert. Woran Josephus dem gegenüber Interesse zeigte, war die Bestimmung des Joseph, wie sie in Josephs Träumen vorhergesagt wurde. Josephus unterstreicht die Begabungen und die Unschuld Josephs. In seiner Nacherzählung konzentriet sich Josephus besonders auf die Träume Josephs und ihre Deutung. Josephs Begabungen machen die Spannungen zwischen ihm und seinen Brüdern unvermeidlich. Was hat diese intensiven Spannungen motiviert? Joseph ben Mattitjahu konnte schlechterdings nicht übersehen, daß er nach Joseph ben Ja'akov benannt worden war. Die Dramatik der biblischen Josephsgeschichte war ihm nur allzu vertraut. Josephus' Verteufelung der Brüder Josephs wird vor diesem Hintergrund besser verstehbar. Wie Joseph wurde Josephus beschuldigt über seine Brüder herrschen zu wollen. Die Ähnlichkeiten zwischen dem Josephus der *Vita* und dem Joseph im Midrasch des Josephus sind auffallend: Josephus verstand sich als ein moderner Joseph. Seine Apologie der Bestimmung des biblischen Josephs zu herrschen, bezeugt seine eigene Unschuld den jüdischen Mitbrüdern gegenüber.

Die Midraschim von Philo und Josephus reflektieren auf diese Weise nicht nur ihre eigenen historischen Gegebenheiten sondern versuchen auch, sie zu gestalten. Philo versucht die Juden zu überzeugen, Josephs Beispiel zu folgen; Josephus versucht, seine jüdischen Mitbürger von seiner Unschuld zu überzeugen.

HERACLEON AND JOHN: REASSESSMENT OF AN EARLY CHRISTIAN HERMENEUTICAL DEBATE

Harold W. Attridge

1. ORIGEN'S *COMMENTARY ON JOHN*

The scriptures of the Christian church have been a source of inspiration and guidance for believers since their composition, but they have also been, from the first, contested territory. A prime piece of that territory was the Fourth Gospel, whose complex Christology and soteriology provided fodder for theologians of various stripes throughout the patristic period.[1] A significant early engagement in that history of contested interpretation was the critique by Origen of the commentary on the text by Heracleon, a controversy that has received considerable attention of late and that may still be instructive.[2]

Origen, the great exegete and theologian of the first half of the third century, was at work on his *Commentary on John* over many years.[3] The work originally encompassed thirty-two books, commenting on the Gospel from the Prologue

---

1. For general works on the interpretation of the Fourth Gospel in antiquity, see Maurice F. Wiles, *The Spiritual Gospel: The Interpretation of the Fourth Gospel in the Early Church* (Cambridge: Cambridge University Press, 1960); T. E. Pollard, *Johannine Christology and the Early Church* (SNTSMS 13; Cambridge: Cambridge University Press, 1970). Most recently, see Titus Nagel, *Die Rezeption des Johannesevangeliums im 2. Jahrhundert: Studien zur vorirenäischen Aneignung und Auslegung des vierten Evangeliums in christlicher und christlich-gnostischer Literatur* (Arbeiten zur Bibel und ihrer Geschichte 2; Leipzig: Evangelische Verlagsanstalt, 2000); and Charles E. Hill, *The Johannine Corpus in the Early Church* (Oxford: Oxford University Press, 2004).

2. The well-known student of gnosticism, Elaine Pagels, devoted her dissertation to the debate (*The Johannine Gospel in Gnostic Exegesis* [Philadelphia: Fortress, 1973]), but the study of Heracleon has been put on totally new footing by the work of Ansgar Wucherpfennig, *Heracleon Philologus: Gnostische Johannesexegese im zweiten Jahrhundert* (WUNT 142; Tübingen: Mohr Siebeck, 2002).

3. In general, see Henri Crouzel, *Origen: The Life and Thought of the First Great Theologian* (trans. A. S. Worrall; San Francisco: Harper & Row, 1989); Charles Kannengiesser and William L. Petersen, *Origen of Alexandria: His World and His Legacy* (Christianity and Judaism in Antiquity 1; Notre Dame, Ind.: University of Notre Dame Press, 1988).

through John 13:33.[4] Origen completed the first six books by the time he left Alexandria for Caesarea, around 231–232 C.E., since Book 6 alludes to the turmoil preceding that move. Work continued into the next decade, ending some time between 244–248 C.E. This diffuse, sprawling work, written, unlike modern commentaries, without a deadline or a strict word limit, shows Origen operating, variously reflective, polemical, analytical, and prayerful.

Some of his commentary seems familiar enough to modern ears, as Origen treats the meaning of words, the genre of "gospel," role of characters in the story, and so on. Some of the commentary operates with what came to be "classical" Christian hermeneutical presuppositions.

Origen very definitely reads the Fourth Gospel canonically. He interprets John by Paul and vice versa, without noting tensions or differences. To cite a few brief examples: *Comm.* 1.1 cites Rom 2:29 to begin a discussion of the meaning of the "true Israel." *Comm.* 1.34–40, discussing the "spiritual" meaning of "gospel," consists of a pastiche of quotations from and allusions to Pauline texts (including Hebrews). *Comm.* 2.191 cites Rom 9:11–14 on the election of Jacob over Esau, but does so in the context of a defense of his notion that John the Baptist is an angel incarnate. The "supplanting," argues Origen, is not unintelligible or a stumbling block to affirming divine justice. It simply recognizes the merit of the supplanter, Jacob, earned in his pre-incarnate state.

Origen also assumes the unity of the Johannine corpus and interprets the Gospel through the images of Revelation and vice versa. Again a few examples: At the very beginning of the commentary (*Comm.* 1.2–8), Origen begins wrestling with the category of "Jew" in the text of the Gospel. His fundamental move is to argue that the "people of Christ" are the tribes of Israel "in a more mystical manner." Although he starts from Rom 2:29, he quickly moves to a discussion, extending to *Comm.* 1.8, of the 144,000 of Rev 7:2–5. *Comm.* 2.42–63 offers a lengthy discussion of the Word (Logos) in Revelation, but Paul, specifically 1 Thessalonians, appears at *Comm.* 2.50.[5]

Origen discusses at length (*Comm.* 1.27–46) the issue of the genre of the gospel, but unlike contemporary discussions, his does not focus on formal questions. He is interested in the contents of the message, particularly its "intelligible and spiritual" dimensions (*Comm.* 1.44).[6]

---

4. Text and French translation: Cécile Blanc, *Origène, Commentaire sur Saint Jean* (5 vols.; SC 120, 157, 222, 290, 385; Paris: Éditions du Cerf, 1966–92). An English translation is available in Ronald Heine, *Origen, Commentary on the Gospel according to John* (2 vols.; Washington, D.C.: Catholic University of America Press, 1989–93).

5. The premise, questionable from a modern critical perspective, leads to an insightful reading. Thus, Origen (*Comm.* 2.61) appropriately interprets the blood-sprinkled garments of the Warrior Messiah and Word in Rev 19:14 as a reference to Christ's passion, which is probably what Revelation intends.

6. The principles of Origen's hermeneutics, articulated in *De Principiis* 4, insist on the importance of the "spiritual sense" of scripture. His hermeneutical principles and exegetical practices have been fre-

Origen reads the scripture with explicit philosophical premises. His Platonic presuppositions are evident in this discussion of the status of the Logos (*Comm.* 1.244):[7]

> But if someone is able to comprehend an incorporeal existence comprised of the various ideas which embrace the principles of the universe, an existence which is living and animate, as it were, he will understand the wisdom of God which precedes all creation, which appropriately says of herself, "God created me the beginning of his ways for his works" (Prov 8:22). It is because of this creation that the whole creation has also been able to subsist, since it has a share in the divine wisdom according to which it has been created, for according to the Prophet David, God made "all things in wisdom" (Ps 103:24).

Origen's association of the Logos and the Platonic realm of forms or "ideas" is hardly new, but has well-known antecedents in Philo.[8] More distinctive perhaps is Origen's philosophical psychology, which famously made room for the preexistence of the soul. That notion, along with an appeal to a mythological tradition about angels, enables Origen at *Comm.* 2.175–192 to deal with the Johannine motif of "sending."

Origen finds subtle theological points in the details of the text. *Comm.* 2.1–33 discusses the opening of the Gospel's Prologue: "And the Word was with God and the Word was God," which leads Origen to worry about the distinction between "the God" and the anarthrous "God" at the end of the verse. His solution appears at *Comm.* 2.17: The God is "very God, wherefore also the Savior says in his prayer to the Father, 'That they may know you the only true God.'" Everything else "participates" (another Platonic notion) in *the* God:

> To be sure, his "firstborn of every creature" (Col 1:15), inasmuch as he was the first to be with God and has drawn divinity into himself, is more honored than the other gods beside him (of whom God is God as it said, "The God of gods, the Lord has spoken, and he has called the earth" [Ps 49:1]). It was by his ministry that they

---

quently treated in recent literature. In addition to Crouzel, *Origen*, 61–84, see R. P. C. Hanson, *Allegory and Event: A Study of the Sources and Significance of Origen's Interpretation of Scripture* (Richmond: John Knox, 1959); Peter Gorday, *Principles of Patristic Exegesis: Romans 9–11 in Origen, John Chrysostom, and Augustine* (Studies in the Bible and Early Christianity 4; New York: Mellen, 1983); Karen Jo Torjesen, *Hermeneutical Procedure and Theological Method in Origen's Exegesis* (Berlin: de Gruyter, 1986); Joseph Wilson Trigg, *Origen: The Bible and Philosophy in the Third-Century Church* (Atlanta: John Knox, 1983).

7. On Origen's debt to middle Platonism, see especially Henry Chadwick, *Early Christian Thought and the Classical Tradition* (New York: Oxford University Press, 1966); Robert M. Berchman, *From Philo to Origen: Middle Platonism in Transition* (Chico, Calif.: Scholars Press, 1984); John M. Dillon, *The Great Tradition: Further Studies in the Development of Platonism and Early Christianity* (Aldershot, England: Ashgate, 1997).

8. For Philo's treatment of creation, see especially Thomas Tobin, S.J., *The Creation of Man* (CBQMS; Washington, D.C.: Catholic Biblical Association, 1983).

became gods, for he drew from God that they might be deified, sharing ungrudgingly also with them according to his goodness.

The principles of Origen's "subordinationism" are clear, and his position is articulated often enough. At *Comm.* 2.21, Origen affirms that the Father is the source of divinity, the Son/Word, the source of reason. Within this framework, he readily interprets the distinction of one God, the Father, and one Lord, Jesus Christ, of 1 Cor 8:5–6 (*Comm.* 2.21). While perhaps deficient from the standpoint of fourth-century orthodoxy,[9] Origen's position was coherent and in dialogue with the Christologies of the period.[10]

2. Heracleon: Origen's Assessment

In the polemical strands of his work, Origen rounded up the usual third-century suspects: Marcionites, Patripassian modalists, and gnostics. Prominent among the latter was Heracleon, whom Origen associated with the second-century teacher Valentinus.[11] Heracleon's commentary on John, the first of its kind, was probably completed some time in the late second century. Origen's frequent citations provide our only access to Heracleon's work.[12]

---

9. The struggle to achieve clarity on Trinitarian questions has been the subject of several important recent studies. See especially R. P. C. Hanson, *The Search for the Christian Doctrine of God: The Arian Controversy, 318–381* (Edinburgh: T & T Clark, 1988). On the Origenist controversies of the fourth and fifth centuries, see Crouzel, *Origen*, 169–79; Elizabeth A. Clark, *Origenist Controversy: The Cultural Construction of an Early Christian Debate* (Princeton: Princeton University Press, 1992).

10. See Alois Grillmeier, *Christ in Christian Tradition* (trans. John Bowden; 2nd ed.; 2 vols.; Atlanta: John Knox, 1975), 1:138–48, on Origen.

11. On whom, see most recently Christoph Markschies, *Valentinus Gnosticus? Untersuchungen zur valentinianischen Gnosis mit einem Kommentar zu den Fragmenten Valentins* (WUNT 65; Tübingen: Mohr Siebeck, 1992). Origen does not spend any time on Valentinus himself, although he clearly knew the Valentinians. There are, by the way, some interesting points of comparison, usually overlooked, with other Valentinian Nag Hammadi texts, including the *Gospel of Truth*. See, e.g., *Comm.* 13.120–122 on being lost in matter, and 13.187–192, the image of the "jars," which are evocative of the *Gospel of Truth* (NHC I,3) 17.5–18.36 and 25.19–26.27.

12. Important earlier literature on Heracleon includes Werner Foerster, *Von Valentin zu Herakleon: Untersuchungen über die Quellen und die Entwicklung der valentinianischen Gnosis* (Giessen: Töpelmann, 1928). An English translation of Foerster's collection of fragments is available in idem, *Gnosis: A Selection of Gnostic Texts* (trans. R. McL. Wilson; 2 vols.; Oxford: Clarendon, 1972–74), 1:162–83. There has been some speculation that at least one Nag Hammadi tractate, the *Tripartite Tractate* (NHC I,5), is a work of Heracleon. For discussion of the suggestion, see Harold W. Attridge and Elaine Pagels, "The Tripartite Tractate," in *Nag Hammadi Codex I (The Jung Codex)* (ed. Harold W. Attridge; Nag Hammadi Studies 22; Leiden: Brill, 1985), 1:178. Despite some interesting parallels between the text and the fragments, there is not enough similarity to be confident of the identification. For an even later dating of the text, see Einar Thomassen, *Traité tripartite (NHC I,5): Texte établi, introduit et commenté par Einar Thomassen* (trans. Louis Painchaud and Einar Thomassen; Québec: Presses de l'Université de Laval, 1989), 11–20.

Scholarly fascination with the controversy between Origen and Heracleon increased with the discovery of the Nag Hammadi library and the consequent reassessment of second-century "Gnosticism." Prior to such revisionism, the exegetical debate was often framed as a conflict between two radically different worldviews. In one corner stood Origen, the self-described "man of the church" (ἐκκλεσιάστικος ἀνήρ), defender of free will and of the intimate connection between creation and redemption; in the other Heracleon, the sectarian, a radical dualist, whose anticosmic presuppositions problematically separated spirit from soul and matter, and the God of Jesus Christ from the God of creation, and whose soteriology was grounded in a determinist anthropology that claimed that "nature" determined the end result of the salvific process. Given such dichotomies, it is clear enough whose reading of the Fourth Gospel would be preferred. Yet the characterization is largely the work of Origen, the lens through which Origen's readers have come to know his erstwhile opponent.

3. HERACLEON: A NEW ASSESSMENT

Theological analysis via polemical caricature is likely to be unsatisfactory, but what more nuanced view should take its place? A more adequate assessment of the debate must begin with the reevaluation of Heracleon's work by Wucherpfennig,[13] who insists that a proper assessment of Heracleon should be grounded in his fragments and not in a reconstruction of the presumed Valentinian background of Heracleon. As the adjective in his title, "Philologus," suggests, the fragments of his work on the Gospel of John give evidence that Heracleon fits nicely into the framework of learned commentary that had developed in the Hellenistic period and was being practiced in educated circles under the Roman Empire.[14]

Heracleon was commenting, apparently for the first time in Christian circles, on what had become a sacred text of the Christian movement. Reexamining the fragments, Wucherpfennig calls attention to the ways in which they exhibit moves typical in early imperial commentators on Homer or other classical texts. Thus, like his philological contemporaries, Heracleon explores *to diorthotikon*, or "text criticism," which includes determining structure and divisions of a work (frag. 11); *to glossematikon*, or the precise meaning of words (frag. 1); *to historikon*, the presumed historical reference or subject of the text (frag. 8). He is careful to determine *to prosopon*, the character or person who is speaking in the text (frag. 3, 14), and frequently uses the technical terminology of literary criticism. He emerges, in other words, as

---

13. See n. 2 above.
14. The social position of the tradents of early Christian literature has been much discussed of late, with a tendency to criticize earlier, somewhat romantic notions of early Christian learned society. See Harlow G. Snyder, *Teachers and Texts in the Ancient World: Philosophers, Jews, and Christians* (London: Routledge, 2000); Kim Haines-Eitzen, *Guardians of Letters* (New York: Oxford University Press, 2000).

a careful student of his text, deploying the tools used by his contemporaries in learned circles of the second century reading the Greek classics.

This characterization holds even when Heracleon's comments wander far from the basic mechanics of reading. People and places in John's Gospel can, according to Heracleon, have a multitude of meanings, not only describing events in the life of Jesus, but also symbolizing cosmological and soteriological truths. Thus the royal officer of John 4 symbolizes the Demiurge, the inferior deity responsible for the creation of the material world.[15] In other places, as Wucherpfennig has persuasively argued,[16] an important register on which Heracleon was reading his text was cosmological. In other words, Heracleon, like Origen and many other ancient readers of classical texts, interpreted them allegorically, with the frame of reference coming from prior metaphysical or cosmological commitments.

4. Origen and Heracleon: Theological Comparison

Where then did Heracleon and Origen differ in their reading of the Fourth Gospel, and how much of their disagreement was based on substantive theological or philosophical positions?

The fragments of and testimonies to Heracleon consist of some fifty passages scattered through the remains of Origen's commentary. Some reveal very little about either of the protagonists. At times, Origen was vaguely bothered or intrigued by Heracleon's views, but did not have the time or energy to construct a critique. To take one example: at *Comm.* 13.164, treating the episode of Jesus and the Samaritan woman, Origen writes: "But consider also Heracleon's assertion. He says that 'the Church received the Christ and was persuaded concerning him that he alone understands all things.'"

Origen offers no critique or indication that he disagrees with Heracleon's assertion. At some points, Origen grudgingly approves Heracleon's position. For example, at *Comm.* 6.126, Origen agrees with Heracleon that the Pharisees acted maliciously. Heracleon and Origen shared a negative assessment of the Pharisees widespread in the second century. At other points, Origen indicates his annoyance with Heracleon, although the substance of his disagreement is not always specified.

Often Origen accuses Heracleon of making arbitrary claims. So, speaking of Heracleon's contention that the Samaritan woman was guilty of fornication "because of her nature," Origen says:

> I do not know how he thought the cause of her fornication was revealed, or how her ignorance [of God] was the cause of her transgressions and neglect of service to

---

15. Frag. 40; *Comm.* 13.416–426.
16. See Wucherpfennig, *Heracleon*, 263–70.

God. He seems to have invented these things at random, without any plausible argument. (*Comm.* 13.93)[17]

Sometimes Origen debates Heracleon on technical points. In the realm of text criticism, Heracleon, with nearly all the manuscripts, prefers Bethania, Origen Bethabara at John 1:28. At the level of narrative construal, Heracleon, like most moderns, assumes that John 1:18 ("No one has ever seen God, etc.") is an authorial comment. Origen construes the verse as testimony of the Baptist (*Comm.* 6.13–14 et al.).

Although Origen, like Heracleon, could also be described as a "Philologus," his dialogue with Heracleon raises significant issues for theology and exegesis. Theologically, the issues at stake cluster around Christology, which involves considerations of God's relationship to the created order, and soteriology, which involves considerations of anthropology. An important part of the difference between the two theological exegetes rests on the way in which they construe the theological relevance of the Johannine text. At several points, Origen's focus seems to differ from that of Heracleon, perhaps because he sees implications of the latter's position that he finds problematic.

5. Origen and Heracleon: Philosophical Comparison

Yet there is something more in the divide between them than a difference of emphasis or an interest in exposing problematic presuppositions. Underlying the debate is a fundamental philosophical difference, which may be crucial to the whole interchange. The debate between Origen and Heracleon sometimes seems to be unproductive because this fundamental issue is never explicitly addressed. As a result, the two opponents occasionally seem to be talking past one another.

The debate between the two exegetes plays itself out primarily in three blocks of fragments: the first in Book 2 of the commentary, where Origen is still treating the Prologue of the Fourth Gospel; the second, in Book 13, treats the Samaritan woman at the well; the third, in Book 20, treats the forensic discourse of John 8 and the claim that the opponents of Jesus in the Gospel have the devil as their father.

The first block provides good examples of what is at stake and will be the focus of this essay.[18] The first passage, *Comm.* 2.100–104, deals with John 1:3: "All things were made through him (δι' αὐτοῦ) and without him was made nothing."[19] Origen begins his debate with Heracleon by clarifying the extension of πάντα, "all things." He argues that Heracleon is wrong to limit the term to the visible cosmos. Things

---

17. For similar critical comments, see *Comm.* 13.249; 13.272.
18. I hope to treat the analogous problems of *Comm.* 13 and 20 (Heracleon, frags. 17–49) in more detail in another study.
19. Origen, over against Heracleon, reads οὐδέν, instead of the emphatic οὐδὲ ἕν.

that transcend the world, as Heracleon puts it, "The Aeon and the things in the Aeon," are excluded (*Comm.* 2.101).

The second point that Origen scores against Heracleon is that the latter has utterly misunderstood the phrase "through him." According to Origen, Heracleon claimed that the Logos is the one "through whom" the Creator of the world received "the cause of making the world" (*Comm.* 2.102). Instead, claims Origen, the prepositional phrase should be understood in its normal, instrumental sense, indicating that the Logos was the agent through whom God made the world.

This debate seems to confirm the correctness of the consensus about the relationship between Origen and Heracleon mentioned previously. More specifically, Heracleon appears to denigrate creation, separating the demiurgic Creator from the redeeming Father. Such a reading misses an important thrust of Heracleon's theological exegesis.

Take the latter point first. In their exegesis of John 1:3 and the prepositional phrase δι᾽ αὐτοῦ, both Heracleon and Origen follow the practice of contemporary philosophy and discuss types of cause using prepositional phrases.[20] Origen sees Heracleon's focus to be the Demiurge and the resultant separation of God and the inferior Creator. Heracleon's attention, however, seems to be instead focused squarely on the Logos.

Heracleon's goal in framing his doctrine of creation is clarified by a statement that Origen quotes, thinking that he is providing clear evidence of his opponent's perfidy: " 'The Word himself,' says Heracleon, 'did not create as though under the impulse of another, that the phrase, 'through him,' should be understood in this way, but another created under his impulse (αὐτοῦ ἐνεργοῦντος).' "[21]

Heracleon's affirmation that the Logos was the ultimate active cause in creation, producing his creative effect through another's agency,[22] in effect, says that the Logos was self-moved, αὐτοκίνητος, not ἑτεροκίνητος. The Logos thus has what would have been assumed to be an important attribute of Deity, independence from any other cause. Heracleon's position about the Logos is analogous to one implied by the

---

20. On the practice, see John Dillon, *The Middle Platonists* (Ithaca, N.Y.: Cornell University Press, 1977), 138–39. For an example in a text from Nag Hammadi, see Harold W. Attridge, "Greek Equivalents of Two Coptic Phrases: CG I,5.65,9–10 and CG II,2.43,26," *Bulletin of the American Society of Papyrologists* 18 (1981): 27–32. See also the full discussion in Wucherpfennig, *Heracleon*, 141–51. Heracleon might have offered an emendation and read δι᾽ αὐτοῦ, making the Logos the final rather than the instrumental cause, which would have achieved a similar end. But he respects the biblical text and reads it, somewhat against the grain, by reconsidering the "agency" expressed by the phrase.

21. See the discussion in Wucherpfennig, *Heracleon*, 151–58.

22. The *Tripartite Tractate* 65.9–10 uses language similar to that of Heracleon's fragment, but seems to affirm that the Son is the "one through whom" the intelligible world of spirit comes into being. Another derivative divine principle, the Logos, is the immediate cause of whatever comes into being outside of the world of spirit (*Tri. Trac.* 77.9–10), and he works through the agency of an archon or ruler of this world (*Tri. Trac.* 100.19–35).

designation of a divine principle in various gnostic[23] texts as αὐτογενής, "self-originate." In these texts, the designation seems paradoxical, since the principle is usually derivative from or an "emanation" from something more fundamental. Yet the divine status of the principle in question is clear.[24]

More important perhaps, the affirmation of John 1:3 that things came to be δι' αὐτοῦ is, for Heracleon, consistent with the affirmation of John 1:1, that the Logos is θεός. Heracleon has, in fact, preserved the coherence of the Prologue's Christology, keeping the Logos firmly within the boundary of what one would want to call divine. He has paid a price: the introduction of a "Demiurge" in the process of creation. Yet this price was small for someone steeped in a tradition that had long amalgamated Platonic and scriptural cosmologies. Heracleon had precedent for his theory of creation in Philo's notion of angelic intermediaries in the creative process, distancing God from the creation of evil (cf. *Op. mundi* 75). In fact, Heracleon's version of creation looks like a very slight modification of the Philonic model, in which the Logos (equated with Wisdom) is the realm of Platonic ideas in the mind of God (*Op. mundi* 17–25) as well as the active extension of the divine presence in the world (*Op. mundi* 8).[25] Origen may have properly criticized Heracleon's move, but he did not do justice to what it accomplished: a consistent reading of John and a philosophically defensible interpretation of the divine status of the Logos.

An analogous set of concerns is at work in the first point at issue between Origen and Heracleon, that "all things" (πάντα), for Heracleon, seems to be limited. Thus, for him, there is something uncreated apart from God. The antiheretical tradition, which delights in describing the cosmologies or maps of the noetic world, focuses on the speculative dimension that lies behind or alongside their affirmation. All the aeons or pleromata in those "gnostic" cosmologies indeed sound strange to

---

23. The term continues to be useful for describing a family of speculative systems of the second century, despite the potential shortcomings of global reconstructions of "Gnosticism" forcefully pointed out by Michael A. Williams, *Rethinking "Gnosticism": An Argument for Dismantling a Dubious Category* (Princeton: Princeton University Press, 1996), and Karen L. King, *What Is Gnosticism?* (Cambridge: Harvard University Press, 2003).

24. See the account of the "Barbeloites" in Irenaeus, *Adv. Haer.* 1.29.2; *The Apocryphon of John*, BG 30.6; NHC III,1.9.17 et al. See Michael Waldstein and Frederik Wisse, *The Apocryphon of John: Synopsis of Nag Hammadi Codices II,1; III,1; and IV,1 with BG 8502,2* (Nag Hammadi and Manichaean Studies 33; Leiden: Brill, 1995). Hippolytus speaks of three sets of teachings that feature the term, a *Gospel of the Egyptians* that apparently distinguishes between a "pre-existent" and a "self-originate" (*Ref.* 5.7.9), a group called the Peratae, distinguishing a "paternal power" from several principles that "originate from themselves" (*Ref.* 5.12.2), and the "Megale Apophasis" (*Ref.* 6.17.3). A similar notion appears in the Nag Hammadi tractate *Zostrianos* (NHC VIII,1), where a visionary on a heavenly ascent is "baptized" into a "self-originate" realm or aeon, thereby assimilating to divinity. More consistently, the *Tripartite Tractate* 56.4 affirms that the first principle alone is "self-begotten." That precision in terminology could be shared by Heracleon, who seems to frame the deity of the Logos/Son in more physical terms of "activity" (ἐνεργοῦντος).

25. So too, Wucherpfennig, *Heracleon*, 141–56.

modern ears, but to describe them may not be the point of the doctrine. Furthermore, the affirmation that there is an uncreated realm seems to compromise the sovereignty of God.

Heracleon's position may in the end be problematic, but its functions deserve greater attention. The affirmation that there is something uncreated serves two ends. The first is again christological. The seriousness of Heracleon's high Christology, evident in the debate about the agency of the Logos, is again clearly visible here. Origen, despite the subordination of his Logos (*Comm.* 2.12–35), may have sympathized with Heracleon's aims. Both Origen and Heracleon wanted to affirm the unique position of the "only begotten Son" (*Comm.* 2.76), and Origen relies on the notion of "begetting" to ensure the Logos/Son's high status. For Origen, only God the Father merited the title of unbegotten (ἀγέννητος). The distinction is even clearer in the case of the Holy Spirit, the third divine "hypostasis," who was, according to Origen, "brought into being" (γενόμενον; *Comm.* 2.75).[26]

We might capture the significance of this debate by thinking about where Origen and Heracleon drew the line between Creator and creature. The heresiological tradition and the modern scholarship dependent on it, focusing on the doctrine of creation, suggest that Heracleon put his line high, separating off an "alien God" from all that is not God, while Origen's God is involved in the muck and mire of the creative act. To frame Heracleon's position in those terms is to miss its anthropological and soteriological thrust. For him, an heir both to the amalgam of Greek philosophy and Jewish wisdom speculation found in Philo and the Wisdom of Solomon,[27] God and the world are not distant, but joined at the hip, through the action of the divine, and uncreated pneuma (spirit). The entirety of the realm of spirit is uncreated and hence divine.

The relationship of God and world through the uncreated spirit which both share is the point at issue in the second fragment of Heracleon, in *Comm.* 2.137–139. The brief exchange between Origen and Heracleon in this fragment reaffirms the fundamental metaphysical commitments evident in the first fragment. It also reveals the philosophical point at stake between the two, which then affects the remaining discussion about anthropology and soteriology.

At *Comm.* 2.137, Origen is commenting on John 1:4, "What was made in him was life." Both Origen and Heracleon associate ὃ γέγονεν with what follows, as most modern commentators tend to do as well. Origen notes:

> But when Heracleon came to the passage 1:4 he took "in him" in a very forced manner to mean "in spiritual men," as though he thought the Word and spiritual men were the same. And, as if to give a reason, he says, "For he himself furnished

---

26. Origen's way of framing his understanding of the Trinity led to accusations that he made the Spirit a "creature." But on the difficulties of pre-Nicene Trinitarian language, see Crouzel, *Origen*, 174–75, 202.
27. See Wis 7:22–27.

their first form at their origin when he brought the things down by another into form and illumination and their own individuality, and brought them forth."

To unpack the cosmological and anthropological details implicit in this quote from Heracleon would require an extensive discussion. The most important point to note here is the affirmation that "spiritual" people, at the same time, *share a nature or substance* with the Logos, but they are also *subject to change*. They grow and develop through a process of individuation that ultimately enables them to relate cognitively to the Father from whom they have come. To use the metaphysics of motion that I suggest underlies Heracleon's conception of the creative function of the Logos: spiritual people are co-substantial with the Logos—they participate in its very being. Yet they are not identical with the Logos; they are not *akinetoi*, unchanging. Because they only "participate in" the nature of the Logos, they are subject to a movement, specifically a movement from potentiality to actuality.

Heracleon then does have a notion of the "essential" identity of God and God's children, but his notion of essence is far from static. No doubt a deep-seated epistemological principle underlies the affirmation: "only like can know like." If this is the case, we must be like God to know God. Again, Heracleon would find ample precedent for the position in the Platonizing appropriation of biblical texts that he inherited from Alexandrian Jewish forebears. But he adds a strong dash of Aristotle to the mix,[28] insisting that the essential relationship of God to God's children is one of potentiality, which must be actualized by an encounter with the Logos.

Origen clearly does not share Heracleon's assumption, particularly when he hears the word "spiritual." If the co-naturality of God and spirit lends the hierarchical cosmos of Heracleon a certain fluidity, because spirit itself is malleable, Origen's riff on the same theme seems more static. Spirit is superior to mortal humans, who participate in it by divine grace. Origen is quite clear on the distinction between spirit and the nonspiritual, as when he cites (*Comm.* 2.138) 1 Cor 2:14–15 on the "spirit of God" that judges all:

> For the spiritual is better than "man," since man is characterized either by soul or body or both of these together, but not also by spirit, which is more divine than these. The spiritual receive this title in accordance with his predominate participation in the spirit.

Origen's critique of Heracleon continues with extensive citations in Book 13,

---

28. On the use of Aristotle in polemics against the "gnostics," see Elizabeth A. Clark, *Clement's Use of Aristotle: The Aristotelian Contribution to Clement of Alexandria's Refutation of Gnosticism* (New York: Mellen, 1977). The Aristotelian distinction between potentiality and actuality, clearly invoked in such passages as Hippolytus, *Ref.* 6.17.1, plays an important, but not widely acknowledged role in several speculative theological projects of the late second century, including those of prominent "gnostics." For its role in the *Tripartite Tractate* (NHC I,5), see Attridge and Pagels, "Tripartite Tractate," 2:247–74.

which treats the episode of the Samaritan woman and its aftermath,[29] and Book 20, which treats John 8. By the time he has come to write those books, in Caesarea after 232, Origen's reading of Heracleon is more pointed and his polemic more focused. Nonetheless, the same slippage between the two, apparent in the treatment of the Prologue, is also evident here. Space precludes a full treatment of these portions of the commentary, but a few key passages will indicate the direction of the debate.[30]

Throughout these books, Origen objects to Heracleon's use of the category of "nature" or "essence" to explain the reactions to the gospel message of characters in John's Gospel and, by implication, people in the real world. Heracleon in frag. 17, on John 4:12–15 (*Comm.* 13.63), is said to have praised the Samaritan women "because she showed the kind of faith that was inseparable from her nature and corresponded to it (τὴν ἀδιάκριτον καὶ κατάλληλον τῇ φύσει ἑαυτῆς)." In frag. 19, on John 4:19–20 (*Comm.* 13:92), Heracleon is said to have noted that the Samaritan woman in acknowledging that Jesus was a prophet "behaved in a way suited to her nature (πρεπόντως τῆς αὐτῆς φύσει), for she neither denied nor explicitly acknowledged her shame." In commenting on the affirmation that those who worship the Father do so in spirit and truth (John 4:24), Heracleon (*Comm.* 13.148) again notes that "those who are of the same nature as the Father (αὐτοὶ τῆς αὐτῆς φύσεως ὄντες τῷ πατρί) are themselves spirit."

Wucherpfennig makes the useful observation that all of the language of "nature" in these fragments appears in introductory material or in Origen's interpretative comments.[31] It may well be that Origen himself has introduced all of this technical language into Heracleon. Alternatively, he could have misconstrued the way in which Heracleon used his philosophical categories.

Origen suggests in his critical comments that such statements on the part of Heracleon are deterministic, since what is something "by nature" precludes change. Consider his comment on the Samaritan woman's request for water in John 4:15 (frag. 17; *Comm.* 13.64): "If therefore he approved her choice (προαίρεσιν), without hinting[32] at her nature as something superior, we would have agreed." But there

---

29. See the thorough study by Jean-Michel Poffet, *La méthode exégétique d'Héracléon et d'Origène: Commentateurs de Jn 4, Jésus, la Samaritaine et les Samaritains* (Fribourg: Éditions Universitaires, 1985).
30. For earlier attempts to clarify Heracleon's theology in these areas, see Ekkehard Mühlenberg, "Wieviel Erlösungen kennt der Gnostiker Herakleon?" *ZNW* 66 (1975): 170–93, and Barbara Aland, "Erwählungstheologie und Menschenklassenlehre," in *Gnosis und Gnosticism: Papers Read at the Seventh International Conference on Patristic Studies (Oxford, September 8–13, 1975)* (ed. Martin Krause; Nag Hammadi Sudies 8; Leiden: Brill, 1977), 165–75. For a useful review of the history of the debate about Heracleon's anthropology, see Wucherpfennig, *Heracleon*, 333–36.
31. Wucherpfennig, *Heracleon*, 338–39. As Wucherpfennig notes, Origen may have derived his understanding of Valentinian determinist anthropology from his heresiological forebears, such as Irenaeus, *Adv. Haer.* 1.6.2.
32. Origen's choice of words here, αἰνιττόμενος, suggests that he may well be reading something into Heracleon.

are abundant indications that Heracleon did not make such an assumption. She does indeed share a "nature" with God, a nature (φύσις) that therefore is "undefiled, pure, and invisible (ἄχραντος γὰρ καὶ καθαρὰ καὶ ἀόρατος)."[33] But that nature does not preclude her having the defect of ignorance (*Comm.* 13.93), which is eliminated by the gift of the "spirit and power" of the Savior (*Comm.* 13.59). Once again, it is clear that for Heracleon, "nature" is a realm of potentiality to be realized, not something fixed and unchanging.

If the Samaritan woman represents the potential that has been realized to the fullest, that has accepted the revealing word of the Savior, and has become a vehicle for the enlightenment of others, the opponents addressed in John 8 represent another possibility, people who have utterly rejected the Savior's message, the "Jews" of the Fourth Gospel.[34] The terms for nature (φύσις) and substance (οὐσία) are particularly common in these chapters and, at first sight, Origen's selections suggest that Heracleon did indeed have a deterministic understanding of "nature" that would stand in tension with the framework evident in the treatment of the Johannine Prologue and the episode of the Samaritan woman.

Heracleon will explain why it is that the word of Jesus "has no place in" the ears of his opponents (John 8:37), because they are unsuitable for it, "either by their substance or by their disposition (ἤτοι κατ' οὐσίαν ἢ κατὰ γνώμην)."[35] He will explain what it means for the Jews to be "of your father the devil" (John 8:44) or "of the substance (ἐκ τῆς οὐσίας) of the devil."[36]

A lengthy fragment 46 (*Comm.* 20.211–218) offers the fullest explanation of Heracleon's terminology. Here appears language that seems to confirm the under-

---

33. Frag. 24, on John 4:24, *Comm.* 13.147. There may be a remote echo of Wis 7:22–23.

34. The Johannine *Iudaioi* have already become for Heracleon, as they have for some modern readers such as Rudolf Bultmann, a symbol of all who have rejected Jesus. The extensive contemporary debate about the original function(s) of the character of the *Iudaioi*, much discussed in the post-Holocaust period, need not detain us here. Among the many treatments of the topic, see C. J. Cuming, "The Jews in the Fourth Gospel," *ExpTim* 60 (1948/49): 290–92; Malcolm Lowe, "Who Were the Ἰουδαῖοι?" *NovT* 18 (1976): 101–30; Wayne Meeks, "Am I a Jew? Johannine Christianity and Judaism," in *Christianity, Judaism, and Other Greco-Roman Cults: Studies for Morton Smith at Sixty* (ed. Jacob Neusner; Leiden: Brill, 1975), 1:163–86; Urban C. von Wahlde, "The Johannine 'Jews': A Critical Survey," *NTS* 28 (1981/82): 33–60; John Ashton, "The Identity and Function of the Ἰουδαῖοι in the Fourth Gospel," *NovT* 27 (1985): 40–75; M. J. Cook, "The Gospel of John and the Jews," *RevExp* 84 (1987): 259–71; R. Alan Culpepper, "The Gospel of John and the Jews," *RevExp* 84 (1987): 273–88; M. Rissi, "'Die Juden' im Johannesevangelium," *ANRW* II/26.3:2099–141; Adele Reinhartz, "The Johannine Community and Its Jewish Neighbors: A Reappraisal," in *Literary and Social Readings of the Fourth Gospel* (vol. 2 of *What Is John?*; ed. Fernando F. Segovia; SBLSymS 7; Atlanta: Scholars Press, 1998), 111–38; idem, "The Gospel of John: How the 'Jews' Became Part of the Plot," in *Jesus, Judaism, and Christian Anti-Judaism* (ed. Paula Frederiksen and Adele Reinhartz; Lousiville: Westminster John Knox, 2002), 99–116; R. Bieringer, D. Pollefeyt, and F. Vandecasteele-Vanneuville, eds., *Anti-Judaism and the Fourth Gospel: Papers of the Leuven Colloquium, 2000* (Jewish and Christian Heritage Series 1; Assen: Van Gorcum, 2001).

35. Frag. 43; *Comm.* 20.54.

36. Frag. 44; *Comm.* 20.168; similarly frag. 45; *Comm.* 20.198.

standing of Origen and of the subsequent heresiological tradition, about the determinist cast of Heracleon's anthropology. Those who are "by nature (φύσει) children of the Devil" are equated with "the Choics"; while the Psychics are those who "have become children of Devil by social convention (θέσει)."[37] Yet one should not move too rapidly from a sociological categorization, which identifies the results of the soteriological process, with the mechanism of that process itself. The Valentinian doctrine of the "three classes" of humankind clearly applies to the former, but is not a key to the latter.

Heracleon provides evidence of how he uses his terminology, in tracing the semantic extension of "children,"[38] which may refer either to children "by nature" who have been begotten by a parent, children by "disposition (γνώμη)," and children by merit (ἀξίᾳ). The former refers to one who "does the will of another person by his own inclination." The latter refers to those who are "known as children of hell, or of darkness and lawlessness." This paragraph represents Heracleon "Philologus" at his best, exploring semantics as a prerequisite to expounding a complex text. That range extends from the literal or primary meaning of the word, its application "in the proper sense (κυρίως),"[39] through two derived meanings, one focusing on interior disposition, another on external estimation. The latter two possibilities allow senses in which some people can come to be "children of the Devil": "Again he (Heracleon) says: 'He (scil. Jesus) calls them children of the Devil, not because the Devil produces any of them, but because by doing the works of the Devil, they become like him.'"[40]

The passage evokes a principle articulated within the Fourth Gospel itself, that what people do determines how they will respond to "the Light" (John 3:20–21). In a reading of Heracleon against the background of an assumed Valentinian anthropology—a reading that begins with Origen—the formulation applies ostensibly only to one class of human beings, the Psychics, who alone actualize one or another inherent potentiality.[41] Yet that reading produces a very odd interpretation of the Gospel, a reading in which the most negative group of those who reject the Revealer are in an "intermediate" position. No, the labels and the rigid anthropology that they import are, as Wucherpfennig suggests, an introduction of Origen.

---

37. Frag. 46; *Comm.* 20.213. C. Blanc (SC 290:263) translates "par adoption"; Foerster (*Gnosis*, 180) "by intent." Both short-circuit the discussion that follows, which will explore what "social convention" means.

38. Frag. 46; *Comm.* 20.215.

39. The term is used at *Comm.* 20.215.

40. *Comm.* 20.218.

41. A disputed phrase in *Comm.* 20.213 may refer to the Psychics, who have a more positive outcome (ἀφ᾽ ὧν τῇ φύσει δύνανταί τινες καὶ θέσει υἱοὶ θεοῦ χρηματίσαι). Foerster translates: "Some who are of this nature may also be called sons of God by intent (θέσει)." Blanc (SC 290:263) more correctly renders: "d'où il résulte qu'on peut être appelé fils de Dieu par nature et par adoption." The prepositional phrase ἀφ᾽ ὧν thus refers to the principles of the previous clause, not to the class of people mentioned in it.

While Heracleon's linguistic scheme lays out the possibility of "natural" children of the devil, the resulting definition of a "nature" functions largely as a conceptual boundary marker, a limiting case. For what the devil marks is unproductive negation, an absolute falsehood that cannot produce truth; his "nature," as Heracleon says, is falsehood.[42] A human "child of the Devil" is one who, as frag. 46 suggests, imitates the negativity of utter falsehood.

6. Conclusion

Heracleon does no more violence to the text of John's Prologue than does Origen and in some particulars, appears to be trying mightily to give a consistent and coherent reading. At stake in their different readings of the text is a fundamental theological disagreement, but the "heretic" seems to be defending a more exalted view of the Logos.

In the fragments that highlight anthropology and soteriology, it is likely that Origen has imposed upon Heracleon an alien scheme. Insofar as "nature" has any role to play in Heracleon's thinking, it is imbued with a distinction between potentiality and actuality. Heracleon's use of the category is thus far more supple and flexible than Origen allows.

Zusammenfassung

Das Johannesevangelium war einer derjenigen Texte, die von den frühen christlichen Theologen genauer behandelt wurden. Herakleon war der erste Denker (2. Jh. n. Chr.), der sich mit diesem Text intensiver systematisch befaßt hat. Sein Werk wurde allerdings als häretisch wahrgenommen. Daher sind die Zitate aus dem Johanneskommentar des Origenes alles, was von Herakleons Werk erhalten geblieben ist. Sein Œuvre wurde allgemein mit Valentin in Verbindung gebracht, und in das System Valentins wurde die Johannesauslegung Herakleons hineininterpretiert. Die neuere Forschung hat sich demgegenüber auf die Analyse der Herakleon-Fragmente selbst konzentriert, anstatt die Polemiken des Origenes zu übernehmen. Die Neuuntersuchung hat gezeigt, daß Herakleon ein umsichtiger Exeget gewesen ist.

In vielerlei Hinsicht ähnelt Origenes Zugang zum Johannesevangelium Herakleons Hermeneutik. Wie in der Antike nicht unüblich, fragten beide nach einem allegorischen Sinn in den Geschichten des Johannesevangeliums. Von der grammatischen Analyse bis zur Textkritik verwendeten beide die kritischen Methoden ihrer Zeit. Im Zentrum ihres Konflikts lagen christologische und soteriologische Themen. Diese theologischen Indikationen wirkten sich auf ihre unterschiedlichen Ansichten über den Menschen und über Gottes Verhältnis zur Welt aus. Die unterschiedlichen philosophischen Begrifflichkeiten dieser beiden Denker sind der hermeneutische Schlüssel zu ihren Differenzen.

Dieser Aufsatz leistet eine detaillierte Analyse der vier Hauptabschnitte jenes Kommen-

---

42. Frag. 47; *Comm.* 20.252–254.

tars des Origenes, der sich mit Herakleons Werk beschäftigt. Ein besonderes Augenmerk liegt dabei auf dem Johannesprolog. Origenes erörtert in diesen Abschnitten die Johannesauslegung Herakleons bezüglich einer Vielzahl exegetischer Fragen. Diese exegetischen Streitpunkte zeigen, wie die beiden Theologen ihre Auslegungsvorhaben jeweils unterschiedlich verstanden. Origenes einerseits wirft Herakleon fehlerhafte Prämissen vor. Herakleon andererseits beschäftigt sich mit zentralen theologischen Problemen, die sich aus dem Text des Johannesevangeliums ergeben und von Origenes entweder übersehen oder heruntergespielt werden. Origenes' Kritik mißversteht das eigentliche Anliegen Herakleons. Herakleon versucht z. B. eine Erklärung für die Göttlichkeit des Logos zu geben, indem er den Logos als selbstbewegt versteht. In diesem Zusammenhang entstellt Origenes Herakleons Argumente, indem er technische Sprache verwendet, die Herakleon selbst nicht gebraucht zu haben scheint—so z. B. im Falle von Herakleons Anthropologie und dem Begriff οὐσία. Origenes interpretiert einen Determinismus in die Begrifflichkeit Herakleons hinein, der letzterem fremd war. Herakleon bediente sich dem gegenüber der Aristotelischen Kategorien der Potentialität und Aktivität. Diese terminologischen Mißverständnisse und Differenzen machen deutlich, wie Origenes und Herakleon den Johannestext von unterschiedlichen philosophischen und theologischen Programmen her betrachten.

The Enscripturation of Philosophy: The Incorporeality of God in Origen's Exegesis

Karen Jo Torjesen

1. Introduction

As a systematic discipline, Christian theology traces its development through the history of philosophy. Philosophical cosmology, terminology, concepts, and modes of argument are the ancestors of Christian theology alongside of scripture. The destinies of these two lineages are intertwined insofar as they each make claims to delineate an ultimate reality. Like philosophers, interpreters of the stories, poetry, and histories of the Bible make claims to reality. Biblical theologians work along the intersection of philosophy and biblical interpretation. Through such a genealogy, both scripture and philosophical notions are subtly transformed. What happens when the rarified beams of philosophical abstraction pass through the denser medium of scripture? Is their light bent? Scriptural language vivifies and, in a process of rhetorical involution, renders poetic the spare concepts of philosophical abstraction.[1] In this process of rhetorical involution, scriptural language exerts a steady pressure on philosophical concepts and slowly reshapes them in its own image. Nowhere is that process more fascinating than in the scriptural elaboration of the philosophical concept of incorporeality by Origen of Alexandria.[2]

Philosophy has contributed well-honed conceptual categories that Christian theologians, in turn, have elaborated and "fleshed out" by using scriptural language. Their intent is to assimilate philosophical claims to describe reality in terms of scripture—scripture encompasses (and embraces) the truth of philosophy. This is simply

---

1. Thomas Csordas uses rhetorical involution to describe the creative process by which religious language is amplified, expanded, and extended within a religious worldview. Rhetorical involution has the effect of creating a fully fleshed-out linguistic cosmos for the believer to inhabit. See Thomas J. Csordas, *Language, Charisma, and Creativity: The Ritual Life of a Religious Movement* (Berkeley: University of California Press, 1997), 78–79.

2. Origen of Alexandria produced the first systematic treatment of Christian teachings. In his *On First Principles*, he devotes an entire section to the term "incorporeality." The term is central to the Platonic framework that he uses to construct Christian theology.

the practical outworking of a process of philosophy's assimilation to and inculturation in the world of scripture.[3] The same process is at work in the more extravagant claims of the apologists, that Plato learned his philosophy from Moses.[4] It is precisely the claims to reality for biblical texts that impel theologians to articulate their theologies using biblical concepts and terminology, but also to think through, and with, biblical texts when working on philosophical problems.

Origen of Alexandria offers an excellent case study for the *enscripturation* of philosophy because it is he who gave Christian theology its earliest systematic philosophical formulation.[5] The Greek patristic theological tradition is built at nearly every point on foundations laid by Origen.[6] Theologians of the West regularly enriched the Latin theological traditions by importing Eastern theologies and spiritualities also built on Origen's legacy. Equally important is the fact that Origen pioneered a thoroughgoing use of allegorical readings. He was the first theologian to write full commentaries on biblical books and the first to work out a systematic process of allegorization.[7] His doctrine of the divine origins of scripture required that every passage yield an allegorical meaning.

2. The Problem of the Incorporeality of God

God without a body was not an easy sell. The notion of the incorporeality of the divine was the fruit of philosophical abstraction. In myth, poetry, and ritual, however, the divine was embodied, if not in images at least in the imagination. Furthermore, the scriptural depiction of a god who acts and intervenes in history did not lend itself to the philosophical notion of incorporeality. In fact, the struggle over God's body in Alexandria dragged on for three centuries. Incorporeality implied the

---

3. See Christopher Stead's magisterial work, *Philosophy in Christian Antiquity* (Cambridge: Cambridge University Press, 1994). For a contemporary discussion of the issues of a divine corporeality, see also Grace Jantzen, *God's World, God's Body* (Philadelphia: Westminster, 1984), 21–35.

4. Within the Roman cultural context, appeals to antiquity established the truth for religious traditions. Critics of Christianity could be dismissive of its teachings as newfangled innovations. Christian apologists defended Christianity by claiming Moses as the founder of Christian teachings and then by "demonstrating" that Plato had learned from Moses. See, for example, *Cohortatio ad Graecos* (*ANF* 1:273), a text commonly attributed to Justin Martyr that is, however, probably from the third century. The arguments so richly developed in this text are echoed in many of the apologists.

5. Origen's synthesis of philosophy and Christian teachings is so thorough that two decades of Origen scholarship have been locked in a debate over whether Origen was primarily a philosopher, driven by philosophical problems to rethink Christian doctrines, or a Christian theologian, cautiously appropriating philosophical notions.

6. The Alexandrian tradition of Didymus, Athanasius, Cyril, and even Arius built on Origen's legacy. Origen's influence on the Cappadocians, Gregory of Nyssa, Basil of Caesarea, and Gregory of Nazianzen is considerable. The tradition of ascetic theology systematized by Evagrius also built on Origen's system.

7. Hippolytus preached and wrote extended commentary on scripture. His works inspired Origen's patron, Ambrosius, to finance a major undertaking of publishing commentaries by providing Origen with a large staff of stenographers.

formlessness of God. Consequently, the struggle to assert the incorporeal nature of God required a frontal attack on biblical anthropomorphism.

A couple of anecdotes will convey a sense of the religious climate on the subject of God's body among Egyptian Christians. An Egyptian monk, Abba Serapion, was visited by a learned deacon from Cappadocia by the name of Photius. Photius was disturbed by the anthropomorphism embedded in the devotional practices of the pious monk and he engaged Serapion in a conversation on the theme of Gen 1:26, "God created man in his own image and likeness." For Abba Serapion, this one passage established a doctrine of God, an anthropology, and a devotional practice. In all of the churches of the East that Photius had visited, each read this passage spiritually, not literally. It is not the embodied human that bears the divine image. Rather, it is some invisible part. Serapion was devastated. The loss of a human shape for the image of God left him despairing. Prostrating himself on the ground, he wept and cried out, "They have taken my God from me and I have now no one to behold, whom to worship and address!"[8] It would take a new devotional piety to create a sense of intimacy with an incorporeal God.

A century later, rioting over the body of God threatened to bring down the bishop of Alexandria and also resulted in the exile of four Egyptian luminaries from monastic Egypt.[9] Theophilus, a bishop and a supporter and patron of the erudite Origenist monks called the Tall Brothers, had taken the occasion of his Easter Festal letter to press the importance of the doctrine of the incorporeality of God. When the letter circulated among the monastic communities with monks like Abba Serapion, it created a furor. Suddenly the bishop found himself confronted by a mob of angry monks threatening violence over his Easter letter. Theophilus, better remembered as a shrewd politician than as a pastor of the flock, judged the anthromorphizing sentiments strong enough and their numbers large enough that he aligned himself with the anthropomorphists. He moved swiftly against the Tall Brothers, exiled them from Egypt, and secured their condemnation again in Constantinople when they sought refuge with the bishop there.

The philosophical debate over the corporeality of God had been simmering for centuries among Cynics, Epicureans, Stoics, and Academics. Each of these groups offered critical popular notions of providence, sacrifice, prayer, as well as anthropomorphic representations of deity.[10] Literati such as Apuleius, Celsus, and Numenius

---

8. John Cassian, *Conferences* X, *LNPF* II/11:401–3. For a discussion of the evidence of the early Christian controversy over the corporeality of God, see David L. Paulsen, "Early Christian Belief in an Incorporeal Deity: Origen and Augustine as Reluctant Witnesses," *HTR* 83 (1990): 105–16.

9. In *The Origenist Controversy: The Cultural Construction of an Early Christian Debate* (Princeton: Princeton University Press, 1992), Elizabeth Clarke provides the most comprehensive analysis of this conflict, weighing political interests alongside theological and ecclesiastical aspects.

10. Harold W. Attridge, "The Philosophical Critique of Religion under the Early Empire," *ANRW* II/16:45–78.

commonly appealed to apophatic language to articulate God's transcendence.[11] The notion of the incorporeality of God had gained a wide following among the intelligentsia.

Among Christians, the crisis was generated by the confrontation of a philosophical conception of divine incorporeality with biblical anthropomorphism. The God who is seen and heard, who is angry and repents, who strikes and succours, resisted any easy assimilation to the abstract categories of the unity, simplicity, formlessness, and incorporeality of the divine. When the irresistible force of philosophical thought collided with the immovable object of anthropomorphizing biblical language, the collision created a different kind of cataclysm. In his fine article "The Incorporeality of God," Guy Stroumsa demonstrates that biblical anthropomorphism was equally dangerous in two quite different aspects. On the one hand, when simple believers read the Bible, the anthropomorphic language made them stubbornly resistant to the fructifying insights of philosophy and the serious claims of rational thought. On the other hand, the insistence on the utter transcendence of God led the gnostics to reject the Old Testament altogether. Stroumsa argues that only allegorical interpretation of biblical anthropomorphism could chart a course between the Scylla of anthropomorphizing and the Charybis of gnostic dualism.[12]

3. The Centrality of Corporeality for Origen's Theology

The crisis for Origen was acute. That God is *asomatos*, without a body, was not only a foundational principle for a Platonist cosmology, it was also a constitutive element of Origen's soteriology. Origen's entire theological system was dependent on this central tenet of Platonic philosophy. Origen's dilemma was that the incorporeality of God was neither a part of apostolic teaching nor a part of the *regula fidei*. In his preface to *On First Principles*, Origen exposed incorporeality as a major theme. "How god himself is to be understood, whether as corporeal or formed according to some shape or of some nature different than bodies is a point which is not clearly in our teachings."[13] Such topics were then necessarily open for investigation, an investigation that employed dialectics and drew heavily on the debates in philosophical circles. Such an investigation was nonetheless located primarily in the linguistic world of scripture.

When laying out the topics and the agenda for his four-volume work *On First Principles*, Origen uses his discussion of incorporeality to function as a fulcrum for

---

11. Guy Stroumsa, "The Incorporeality of God: Context and Implications for Origen's Position," *Religion* 13 (1983): 345. Stroumsa shows that *Allogenes*, the *Apocryphon of John*, and the *Tripartite Tractate* blend the poetic and the philosophical in the richly elaborated apophatic language for God.

12. Ibid., 349.

13. Origen, *De Principiis*, Preface 9. In *On First Principles* (trans. G. W. Butterworth; Gloucester, Mass.: Peter Smith, 1973). (References to this work indicate paragraph, rather than page number. Citations of this work refer to the Butterworth translation.)

leveraging his treatment of each of the major doctrines. Origen begins his preface by listing each of the topics that he will take up in Books I–III. He calls these topics the teachings of Christ delivered in "an unbroken succession from the apostles [that] have been delivered in the plainest terms": the one creator God, the incarnate Christ, the divine Spirit sharing in the divinity of Father and Son, the free will of the soul, its rewards and punishments, the angels and the opposing powers, the creation and dissolution of the world of matter, and finally the doctrine of scripture's hidden meanings.[14] Origen then proceeds to engage these topics in the above order. Before he concludes his introduction, however, he takes up the problem of the concept of incorporeality and its problematic absence from the language of scripture.

More critical than the problem that the incorporeality of God is not part of apostolic teaching is the problem that no scriptural language affirms the incorporeality of God. Origen states this problem in unequivocal terms: "The term incorporeal is unknown, not only to the majority of Christians but also to the scriptures."[15]

Even when Christians employed the word *asomatos*, they often understood the term to mean a refined corporeality. This idea is similar to the Stoic notion of *pneuma*, or spirit, as the divine, the purest and finest essence, a divine form of corporeality. It is this notion of corporeality that informed the Christians' interpretation of John 4:24: "God is Spirit and they that worship him must worship him in spirit." Origen acknowledges that even in view of this passage, Christians attribute some form of corporeality to God. Origen acknowledges this attribution and then takes some time to discount this popular use of incorporeality by discrediting the appeal to the *Preaching of Peter*, a book whose apostolic authority was challenged in his age. He does this to clear the way for a thoroughgoing Middle Platonic understanding of *asomatos*.[16]

Origen concludes his preface by making the rigorous philosophical concept of incorporeality the leading topic for his ensuing discussions of God, Christ, the Holy Spirit, and the creation of rational beings:

> Nevertheless we shall inquire whether asomatos (incorporeal) is found in the scriptures under a different name. We must also seek to discover how god himself is to be conceived whether as corporeal and fashioned in some shape or as having a different nature from bodies. A point which is not clearly set forth in the teaching.

---

14. Ibid.
15. Ibid., Preface 8. Butterworth uses Koetschau's edition that favors the Greek text. Rufinius' Latin translation offers a milder version of the same sentiment. Koetschau finds this interpretation in a fragment attributed to Antipater of Bostra and preserved in John of Damascus' writings. See PG 96:501.
16. In "Early Christian Belief in an Incorporeal Deity," Paulsen makes the interesting case that notions of the corporeality of God proved surprisingly resistant to a Platonizing transcendence (105–16).

The same inquiry must be made in regard to Christ and the Holy Spirit and indeed in regard to every soul and every rational nature also.[17]

The concept of the incorporeality of the divine is essential for Origen's elaboration of the doctrines of God, Christ, and the Holy Spirit. In addition to its importance for the Christian doctrine of God, Origen also appeals to the incorporeality of the divine in order to explain the creation of the rational beings, angels, daimons, and the human soul. In order to be given the status of an article of faith, however, this philosophical concept must be clothed in scriptural language. Indeed, it must be embedded in the scriptural meanings themselves. Hence Origen proposes to "inquire whether the actual things the Greek philosophers call *asomatos* is found in the Holy Scriptures under another sense."[18] This is the overriding concern of the first book of *On First Principles*; Origen's introduction of the term *asomatos* at the end of his preface allows him to begin his treatment of the doctrines of God, Christ, and the Holy Spirit with a discussion of the incorporeal nature of the divine.

4. Allegory as a Strategy for Bending Biblical Language

Origen insists again and again that the scriptures are the oracles of God. As a result, the language and vocabulary of scripture carry a value beyond the capacity to convey meaning. The choice of words is the key element in the process of inspiration. More than any others, the allegorical interpreters invest the language of scripture with a unique potency because it is the only language and the only vocabulary that opens up higher, spiritual meaning.[19] No other language has this capacity. Origen is reluctant to articulate theological ideas in any other language than scriptural language.

While it is the allegorical interpreter's high valuation of scriptural language that creates the original dilemma, namely that the incorporeality so central to Origen's Christian theology is absent from biblical language, it is also allegory that gives the solution.[20] It is the rhetorical involution that makes it possible to wed the meaning of *asomatos* to biblical language. For each passage using a biblical metaphor such as God's eye, hand, foot, the allegorist applies the doctrine of the incorporeality of God. Further, each new scriptural elaboration of the doctrine of the incorporeality

---

17. Origen, *De Princ.*, Preface 8–9.
18. Ibid., Preface 9.
19. Because Origen considers the language of scripture to be oracular—prophecy in its fullest sense—the words themselves carry a particular potency. Furthermore he shares with his culture a sense of the intimate connection between the sound of a word and the essence of the thing to which it refers.
20. Stroumsa has argued that it was precisely the dilemma of an anthropomorphizing scripture that led gnostic Christians to reject scripture in favor of theological myth. In allegorical interpretation, Origen found a middle ground between the gnostic rejection of scripture and the acceptance of a sacred text ("Incorporeality," 349).

of God drags a string of verses in its wake, drawn into the exegetical process to clarify the first metaphor that was implied in the notion of God's incorporeality.

Allegorical interpretation overlays new sets of meanings onto scripture and transforms spiritual meaning into a palimpsest of the original text. Unlike the palimpsest printed on papyri, however, the palimpsest created by allegorical interpretation is dynamic and fluid because the actual scriptures' words have a life and force of their own that exert a pressure on the meanings the allegorist has overwritten. The power of the actual words of scripture (in the allegorical framework we can talk about the power of the literal sense) should not be underestimated precisely because allegorical interpretation pays such minute attention to the actual words in their grammatical, literal, and historical senses.

5. Interpretative Strategies

5.1. The First Strategy:
Conducting Philosophical Arguments in Biblical Language

Origen's first strategy is to rely primarily on scriptural language to articulate and even solve philosophical problems. For example, Origen argues for philosophical distinctions by quoting scriptural authority.[21] It is not that he does not make the same arguments that other philosophers do. Rather it is that he argues his claims through and in the medium of scriptural language. In his opening chapter of Book I on the divine nature, Origen's argument for the incorporeality of God appeals to biblical books from the Gospel of John to Letters of Paul, from Deuteronomy and Exodus to Proverbs.[22]

This practice giving scripture a primacy in Christian philosophical schools had no parallels in other philosophical schools. Philosophers from time to time would cite the authority of the poets, but their arguments could and did stand alone, independent of the poets. By the time Origen introduces the familiar doctrine of the incorporeality of God in Book I of *On First Principles,* he has performed an erudite exegesis of "God is Spirit," "God is light," and "Our God is a consuming fire."[23] He positions the philosophical doctrine of the incorporeality of God as flowing directly from scripture. The result is that when referring to God, scriptural vocabulary of light, spirit, and fire now functions as a key signifier for God's incorporeality. Scrip-

---

21. One of the most common elements in rhetorical composition, *inventio*, was the citation of authorities. In the Hellenistic tradition in which Origen stands, these authorities came from the body of classical literature. His use of scriptural citations follows this rhetorical pattern. In doing so, however, he is consciously supplanting classical literature with scripture as well as investing scripture with the homogenizing, cultural function of classical literature.

22. In the Preface, Origen uses John 1:3; 1:17; 14:6; Heb 1:1; 11:23; 1 Cor 15:42; 2 Cor 13:3. In Book I.1, he uses Deut 4:24; Matt 5:8; 11:27; John 1:18; 4:20, 22, 23, 24; 14:23; Col 1:15; 1 John 1:5; 1 Cor 3:6, 12; Heb 8:5.

23. John 4:24; Ps 34:10 (LXX); Deut 4:24.

tural language is made the bearer and revealer of philosophical categories. From his exegesis, Origen concludes that "God therefore must not be thought to be any kind of body, nor to exist in a body, but to be a simple intellectual existence."[24] Simplicity and unity are the hallmarks of the incorporeality of God. Neither space nor physical magnitude is an appropriate category for the incorporeal mind. As soon as Origen provides the synopsis of divine incorporeality that he derives from scripture, he returns to scripture. "But these assertions may perhaps seem to be less authoritative to those who desire to be instructed in divine things from the holy scriptures and who seek to have it proved to them from that source how God's nature surpasses the nature of bodies."[25] By the time he has finished, the scriptural language claiming that God is light, God is fire, God is Sprit, and Christ is the image of the invisible God teaches the doctrine of the incorporeality of God. Origen creates intertextuality between philosophy and scripture in which poetic metaphors become the medium for philosophical clarity and precision. The result is a rhetorical fusion of scriptural language with philosophical meaning.

5.2. THE SECOND STRATEGY: BIBLICAL INTERTEXTUALITY

An internal intertextuality of scripture is key to Origen's incorporation of philosophical notions into biblical texts. Origen's use of exegesis to expound on philosophical ideas follows a recognizable pattern of five steps. The first is a direct challenge to an anthropomorphic reading of a biblical text. The second step is to bring another scripture, scripture "B," into the interpretation of scripture "A" on the basis of a common term. The third step is to argue (often employing dialectic) that scripture "B" clearly implies the incorporeality of God. The fourth step is to read from a clear meaning of scripture (which affirms the incorporeality of the divine) to a similar meaning of scripture "A" on the basis of the common term. The fifth, and perhaps most important move, is to graft onto scripture "B" a religious meaning or religious obligation nested in the concept of the incorporeality of God. The result is that both scriptural passages "A" and "B" are understood to confirm the incorporeality of God and, at the same time, are invested with an important significance for the Christian life. For Origen, theology is inseparable from soteriology.[26]

The most interesting examples of this five-step process are found in Origen's refutations of readings that assume God's embodiment in a fine, ethereal materiality for such passages as: "God is a consuming fire"(Deut 4:24), "God is Spirit" (John 4:24), and "God is light" (1 John 1:5). Origen challenges the readings that imply God's embodiment—fire requires fuel, *pneuma* can increase density; how can these

---

24. Origen, *De Princ.* I.1.
25. Ibid.
26. The concern for the soteriological process of transforming the hearer or reader is the key element in Origen's allegorical exegesis. No allegorical interpretation is complete until the hearer is brought into the circle of the spiritual allegorical meaning derived from the literal sense. See Karen Jo Torjesen, *Hemeneutical Procedure and Theological Structure in Origen's Exegesis* (Berlin: de Gruyter, 1985), 138–47.

passages be read literally?[27] The following illustrates the five-step interpretative process:

1. Origen moves from "God is light" in 1 John 1:5 to Ps 35:10: "In thy light shall we see light."

2. The Psalmist cannot be understood as referring to material light, since what is implied here is the intellectual act of knowing. Origen's *Commentary on John* makes the point more clearly. Material light is a metaphor for the invisible and incorporeal light; light is intelligible and spiritual.[28] Thus light needs to be understood as a spiritual power that enlightens the understanding.

3. To bring light is not to penetrate a material darkness, but to enlighten the understanding. According to both Ps 35 and 1 John, light is therefore the spiritual power that causes the human to see clearly the truth of all things.

4. The hearer or reader who has diligently meditated on the meaning of scripture is persuaded that spirit, fire, and light cannot refer to God's mode of corporeal being but to the spiritual powers that enlighten the mind and to the fire that "consumes evil thoughts and shameful deeds and longings after sin."[29]

5. A similar operation performed on John 4:24 ("God is Spirit") and 2 Cor 3:15 ("Where the Spirit of the Lord is there is liberty") results in the reader's understanding that spirit refers to the intellectual or noetic realm. In this case, the Spirit is the one who reveals spiritual knowledge. All of these interpretations remain in the arena of the noetic—spirit, fire, and light.

5.3. The Third Strategy: Exegetical Preaching

Thus far we have considered Origen's use of scripture to elaborate a Christian philosophy in his definitive work, *On First Principles*. A third strategy for the enscripturation of philosophy, and certainly the most influential, was Origen's exegetical preaching. In exegetical preaching, key scriptural passages convey philosophical meanings.

For the proponents of the incorporeality of God, the most troublesome scriptural passage was Gen 1:26: the human was created in the image and likeness of God. Origen often reiterates that when scripture says that the human was created in the image of God, it is essential to understand that the passage refers to the inner person, which is incorporeal, incorruptible, and immortal.[30] Origen's homilies on

---

27. Origen, *Comm. Jo.* 13.129.
28. Ibid., 13.132.
29. Origen, *De Princ.* I.1.
30. Origen, *Gen. Hom.* 1.13. In *Origen, Homilies on Genesis and Exodus* (trans. Ronald Heine; Washington, D.C.: Catholic University Press, 1982). (Citations of this work refer to the Heine translation.)

Genesis tackle the allegedly self-evident implications that Abba Serapion would draw from this passage by linking Gen 1:26 to Isa 66:1: "Heaven is my throne, earth is my footstool." "Is God so huge," Origen baits his Caesarean congregation, "that his body fills the heavens? What do heavens mean here?"[31] Again Origen brings into play an intertextuality of scripture that he creates between Phil 3:20 and Eph 2:6. Origen interprets the passage "For those who have their conversation in heaven" (Phil 3:20) to mean that God resides in those who have become heavenly through the perfection of life and of depth of thought.[32]

It was the words of scripture along with their interpretations that echoed and reechoed in the lives and memories of early Christians. Liturgical readings of scripture were constitutive elements of every Christian gathering; the office of reader was among the earliest Christian offices. Early Christian preaching often followed a program for the reading and hearing of the entire scripture.[33] The Psalms were the hymnal of the early church, and pedagogical and devotional practices encouraged committing large portions of scripture to memory. Exegetical preaching is obviously an earlier form of the enscripturation of theology in which particular theological understandings are embedded in particular textual readings. When the text is read, a distinct theological "take" is heard. In this way, the philosophical concept of the incorporeality of God penetrates scripture and passes through scripture to the Christian understanding of God.

5.4. THE FOURTH STRATEGY: APPEALS TO RELIGIOUS PIETY

Incorporated into exegetical preaching was a fourth strategy for asserting the incorporeality of God in the face of anthropomorphizing scriptures. It is what I call a rhetorical manipulation of religious sensibilities. Here, Origen invokes what Guy Stroumsa terms "the rationalist criticism of religious sensibilities directed at popular religious piety."[34] Generally the intellectual critique of popular anthropomorphism did not aim to discredit the gods and goddesses of the Homeric myths, but to redirect personal piety toward the principles that the deities represented. Origen's critique of anthropomorphic readings touches a nerve when he implies that such readings are an act of impiety. To believe that God is angry, jealous, or vengeful by virtue of a literal reading of the Old Testament is equivalent to slander. Simple believers who accept such literal statements seem to be willing to believe of God things "that they would not believe of the most unjust and savage of men."[35]

When preaching on Gen 1:26, Origen explains that it would be an impious,

---

31. Ibid.
32. Ibid.
33. On the basis of Origen's preaching in Caesarea, Pierre Nautin has reconstructed a liturgical cycle for reading the entire scriptures in a three-year period. See Nautin, *Origène* (Paris: Beauschesne, 1977), 389–409.
34. Stroumsa, "Incorporeality," 345.
35. Origen, *De Princ.* IV.2.1.

slanderous way to think about God if the image of God were to refer to the flesh of the human being "fashioned from the slime of the earth."[36] This rhetorical strategy, however blandly stated, accuses the devout believer of impiety, of defaming, and of dishonoring the object of worship precisely in the act of worship itself. Religiously, this is a far more potent critique than it is philosophically. When Origen takes on a fellow philosopher Heracleon, the accusation of impiety takes on the tone of invective: "It is the worst impiety (the notion of humans being consubstantial with the divine), the consequences which flow from their teachings are sacrilegious, impious and blasphemous."[37]

Origen's criticism of anthropomorphism has much in common with that of the philosophers. With them, he shares the conviction that a purified conception of the divine forms the basis for true piety.[38] In the words of the Epicurean Diogenes of Oneoanda, "the essence of piety is not external worship, but the proper conception of God," or according to Apollonius of Tyana, "true piety is to recognise the unity and transcendence of God."[39] Origen differs from these opinions by connecting his philosophy to scripture. Scripture is foundational for the church, but even more for Origen who is persuaded of its oracular character. In the end, with the aid of allegorical and interlinear exegesis, "the natural and purified piety" of the philosophers was mediated by the anthropomorphic language of scripture itself. Allegorical readings of scripture overlaid scriptural language with a philosophical piety such that even when anthropomorphic language was preached, what was understood was the incorporeality of God.

ZUSAMMENFASSUNG

Philosophische Weltbilder, Terminologie, Konzepte und Argumentationsweisen sind oft die Vorläufer christlicher Theologien. Die Philosophie steuert konzeptionelle Kategorien bei, die mit Hilfe von Schrift-Sprache (*scriptural language*) ausgearbeitet und vervollkommnet werden. Schrift-Sprache belebt die kahlen Konzepte philosophischer Abstraktion und überträgt sie ins Poetische. In diesem Prozess übt die Schrift-Sprache einen ständigen Druck auf philosophische Konzepte aus und gestaltet sie in ihr eigenes Ebenbild um. Dieser Prozess ist nirgends faszinierender als in der biblischen Ausarbeitung des philosophischen Konzepts der Körperlosigkeit in der Theologie und Exegese Origenes' von Alexandrien.

Gott ohne Körper ist nicht einfach vorstellbar. Körperlosigkeit war ein Ergebnis philosophischer Abstraktion, aber im zeitgenössischen Mythos und Ritual sowie in der zeitgenössischen Poesie wurde das Göttliche verkörpert—wenn nicht in der Bildsprache, dann zumindest in der Vorstellung. Die Schrift-Sprache eines Gottes, der in der Geschichte handelt und in die Geschichte eingreift, eignet sich nicht für das philosophische Konzept der

---

36. Origen, *Gen. Hom.* 1.13.
37. Origen, *Comm. Jo.* 13.148–150.
38. In "The Philosophical Critique of Religion under the Early Empire" (64), Attridge provides a framework for the religious sensibilities of the age, to which Origen appeals here.
39. Ibid., 53.

Körperlosigkeit. In der Tat zog sich der Streit um Gottes Körper in Alexandrien über drei Jahrhunderte hin. Die Tumulte um den Körper Gottes drohten Theophilos, den Bischof von Alexandrien, zu stürzen und verbannten vier der Leuchten des monastischen Ägyptens.

Das ganze theologische System des Origenes hängt von dieser zentralen philosophischen Lehre ab. Origenes' Dilemma war, daß die Schrift nirgendwo die Körperlosigkeit Gottes bestätigt. Um ein Glaubensgegenstand zu werden, muß dieses philosophische Konzept jedoch in Schrift-Sprache gekleidet werden, ja es muß in die Bedeutung der Schrift selbst einverleibt werden.

Origenes besteht immer wieder darauf, daß die Schriften Prophetien Gottes seien. Für allegorische Exegeten sind Sprache und Vokabular der Schrift über ihre Fähigkeit, Bedeutung zu vermitteln, hinaus sinntragend. Die Wortwahl selbst ist das Zentrum des Inspirationsprozesses. Mehr als alle anderen sprechen die allegorischen Ausleger der Schrift-Sprache ein einmaliges Potential zu, denn nur die Sprache und das Vokabular der Schrift öffnen den Weg zu ihrer geistlichen Bedeutung. Keine andere Sprache ist dazu in der Lage. Origenes ist daher unwillens, theologische Ideen in einer anderen als der Schrift-Sprache zu artikulieren. Infolge dessen ist es für Origenes besonders problematisch die Körperlosigkeit Gottes auszudrücken.

Origenes hat zwei Strategien zur Ver-Schriftlichung (*enscripturation*) entwickelt. Einerseits stützt er sich ganz auf Schrift-Sprache, um philosophische Probleme nicht nur zu artikulieren sondern auch zu lösen. Er argumentiert für philosophische Unterscheidungen, indem er die Schrift zitiert. So verwendet er z. B. eine Aussage Jesu aus seinem Gespräch mit der samaritanischen Frau ("Gott ist Geist, und die ihn anbeten, die müssen ihn im Geist und in der Wahrheit anbeten"; Joh 4,24), um dem Geist den Körper und der Wahrheit das Bild gegenüberzustellen. Auf diese Weise interpretiert Origenes die Körperlosigkeit Gottes in die Lehre Jesu hinein.

Die exegetische Predigt andererseits ist eine zweite Strategie der Ver-Schriftlichung, in der Origenes Passagen der Schrift mit Hilfe allegorischer Auslegung philosophische Bedeutungen verleiht. Durch kontinuierliche Predigt wurden spezielle theologische Deutungen in individuelle Textlesungen eingetragen, so daß eine besondere theologische Perspektive anklingt, wenn der Text gelesen wird.

PART 2

Philosophical Interpretation

THE DEMOCRATIZATION OF MESSIANISM
IN MODERN JEWISH THOUGHT

Marvin A. Sweeney

I

One of the issues raised in relation to the development of Jewish biblical theology is the extent to which theological interpretation of the Tanakh will interact with later Jewish tradition.¹ Although there is a long tradition of Jewish interpretation of the Bible from antiquity to the present, the impact of modern historical critical scholarship and comparative Near Eastern studies has prompted many Jewish (and non-Jewish) biblical scholars to contend that biblical interpretation should focus only upon the biblical text itself and not upon the later rabbinic traditions of Judaism (or for Christian interpreters, the New Testament).² There is indeed a certain justification for studying and maintaining the integrity of the Bible's own presentation of its theological ideas, particularly since modern scholars are acutely aware of the role that later tradition has played in shaping and often changing or distorting interpreters' understandings of the biblical text. Nevertheless, there is also a

---

1. E.g., Jon D. Levenson, "Why Jews Are Not Interested in Biblical Theology," in *Judaic Perspectives on Ancient Israel* (ed. Jacob Neusner, Baruch A. Levine, and Ernest M. Frerichs; Philadelphia: Fortress, 1987), 281–307, esp. 286–87; repr. in idem, *The Hebrew Bible, the Old Testament, and Historical Criticism: Jews and Christians in Biblical Studies* (Louisville: Westminster John Knox, 1993), 33–61, 165–70, esp. 39; Marvin A. Sweeney, "The Emerging Field of Jewish Biblical Theology," in *Academic Approaches to the Teaching of Jewish Studies* (ed. Zev Garber; Lanham, Md.: University Press of America, 2000), 83–105, esp. 99–101. For overview discussion of the field of Jewish biblical theology, see in addition to Sweeney, Gerhard Hasel, "The Emerging Field," in *Old Testament Theology: Basic Issues in the Current Debate* (4th ed.; Grand Rapids: Eerdmans, 1991), 7, 34–37; James Barr, *The Concept of Biblical Theology* (Minneapolis: Fortress, 1999), 286–311. See also Alice Ogden Bellis and Joel S. Kaminsky, eds., *Jews, Christians, and the Theology of the Hebrew Scriptures* (SBLSymS 8; Atlanta: Society of Biblical Literature, 2000).

2. See, e.g., Mattityahu Tsevat, "Theology of the Old Testament—A Jewish View," *HBT* 8 (1986): 33–50; Moshe Goshen-Gottstein, "Tanakh Theology: The Religion of the Old Testament and the Place of Jewish Biblical Theology," in *Ancient Israelite Religion* (ed. Patrick D. Miller Jr., Paul D. Hanson, and S. Dean McBride; Philadelphia: Fortress, 1987), 617–44.

certain justification for asking how the Bible relates to subsequent Jewish tradition, including the understanding(s) of the biblical text in later tradition and its conceptualization of Judaism and Jewish thought at large. One might point, for example, to the role that the modern experience of the *Shoah* (Holocaust) has played in prompting interpreters to direct some very important questions to their reading of the biblical text that were either overlooked or deemphasized by earlier interpreters, such as the potential for divine absence, complicity, or sorrow in the face of evil; or the theological significance of the establishment of modern Israel in the aftermath of the Shoah.[3] Indeed, with the postmodern emphasis on the contextualization of biblical interpretation, the question of the relation of the Bible to subsequent Jewish tradition is essential to the development of Jewish biblical theology.[4]

It is with this in mind that I would like to address the conceptualization of messianism in several modern strands of Jewish thought. Biblical texts frequently speak of a Davidic monarch, who will deliver Israel/Judah from oppression and play a role in inaugurating an ideal age of peace and restoration for the people of Israel/Judah and indeed the world at large.[5] Such an understanding of a personal messiah has loomed large in the development of Christianity, and it has also played a role in

---

3. E.g., Emil Fackenheim, *Reading the Jewish Bible after the Holocaust: A Rereading* (Bloomington: Indiana University Press, 1990); idem, *G-d's Presence in History: Jewish Affirmations and Philosophical Reflections* (New York: Harper Torchbooks, 1972); Richard Rubenstein, *After Auschwitz: Radical Theology and Contemporary Judaism* (Indianapolis: Bobbs-Merrill, 1966); Eliezer Berkovits, *Faith after the Holocaust* (New York: Ktav, 1973); Zev Garber, *Shoah: The Paradigmatic Genocide. Essays in Exegesis and Eisegesis* (Studies in the Shoah 8; Lanham, Md.: University Press of America, 1994); Zachary Braiterman, *(G-d) After Auschwitz: Tradition and Change in Post-Holocaust Jewish Thought* (Princeton: Princeton University Press, 1998); Tod Linafelt, ed., *Strange Fire: Reading the Bible after the Holocaust* (Biblical Seminar 71; Sheffield: Sheffield Academic Press, 2000); Clark M. Williamson, *A Guest in the House of Israel: Post-Holocaust Church Theology* (Louisville: Westminster John Knox, 1993).

4. Marvin A. Sweeney, "Why Jews Should Be Interested in Biblical Theology," *CCARJ* 44 (winter 1997): 67–75; idem, "Reconceiving the Paradigms of Old Testament Theology in the Post-Shoah Period," *BibInt* 6 (1998): 142–61; repr., Bellis and Kaminsky, *Jews, Christians, and the Theology of the Hebrew Scriptures*, 155–72; Isaac Kalimi, "History of Israelite Religion or Hebrew Bible/Old Testament Theology? Jewish Interest in Biblical Theology," in *Early Jewish Exegesis and Theological Controversy: Studies in Scriptures in the Shadow of Internal and External Controversies* (Assen: Van Gorcum, 2002), 107–59.

5. For overview discussion of the texts and concepts of messianism in the Hebrew Bible, see esp. Marinus de Jonge, "Messiah," *ABD* 4:777–78; Joseph Klausner, *The Messianic Idea in Israel from Its Beginning to the Completion of the Mishnah* (New York: MacMillan, 1955); Sigmund Mowinckel, *He That Cometh* (trans. G. W. Anderson; Nashville: Abingdon, 1956); Raphael Patai, *The Messiah Texts* (Detroit: Wayne State University Press, 1979). For a discussion of messianism in the general history of Judaism and Jewish thought, see Harold Louis Ginzberg et al., "Messiah," *EncJud* 11:1407–17; Haim Hillel Ben-Sasson, "Messianic Movements," *EncJud* 11:1417–27; "Messiah," *The Oxford Dictionary of the Jewish Religion* (ed. R. J. Zwi Werblowsky and Geoffrey Wigoder; Oxford: Oxford University Press, 1997), 458–60; William Scott Green and Jed Silverstein, "The Doctrine of the Messiah," in *The Blackwell Companion to Judaism* (ed. Jacob Neusner and Alan J. Avery-Peck; Oxford: Blackwell, 2000), 247–67; Harris Lenowitz, *The Jewish Messiahs: From the Galilee to Crown Heights* (Oxford: Oxford University Press, 1998).

Judaism at various points throughout its history, but the concept of an ideal messianic age in which a royal Davidic figure is absent or serves only in a marginal role appears to be far more influential in the various movements of modern Judaism. Indeed, a number of biblical texts portray such an ideal age either without the presence of a messiah or with the marginal involvement of such a messianic figure (e.g., Isa 2:2–4; 35; 49–54; 55; 60–62; 65–66; Ezek 40–48; Hos 14:2–9; Joel 3–4; Zeph 3:14–20; Zech 12–14). The book of Isaiah is particularly important in this regard. The first part of the book contains several important messianic texts that articulate the notion of an ideal Davidic monarch (e.g., Isa 9:1–6; 11:1–16; 32:1–8), and the second part of the book announces the Persian king Cyrus as the messiah and Temple builder (see Isa 44:28; 45:1) and later even G-d as the true royal figure (see Isa 66:1–24) while applying the Davidic covenant to the people of Israel at large (see Isa 55:1–13, esp. v. 3).[6] Although the significance of this "democratization" of the Davidic covenant has been discussed extensively in relation to its biblical context, either within the book of Isaiah itself or in relation to the larger framework of the Bible as a whole, relatively less attention has been paid to the role of such a concept in modern Jewish thought.[7]

This essay therefore provides a cursory examination of the notion of a "democratized" messianic age in several major streams of modern Judaism and Jewish thought. It focuses especially on the role of Kabbalistic thought in articulating the interrelationship between G-d and human beings and in laying the foundation for modern notions of a messianic age. In presenting such an examination, it provides the basis for relating the notion of a democratized Davidic covenant in the book of Isaiah to modern expressions of the role of Jews and Judaism at large in bringing about an ideal messianic age.

---

6. Marvin A. Sweeney, "Multiple Settings in the Book of Isaiah," in *Society of Biblical Literature 1993 Seminar Papers* (ed. Eugene H. Lovering Jr.; Atlanta: Scholars Press, 1993), 267–73; idem, *Isaiah 1–39, with an Introduction to Prophetic Literature* (FOTL 16; Grand Rapids: Eerdmans, 1996).

7. See Marvin A. Sweeney, "The Reconceptualization of the Davidic Covenant in Isaiah," in *Studies in the Book of Isaiah: Festschrift W. A. M. Beuken* (ed. J. van Ruiten and M. Vervenne; BETL 132; Louvain: Louvain University Press and Peeters, 1997), 41–62; Otto Eissfeldt, "The Promises of Grace to David in Isaiah 55:1–5," in *Israel's Prophetic Heritage: Essays in Honor of James Muilenburg* (ed. Bernhard W. Anderson and Walter Harrelson; London: SCM, 1962), 196–207; H. G. M. Williamson, "'The Sure Mercies of David': Subjective or Objective Genitive?" *JSS* 23 (1978): 31–49; Joseph Blenkinsopp, *Isaiah 40–55* (AB 19A; New York: Doubleday, 2002), 366–73; Brevard S. Childs, *Isaiah: A Commentary* (OTL; Louisville: Westminster John Knox, 2001), 431–38.

II

I would like to begin by quoting a story told about the Baal Shem Tov, the Podolian Rabbi and mystic faith healer, who founded the modern Hasidic movement in eastern Europe in the eighteenth century:[8]

> One day (the Baal Shem Tov) promised to show (his disciples) the Prophet Elijah. "Open your eyes wide," he said.
> A few days later they saw a beggar enter the House of Study/Beit Midrash and emerge clutching a book under his arm. Shortly thereafter they watched him leaving a ceremony, taking along a silver spoon. The third time, he appeared to them disguised as a soldier on a horse, asking them to light his pipe.
> "It was he," said the Baal Shem, "The secret is in the eyes."[9]

The point of this story is to teach that the prophet Elijah, who will precede the Messiah, could be anyone and everyone. By portraying the prophet, first as a common thief who steals a book from the Beit Midrash and later a silver spoon from a celebration and then as a Russian soldier who was always perceived as a threat by Jews, the Baal Shem Tov emphasizes the Hasidic teaching that every human being possesses a spark of the divine within, and that every human being is therefore capable of being recognized as the prophet Elijah. By stating that "the secret is in the eyes," the Baal Shem Tov emphasizes the need for his disciples to recognize the holiness of divine presence that is inherent in the world of creation at large and, indeed, in themselves in particular.

Although rooted in the Hasidic tradition, such a story well illustrates the general view of messianism that pervades most movements of modern Judaism, namely, the messiah is not a supernatural individual, whose appearance in the world will inaugurate the new age of the kingdom of G-d. Indeed, such a conceptualization of the messiah appears to be characteristic of the Christian tradition in general. Judaism, however, has experienced a number of would-be messiahs, Zerubbabel ben

---

8. For discussion of Israel ben Eliezer (the Baal Shem Tov) and the foundation of Hasidic Judaism, see Gershom Scholem, *Major Trends in Jewish Mysticism* (New York: Schocken, 1962), 325–50; idem, "The Neutralization of Messianism in Early Hasidism," in *The Messianic Idea in Judaism, and Other Essays on Jewish Spirituality* (New York: Schocken, 1972), 176–202; Simon Dubnow, "The Beginnings: The Baal Shem Tov (Besht) and the Center in Podolia," in *Essential Papers on Hasidism: Origins to Present* (ed. Gershon David Hundert; New York: New York University Press, 1991), 25–57; Benzion Dinur, "The Origins of Hasidism and Its Social and Messianic Foundations," in Hundert, *Essential Papers on Hasidism*, 86–208.

9. Adapted from Elie Wiesel, *Souls on Fire: Portraits and Legends of the Hasidic Masters* (New York: Summit, 1972), 27.

Shealtiel,[10] Jesus of Nazareth,[11] Shimon bar Kosiba/bar Kochba,[12] Shabbetai Zvi,[13] Shukr Kuhayl I and Shukr Kuhayl II of Yemen,[14] and even the very recent implicit claims concerning the late Lubavitcher Rebbe, Menahem Schneerson,[15] but every one of them has failed to realize the biblical expectations of the world of creation at peace in which all nations will recognize G-d at the holy Temple in Jerusalem. Although there is still room for a personal messiah in some elements of Judaism, as the last-cited example of the Lubavitcher Rebbe indicates, modern Judaism tends to think in terms of a messianic age in which all Jews—and indeed all human beings—have the divinely ordained responsibility to work for the sanctification of the entire world of creation.

In order to illustrate this contention, the remainder of this essay discusses three basic movements and individuals that have played constitutive roles in defining the outlook of modern Judaism and its perspectives on the messianic age, namely, Kabbalistic thought as taught by the sixteenth-century mystic of Safed, Isaac Luria; modern Jewish philosophy as taught by the eighteenth-century Berlin rationalist, Moses Mendelssohn; and modern Zionism as conceived by the late-nineteenth- and early-twentieth-century thinker Asher Ginzberg, better known by his pen name, Ahad Ha-`Am.

III

Although much of modern nineteenth-century Jewish scholarship castigated Jewish mysticism as an illegitimate expression of Jewish superstition that had rejected the principles of modern rationalism,[16] twentieth- and now twenty-first-century interpreters of Judaism have begun to recognize the foundational role that Jewish mysticism plays in the conceptualization of modern Jewish thought.[17] Gershom Scholem, the late historian of Jewish mysticism, almost single-handedly demonstrates that Jewish mysticism was not a deviant or heretical offshoot of Judaism, but instead it plays a crucial role in defining modern Judaism's view of G-d,

---

10. See Hag 2:20–23; Marvin A. Sweeney, *The Twelve Prophets* (2 vols.; Berit Olam; Collegeville, Minn.: Liturgical Press, 2000), 2:549–55.

11. See Lenowitz, *Jewish Messiahs*, 34–49.

12. See Richard G. Marks, *The Image of Bar Kochba in Traditional Jewish Literature* (University Park: Pennsylvania State University Press, 1994); Lenowitz, *Jewish Messiahs*, 49–59.

13. For a detailed study of Shabbetai Zvi, see Gershom Scholem, *Shabbetai Sevi: The Mystical Messiah (1626–1676)* (Princeton: Princeton University Press, 1973); cf. Lenowitz, *Jewish Messiahs*, 149–65.

14. See Bat-Zion Eraqi Klorman, *The Jews of Yemen in the Nineteenth Century: A Portrait of a Messianic Community* (Leiden: Brill, 1993), esp. 104–58; Lenowitz, *Jewish Messiahs*, 235–56.

15. Lenowitz, *Jewish Messiahs*, 215–23.

16. See, e.g., Heinrich Graetz, *A History of the Jews* (6 vols.; Philadelphia: Jewish Publication Society, 1891–98), 3:522–62, esp. 546–57.

17. For general studies of Jewish mysticism, see esp. Scholem, *Major Trends*; Moshe Idel, *Kabbalah: New Perspectives* (New Haven: Yale University Press, 1988).

human beings, and the world. Indeed, he very perceptively demonstrates that concepts from Jewish mysticism underlie modern Reform Judaism and the modern Haskalah, or Jewish Enlightenment of eastern Europe.[18]

Scholem traces the influence of Jewish mysticism on modern Jewish thought through the experience of the false messiah, Shabbetai Zvi (1626–1676), who proclaimed himself to be the messiah in 1665, but converted to Islam some two years later when he was arrested by the Ottoman Turks and threatened with death if he did not renounce his claims.[19] Scholem demonstrates that Shabbetai Zvi's experience, particularly the claim that he was a hidden messiah whose conversion marked his willingness to descend into the deepest depths of sin in order to redeem the world, was instrumental in the foundation of modern Hasidism a century after his death. But in fact, the foundations for Shabbetai Zvi's claims and the worldview of modern Hasidism owe much to the Kabbalistic system of thought devised by Isaac Luria (1534–1572).

Isaac Luria was born in Jerusalem, brought up in Egypt, and taught a group of mystic disciples in the city of Safed from 1570 until his death from the plague in 1572.[20] In true mystical fashion, he wrote no literary works, but his disciples recorded his teachings after his death. Luria lived in a desperate time for the Jewish people, immediately following the expulsion of the Jewish population of Spain by King Ferdinand and Queen Isabella in 1492. The exile and destruction of Spanish Jewry had tremendous repercussions throughout the Jewish world, since Spanish Jewry had emerged as the premier Jewish community of the medieval world, known for both its advances in Jewish learning and its high standing in Muslim and later Christian Spain.

The exile of Spanish Jewry posed the fundamental question of evil to Jewish thinkers of the day, much as the Shoah or Holocaust challenges modern Jewish—and Christian—theology. How could G-d stand by and allow the destruction of the world's preeminent Jewish community? Drawing upon earlier Kabbalistic concepts of the ten sephirot, that is, the ten emanations or qualities of G-d that permeate the world and every human being within it,[21] Luria and his disciples devised a theolog-

---

18. See his essay "Redemption through Sin," in *The Messianic Idea in Judaism*, 78–141.
19. See also Scholem's larger study of Shabbetai Zvi, noted above, and *Major Trends*, 287–324.
20. For discussion of Isaac Luria and the development of Lurianic Kabbalah, see Scholem, *Major Trends*, 244–86; Solomon Schechter, "Safed in the Sixteenth Century: A City of Legists and Mystics," in *The Jewish Expression* (ed. J. Goldin; New Haven: Yale University Press, 1976), 258–321; R. J. Zwi Werblowsky, "The Safed Revival and Its Aftermath," in *Jewish Spirituality from the Sixteenth Century Revival to the Present* (ed. Arthur Green; New York: Crossroad, 1989), 7–33; Lenowitz, *Jewish Messiahs*, 125–47.
21. For discussion of the ten sephirot of Kabbalistic thought, see Marvin A. Sweeney, "Ten Sephirot," *Dictionary of Deities and Demons in the Bible* (ed. Karol van der Toorn, Bob Becking, and Pieter W. van der Horst; 2nd ed.; Leiden: Brill; Grand Rapids: Eerdmans, 1999), 837–43; Scholem, "Kabbalah," *EncJud* 10:489–653, esp. 556–79, 588–601.

ical system that attempted to discern the character of G-d and the nature of the world of creation that G-d had produced. The ten sephirot included abstract qualities, such as the will, wisdom, understanding, the capacity for lovingkindness, the capacity for punishment, dynamism in the material world, and stability in the material world, that pointed to qualities shared by human beings, G-d, and the world at large. Luria argues that it was the interaction of these qualities within the personality of G-d that prompts G-d to create the world. Although G-d is infinite, G-d's lovingkindness prompts G-d to create the world. But the creation of a finite world limits the infinite character of G-d, and calls forth the quality of punishment or evil that is inherent in G-d and the world created by G-d. Luria expresses the creation metaphorically as G-d's pouring divine light into ten earthenware jars. Of course, such a metaphor points to an effort to contain the infinite nature of G-d in finite vessels. In Luria's thought, the finite vessels are unable to contain the light of G-d. Seven of them shattered, and thereby scattered divine sparks of light mixed together with the finite pieces of the shattered jars throughout the world of creation. Such a metaphor points to the conceptualization of human beings, each of whom possesses a spark of divine light within that is encased in a finite vessel. Insofar as every human being possesses such a spark of divine light within, Luria argues that every human being has the responsibility to recognize that divine light and to act upon or to actualize that divine spark within in order to carry out the human responsibility to act as partners with G-d to sanctify the world in which we live. In this manner, Luria metaphorically claims that human beings must gather the sparks of divine light from among the broken shards of the shattered vessels, reassemble them, and thereby restore the holy divine presence in the world of creation. Indeed, such a reconstitution of the holy presence in the world constitutes the repair of the world or *Tikkun Olam* in Luria's thought. Because Jews were designated by G-d to bring knowledge of the holy presence to the world at large, Luria argues that the exile of Jews throughout the world is intended to play a role in sanctifying the world. In short, the evil of exile became the platform by which the goodness of divine holiness would be realized in creation at large.

Luria's conceptualization of the repair of the world, or Tikkun Olam, has implications for understanding the nature of messianism in Jewish thought. Every Jew and every human being possesses the divine spark within and has both the capacity and the responsibility to act upon that spark to bring about Tikkun Olam. In this respect, anyone and everyone represents a potential messiah for the world. It is this principle that underlies Shabbetai Zvi's claims to be the messiah—although the results hardly brought about the Tikkun Olam that Lurianic Kabbalah envisions, and it is this principle that underlies modern Hasidism of all varieties. Indeed, for modern Hasidism, particularly the Habad movement, a holy life begins with the mental sephirot or divine qualities, that is, *Hokhmah*, "wisdom," *Binah*, "understanding," and *Da'at*, "knowledge," that is, HaBaD, that then actualize the moral sephirot of lovingkindness and judgment and the material sephirot of dynamism and stability in the lives of human beings.²² Through the manifestation of holiness in one's mental, moral, and material life, one may live a holy life and bring about Tikkun Olam.

IV

As noted above, Scholem argues that Jewish mysticism, under the influence of the career of Shabbetai Zvi, plays an important role in laying the groundwork for the emergence of Reform Judaism in western Europe. Scholem's argument is based in large measure on the Shabbatean contention that the coming of the messiah entails the abrogation of Torah; namely, Shabbetai Zvi early in his career began to violate precepts of the Torah publicly in order to affirm his messianic status, and his later conversion to Islam was taken as a proof of his role in bringing about the sanctification of the entire world. Insofar as early Reform Judaism in the nineteenth century would call for the end of traditional Jewish observances that purportedly had no place in the modern world, Scholem sees a link between the Shabbatean experience and modern Reform.²³ And yet, such a characterization of the link misconstrues the issue. The crucial question in Reform Judaism is not the abrogation of Torah; it is in fact the question of the place and role of Jews in the modern world.²⁴ Indeed, the same question underlies the formulation of modern Orthodox Judaism in Germany during the same period.²⁵ We might also observe that the recent moves of the Reform movement to more traditional forms of observance point to a fundamental concern with the question of what constitutes Torah and its observance in the modern world.²⁶

Modern Reform Judaism and modern Orthodoxy share the contention that Judaism serves as a means to bring knowledge of G-d to the world at large. They

---

22. For discussion of Habad Hasidism, see Rachel Elior, *The Paradoxical Ascent to G-d: The Kabbalist Theosophy of Habad Hasidism* (Albany: SUNY Press, 1993); idem, "The Contemplative Ascent to G-d," in *Jewish Spirituality from the Sixteenth Century to the Present*, 157–205.

23. See Scholem, "Redemption through Sin," esp. 84.

24. For discussion of the emergence of Reform Judaism in Germany and the development of early Reform theology, see Michael A. Meyer, *Response to Modernity: A History of the Reform Movement in Judaism* (New York: Oxford University Press, 1988), 10–224; Jakob J. Petuchowski, *Prayerbook Reform in Europe: The Liturgy of European Liberal and Reform Judaism* (New York: World Union for Progressive Judaism, 1968).

25. Note, for example, Samson Raphael Hirsch's adaptation of the principle Torah im Derekh Eretz, "Torah with the Way of the World," which expresses his call for traditional Jewish observance while living in the modern world (for discussion, see Robert M. Seltzer, *Jewish People, Jewish Thought: The Jewish Experience in History* [New York: MacMillan, 1980], 584–90, esp. 586; Meyer, *Response to Modernity*, 77–79; Noah H. Rosenbloom, *Tradition in an Age of Reform: The Religious Philosophy of Samson Raphael Hirsch* [Philadelphia: Jewish Publication Society, 1976]).

26. See Dana Evan Kaplan, "Reform Judaism," in Neusner and Avery-Peck, *Blackwell Companion to Judaism*, 291–310, esp. 305–6.

differ markedly in their views on how this is accomplished, but both are grounded in the view that G-d's Torah was revealed to Israel at Mount Sinai, outside of the land of Israel, and that the designation of Israel/Judaism as a holy people was an event of worldwide significance intended to reveal G-d to the world at large. Both contend that Jews play an instrumental role in sanctifying the world, and thereby in bringing about the messianic age of peace and holiness in the world as all come to recognize G-d. We might note the basis for such a contention in Lurianic Kabbalah's understanding of exile and Tikkun Olam, but we must also consider the work of the Enlightenment Jewish philosopher Moses Mendelssohn (1729–1786), who laid the foundation in Jewish thought for the emergence of both modern Reform and modern Orthodox Judaism.[27]

Moses Mendelssohn was the son of a poor Torah scribe named Mendel in the city of Dessau. He was a child prodigy, having mastered Talmud and Maimonides by the age of 14. When his teacher, R. David Fränkel, left Dessau in 1743 to accept an appointment as chief rabbi of Berlin, young Moses followed. In Berlin, Mendelssohn became one of the first Jews to study in the university, and he quickly mastered philosophy, aesthetics, mathematics, and languages, such as German, Greek, Latin, French, and English. Indeed, Mendelssohn was an anomaly for his time, an educated and enlightened Jew, which most in Christian society thought to be impossible. Young Mendelssohn achieved great stature in Berlin as a leading intellectual, particularly after he won first prize in an essay competition sponsored by the Berlin Royal Academy, beating the young Immanuel Kant.

Mendelssohn adhered to the general principles of reason that were characteristic of the day and spent much of his career writing in the areas of philosophy and aesthetics. His treatise, *Phaedon*, argues for the principles of rational religion in the Enlightenment world, namely, G-d's existence, divine providence, and immortality of the soul, each of which could be demonstrated by rational argumentation.[28] Although he was viewed as a modern Socrates, Mendelssohn was frequently challenged by Christian intellectuals to defend his adherence to the "backward" Jewish religion or to convert to Christianity, which was conceived at the time as a religion of natural reason. As a result of these challenges, Mendelssohn in 1783 published his classic work, "Jerusalem, or On Religious Power and Judaism," which is widely recognized as the foundation for modern Jewish thought.[29] It is a work concerned

---

27. For studies of the life and thought of Moses Mendelssohn, see David Sorkin, *Moses Mendelssohn and the Religious Enlightenment* (Berkeley: University of California Press, 1996), and Alexander Altmann, *Moses Mendelssohn: A Biographical Study* (Philadelphia: Jewish Publication Society, 1973). For a study of Mendelssohn's principles of biblical interpretation in relation to Enlightenment thought, see Edward Breuer, *The Limits of Enlightenment: Jews, Germans, and the Eighteenth-Century Study of Scripture* (Cambridge: Harvard University Press, 1996).

28. For discussion of *Phaedon*, see esp. Altmann, *Moses Mendelssohn*, 140–58.

29. Moses Mendelssohn, *Jerusalem, or On Religious Power and Judaism* (trans. Allan Arkush; introduction and commentary by Alexander Altmann; Hanover, N.H.: University Press of New England, 1983).

fundamentally with the place and role of Jews in modern Enlightenment society, and it articulates a philosophy of Judaism that defines Judaism as a modern religion of reason. It begins with the question of the right of religious authorities to excommunicate adherents for heresy. Mendelssohn argues that the right of coercion belongs only to the state, not to religion, and that the state has no right to apply coercion in matters of conscience. Religion is a matter of reason, and a true religion of reason properly holds to three essential rational truths, belief in G-d, divine providence, and immortality of the soul, because each can be demonstrated by rational arguments. In this respect, Judaism is a true religion of reason, as is any other tradition that holds to these principles, such as Christianity. But Mendelssohn rejects the notion of supernatural revelation; all people have an innate ability to discover the rational truth of G-d. To make G-d dependent upon a supernatural revelation suggests that G-d is not omnipotent, since G-d would be unable to give humans the capacity to discern G-d themselves. For Mendelssohn, the revelation at Sinai is not the revelation of religion—for G-d was already known prior to Sinai—but the revelation of Mosaic law, which is designed to form Israel into the holy Jewish people and thereby to stimulate reflection and contemplation that would facilitate recognition of G-d. Although Jews had been formed originally as a nation, the end of that nation meant that Jews could go out into the world, and bring knowledge of G-d or rational religion to the world at large. Practically speaking, Mendelssohn's conception of Judaism as a rational religion meant that Jews could live simultaneously as loyal and productive citizens of the modern European nation and as faithful and observant adherents of the Jewish religion. To that end, Mendelssohn calls upon Jews to learn German, to learn secular knowledge, and to live as full citizens of the Gentile societies of the time, in order to demonstrate knowledge of G-d to the world and to play their roles in bringing that world to its ultimate perfection. For Mendelssohn, such perfection is encapsulated in his contention that G-d intends not a single religion, but a diversity of religions in which human beings would learn to accept and respect the beliefs of others while adhering to their own.

Indeed, Mendelssohn's principles stand at the basis of modern Reform and Orthodox Judaism insofar as each defines itself in religious terms so that Jews may live in the Diaspora. Abraham Geiger, the primary architect of nineteenth-century Reform Judaism in Germany, for example, calls for the modernization of Judaism so that Jews could live legitimately as citizens of the modern European state.[30] Samson Raphael Hirsch, the primary architect of modern Orthodox Judaism, articulates the Talmudic principle of Torah im Derekh Eretz, that is, "Torah with the Way of the World," so that Jews could adhere to traditional observance of Torah while living in

---

30. For discussion of Geiger, see Seltzer, *Jewish People, Jewish Thought*, 591–97; Meyer, *Response to Modernity*, 89–99; idem, "Abraham Geiger's 'Historical Judaism,'" in *New Perspectives on Abraham Geiger: An HUC-JIR Symposium* (ed. Jakob J. Petuchowski; New York: Ktav, for Hebrew Union College–Jewish Institute for Religion, 1975), 3–16.

the modern secular state.³¹ Both see the role of Jews in the world as models of holiness that call upon human beings to recognize the reality of G-d and thereby to bring about the sanctification or perfection of the world at large.

V

Scholem also argues that the Shabbatean movement plays a role in laying the foundations for the Haskalah movement, that is, the Jewish Enlightenment, that was known initially in western Europe, but ultimately found its deepest and most widespread expressions in eastern Europe. Again, Scholem points to the nihilism of the Shabbateans as a primary contributing factor in the development of the Haskalah, particularly since the Haskalah gives expression to Jewish secularism and the abandonment of traditional Jewish observance in its calls for Jews to enter the modern age.³² And yet here, too, the religious dimensions of Jewish mysticism cannot be ignored. Although eastern European Hasidism began with an anti-intellectual outlook that rejected traditional Jewish practice and learning in favor of individual spiritual expression, Hasidism very quickly adapted itself to traditional Torah study and practice as the Hasidic rebbes came to understand that the development of the mind or inner divine essence was crucial to the expression of Jewish spirituality in the moral and material realms of Jewish life.³³ As noted above, the focus on the mental aspects of the divine emanations in the human being and the world at large produced Habad Hasidism, which emphasizes Hokhmah (Wisdom), Binah (Understanding), and Da`at (Knowledge) as the fundamental basis for both the divine and human personality and sense of self-consciousness. It is this sense of self-consciousness that motivates modern Hasidism in its efforts to promote holy life and thereby to sanctify the world.

And yet the Kabbalistic/Hasidic interest in the mental qualities of the divine/human personality was not limited only to religious forms of Jewish expression. The secular, rationalistic orientation of the Haskalah in eastern Europe was also profoundly interested in the question of the Jewish mind or spirit that stood at the core of the Jewish individual and the Jewish people as a whole. Indeed, the question of the Jewish spirit stands at the basis of modern Zionism, the political movement of Judaism that calls for the reestablishment of a Jewish nation.³⁴ Although we fre-

---

31. See n. 25 above. See also Benjamin Brown, "Orthodox Judaism," in Neusner and Avery-Peck, *Blackwell Companion to Judaism*, 311–33.

32. Scholem, "Redemption through Sin," 84.

33. See Scholem, *Major Trends*, 340–43; Elior, *Paradoxical Ascent;* idem, "HaBaD: The Contemplative Ascent to G-d."

34. For studies of the history and intellectual outlook of modern Zionism, see Shlomo Avineri, *The Making of Modern Zionism: The Intellectual Origins of the Jewish State* (New York: Basic, 1981); Walter Laqueur, *A History of Zionism* (New York: Holt Rinehart, 1972); Arthur Hertzberg, *The Zionist Idea* (New York: Athenaum, 1979), esp. 15–100.

quently think of Theodor Herzl as the founder of modern Zionism, he was a highly assimilated Austrian Jew who had little formal Jewish education or sense of Jewish identity. He tended to be an effective organizer and publicist for modern Zionism, but he was not a major theoretician.[35] That role is more properly assigned to his eastern European counterpart, Asher Ginzberg, better known by his pen name, Ahad Ha-'Am, "One of the People," who worked out the theoretical foundations of modern Zionism and its understanding of the character of the Jewish state and the Jewish people.[36] Insofar as he defines the national character of the Jewish spirit as the basis for Jewish national self-identity, it is apparently no accident that he started life as a traditional Hasidic Jew.[37]

Asher Ginzberg was born to a traditional Hasidic family in the Ukraine in 1856 and achieved a reputation as a brilliant young Hasidic Talmud scholar. When his family was forced by the Russian May Laws to move to the city of Odessa in 1884, young Ginzberg encountered a city in which the secular Haskalah was in full swing. Influenced by the Haskalah, the general intellectual atmosphere of Odessa, and the openly anti-Semitic policies of the Russian government, Ginzberg quickly emerged as the leading figure in the Hovevei Zion movement, which called for Jews to return to the land of Israel since Jewish life in Russia—and indeed in Europe in general—was becoming untenable.

Under the pen name Ahad Ha-'Am, Ginzberg calls for the recognition of the Jewish spirit or Jewish national character as the basis for cultural Zionism. He argues that the Jewish people, like all nations, possess a distinctive culture and spirit that defines its national character and that prompts the continued development and progressive outlook of the Jewish people through history and into the future. Of course, one sees the influence of Kabbalistic/Hasidic thought insofar as the intangible divine emanations or qualities stood at the core of both G-d and the individual human being, much as the intangible Jewish spirit stood at the core of Jewish culture and national character. Because of his notions of historical progression, Ahad Ha-'Am believes that the period of national religious expression has come to an end, but that the core of the Jewish personality has been defined by its keen sense of ethics and absolute justice throughout its history. He argues that this sense of ethics and justice had developed during the origins of Jewish national history in the land of Israel, and that it is rooted in the outlook of the prophets of the Hebrew Bible, who continu-

---

35. See esp. Avineri, *Modern Zionism*, 88–100; Laqueur, *History of Zionism*, 84–135.

36. See esp. Avineri, *Modern Zionism*, 112–24; Jacques Kornberg, "Ahad Ha-Am and Herzl," in *At the Crossroads: Essays on Ahad Ha-'Am* (ed. Jacques Kornberg; Albany: SUNY Press, 1983), 106–29. For a collection of his writings, see Ahad Ha-'Am, *Selected Essays* (trans. Leon Simon; Philadelphia: Jewish Publication Society, 1948). Note especially his essay "Flesh and Spirit," 139–58.

37. For a background study of the interrelationships between Hasidism and the Haskalah in eastern Europe, see esp. Raphael Mahler, *Hasidism and the Jewish Enlightenment: Their Confrontation in Galicia and Poland in the First Half of the Nineteenth Century* (Philadelphia: Jewish Publication Society, 1985).

ally call for justice and ethics in ancient Jewish society. Bear in mind that Moses was a prophet, and that Mosaic law is fundamentally concerned with the questions of justice and ethics as well. In Ahad Ha-`Am's estimation, this distinctive Jewish character is the product of Jewish life in the land of Israel as the Jewish sense of self-identity is formed as a part of its national character. For Ahad Ha-`Am, life in the land of Israel forms the Jewish national spirit, and continued life in the land of Israel is essential to the continued development of that Jewish spirit and a distinctive Jewish culture. Life in exile, in which Jews had suffered under the oppression of the nations, had deprived Jews of the freedom necessary to develop Jewish national culture. A return to the land of Israel is an absolute necessity for the future of the Jewish people, because only in Israel would Jews have the freedom from persecution to define their own national life and character.

And yet Ahad Ha-`Am recognizes fully well that the historical experience of the Jewish nation includes some seventeen hundred years of exile in foreign lands following the destruction of the Jerusalem Temple in 70 C.E. and the failure of the Bar Kochba Revolt against Rome in 135 C.E. To that end, he notes how life among the nations had provided Jews with the opportunity to learn about and participate in the advances that were being made throughout the world, in technology, in social thought, in the arts, politics, and so on. One might note here the Lurianic reinterpretation of exile, since Ahad Ha-`Am looks for the positive aspects of a very negative experience. Despite the threat of anti-Semitism, life in the Diaspora enabled Jews to adapt the more progressive elements of the world in their efforts to ensure the continued development and progress of the Jewish nation. To that end, Ahad Ha-`Am calls for a close relationship between Jews living in the Diaspora and Jews living in the land of Israel. Jews living in Israel would develop the distinctive national character of Judaism through life in the land, and Jews living in the Diaspora would develop the progressive notions of human advancement in the modern world. Through such interaction, Ahad Ha-`Am maintains that the Jewish nation would serve as an example for the other nations of the world in its emphasis on absolute justice and ethics as the quintessential core of the Jewish national character. Again, we might note that the emphasis on justice and ethics as the core quality of Jewish culture builds upon earlier Kabbalistic/Hasidic notions that the divine/human personality is obligated to bring about Tikkun Olam, "Repair of the World." Although we no longer have a holy center for the world of creation, we have in Ahad Ha-`Am's thought an ethical center for the world of the nations. In his estimation, it is a Jewish obligation to develop the ethical core articulated by the prophets as the basis for the Jewish national personality.

It is this understanding of the distinctive national character of the Jewish people, based in the ethics and justice of the prophets, that stands at the core of modern Zionist thought and the self-understanding of the modern state of Israel. We might also note that the notions of a distinctive Jewish people or nation likewise stand at the core of modern Conservative Judaism and its offshoot, Reconstructionist

Judaism.³⁸ Although modern Americans are very accustomed to thinking in terms of the separation of church and state, the foundations of the modern Jewish state are very much rooted in the religious traditions of Jewish mysticism.

VI

In conclusion, it seems clear that messianism has had a profound impact on modern Jewish thought. Although there is still a place, at least in some circles, for a personal messiah, modern Jewish thought in general has moved to a collective understanding of a messianic age in which Jews in general have the responsibility to work for the continued improvement and, ultimately, the perfection of the world in which we live. Insofar as the book of Isaiah—and in particular, Isa 55:3—points to a democratized understanding of messianism in which Jews and Judaism in general stand as heirs to the Davidic covenant while G-d ultimately functions as the righteous king, Jewish biblical theology would best illustrate its contemporary relevance by pointing to the influence of such a concept in the articulation of modern Jewish thought. In this regard, it should be noted that Judaism does not envision a world in which all human beings become Jewish. Instead, it envisions a world in which Jews play a role in bringing knowledge of G-d to the world at large, but in which Gentiles will develop their own distinctive religious traditions that will express that knowledge. The so-called Noachide laws in the Babylonian Talmud (*b. Sanhedrin* 56–60) call upon Jews to observe the entire Torah, but they call upon Gentiles to observe seven precepts, namely, to avoid idolatry, blasphemy, bloodshed, sexual sins, theft, eating from a living animal, and to establish legal systems.³⁹ In such a conceptualization, the vision of the messianic age announced by the prophets in which all nations would stream to Zion to give up war and to learn the teachings or Torah of G-d would also entail the recognition by all nations of their obligation to develop their own distinctive approaches to bringing about Tikkun Olam or the Repair of the World while simultaneously recognizing the right and responsibility of other nations to work toward the same end.⁴⁰

---

38. For studies of modern Conservative and Reconstructionist Judaism and their distinctive theologies or worldviews, see Marc Lee Raphael, *Profiles in American Judaism: The Reform, Conservative, Orthodox, and Reconstructionist Traditions in Historical Perspective* (San Francisco: Harper & Row, 1984), 81–111, 179–87; Mordecai M. Kaplan, *The Greater Judaism in the Making: A Study of the Modern Evolution of Judaism* (New York: Reconstructionist Press, 1967), 350–80, 450–511; Daniel Gordis, "Conservative Judaism: The Struggle between Ideology and Popularity," in Neusner and Avery-Peck, *Blackwell Companion to Judaism*, 334–53; R. G. Goldy, *The Emergence of Jewish Theology in America* (Bloomington: Indiana University Press, 1990).

39. See Steven S. Schwarzschild and Saul Berman, "Noachide Laws," *EncJud* 12:1189–91.

40. This is a revised form of a lecture presented at the Jewish-Christian Dialogue Series, Palm Beach Atlantic University, West Palm Beach, Florida, on March 30, 2003. I would like to thank Professor Dan Goodman and Acting Dean Joseph Webb for the invitation to present this lecture and for their hospitality during my stay in West Palm Beach. I would also like to thank my former colleague at the University of Miami, Professor Henry A. Green, who suggested many years ago that I write on this topic.

Zusammenfassung

Der vorliegende Aufsatz behandelt unter Betonung der Kontinuität von Hebräischer Bibel und nachbiblischem jüdischen Gedankengut die Idee eines "demokratisierten" messianischen Zeitalters in den kabbalistischen Lehren Isaak Lurias, in der rationalen Philosophie von Moses Mendelssohn und im zionistischen Gedanken von Asher Ginzberg bzw. Ahad Ha-`Am. Der Aufsatz will eine Basis schaffen, auf Grund derer die Idee eines demokratisierten David-Bundes, wie sie sich im Jesajabuch findet, mit modernen Erwägungen über die Rolle der Juden bei der Herbeiführung des messianischen Zeitalters in Beziehung gesetzt werden kann. Auf diese Weise hoffen wir neue Einsichten zu gewinnen, wie die Bibel mit der ihr nachfolgenden jüdischen Tradition zusammenhängt. Dabei werden ausdrücklich auch die Auslegung(en) des Tanakh der späteren jüdischen Tradition und deren Konzeptualisierung des Judentums und der jüdischen Philosophie im ganzen miteinbezogen.

Eine solche Untersuchung ist aus drei Gründen berechtigt und notwendig: 1. Im akademischen Kontext wurde die Idee eines demokratisierten messianischen Zeitalters nur in biblischen Zusammenhängen diskutiert, während die Rolle dieser Idee in der modernen jüdischen Philosophie vernachlässigt wurde. 2. Postmoderne Einsichten über die kontextuelle Natur biblischer Exegese legen nahe, daß die Beziehung des Tanakh zur nachbiblischen jüdischen Tradition für die Entwicklung einer jüdischen biblischen Theologie essentiel ist. Der Aufsatz geht daher von der Annahme aus, daß die zeitgenössische biblische Theologie nicht nur die Integrität biblischer Themen und Vorstellungen zu bewahren hat, sondern daß sie auch modernen Kontexten und Erfahrungen adäquat sein muss. Zusammengenommen deuten diese beiden Punkte auf einen weiteren Punkt hin, nämlich 3., daß historisch-kritische Textzugänge, die sich allein auf biblische Kontexte konzentrieren, schlecht dazu geeignet sind, Fragen der modernen jüdischen Theologie zu behandeln. Gute Beispiele sind die Bibelauslegung nach der Schoah und die Interpretation der Bibel im Licht des modernen Diaspora-Judentums.

Unter Betrachtung dieser Vorüberlegungen wird dieser Essay eine skizzenhafte Untersuchung vorlegen, wie Luria, Mendelssohn und Ahad Ha-`Am das Konzept eines demokratisierten Messianismus aus dem Jesajabuch (s. bes. Jes 55,3) erweitert haben. Unter den genannten Messianismus-Konzepten ragt besonders jenes Konzept heraus, das die Rolle einer einzelnen übernatürlichen Figur, deren Erscheinen in der Welt das neue messianische Zeitalter inauguriert, herunterspielt. Stattdessen findet sich in den Konzeptionen Lurias, Mendelssohns und Ahad Ha-`Am in jeweils spezifischer Weise das jesajanische Messianismus-Konzept wieder, nach dem alle Menschen sowohl die Fähigkeit als auch die göttlich festgesetzte Verpflichtung haben, mit G-tt als Partner die Heiligung an der Schöpfung zu arbeiten. In dem er sich auf die kabbalistische Idee von Tikkun Olam oder "Instandsetzung der Welt" konzentriert, zeichnet der vorliegende Essay die Art und Weise nach, in der diese prägenden Denker sich wohl den jüdischen als auch den nichtjüdischen Beitrag zum idealtypischen messianischen Zeitalter vorgestellt haben. Dabei ensteht eine Messianismus-Konzeption, die auf verschiedenen Ebenen "demokratisch" ist. In dieser Vorstellungswelt können jeder und alle ohne Rücksicht auf religiöse, nationale oder soziale Ausrichtung potentiel sowohl ein Vorbild an Heiligkeit als auch ein Weg sein, auf dem die Erkenntis G-ttes in die Welt gelangt.

Verkündigung in Übereinstimmung mit der Vernunft: Fichtes Auslegung des Johannesevangeliums

Stephan Grätzel

1. Die überzeitliche Wahrheit und ihre Genese

Der grundsätzliche Anspruch von Kant und seiner Kritischen Philosophie war es, Vernunftwahrheiten zu formulieren, die unabhängig von natürlichen oder kulturellen Bedingungen gegeben sind. Im Unterschied zu den bedingten Einsichten sollten allein die apriorischen Vernunfteinsichten die Würde des Menschen begründen können, da nur sie die autonome Freiheit bezeugen zu können in der Lage seien. Die Vernunft, die wichtigste Autorität der Aufklärung, sollte weder von Gott noch von der Natur abhängig sein oder in dieser Abhängigkeit gedacht werden müssen.

Mit der Apriorität der Vernunfteinsichten war aber zugleich ihre überhistorische Gültigkeit verbürgt. Apriorische Einsichten sind demnach auch keinem geschichtlichen Wandel unterworfen, sie sind auch keine Produkte, die einer bestimmten geschichtlichen Gegebenheit geschuldet sind. Gerade diese unhistorische Einstellung sollte um die Wende zum 19. Jahrhundert eine Kritik erfahren. Hier war es vor allem Hegel, der in seiner *Phänomenologie* nachzuweisen glaubte, dass der Kern der Vernunfteinsicht, das Selbstwissen, das Produkt einer geschichtlichen "Entwicklung" sei, die ein innerlich angelegter Kern der Vernunft in der geschichtlichen Entfaltung hervorbringt. War hier das Selbstwissen in sich geschichtlich angelegt, so sollte sich dieses Verhältnis von Selbstwissen und seiner Geschichte bis zum Ende des 19. Jahrhunderts vollständig verkehrt haben, indem die Vernunft und ihr Zeitalter zur ideengeschichtlichen Episode erklärt wurde. Diese Selbstrelativierung der Vernunft war am Anfang bei den Entdeckern des Geschichtlichen noch nicht zu finden, sie konnte erst Fuß fassen mit der Zugrundelegung naturwissenschaftlicher Zeit- und Entwicklungsvorstellungen, in die auch die Vernunft einbezogen wurde. Nicht die Geschichte der Entwicklung der Vernunft war dann mehr gefragt, sondern die Entwicklung der Vernunft in der Geschichte.

Mit dieser relativierenden Kehre gegen sich wurde die Vernunft zum kulturellen oder evolutionären Epiphänomen.

Diese Folgen des geschichtlichen Prinzips hatten seine Väter nicht intendiert, was für das heutige Verständnis ihrer Gedanken erhebliche Schwierigkeiten bereitet. Die Genesis der Vernunft aus ihrem Anfang heraus ist für sie zwar ein zeitliches Phänomen, aber kein Phänomen in der Zeit. Die Zeit selbst und damit die Geschichte und ihre Epochen ist ein Produkt der Entwicklung des Sichwissens und seiner allmählichen Selbstdurchdringung. Dieses Konzept der Vernunft findet sich neben Schelling und Hegel vor allem bei Fichte. Auch er sieht eine Genesis der Vernunft in den ihr eigenen Möglichkeiten der Selbsterkenntnis. Einfacher als Hegel formuliert er fünf Entwicklungsstufen der Vernunft, die sich in den moralischen Standards der jeweiligen Epoche ausdrücken. Beginnend mit dem Zeitalter der Sinnlichkeit, das noch die physische Verhaftetheit der Vernunft kennzeichnet, bringen Ordnung, Sittlichkeit, Religion und letztlich die Wissenschaft den Freiraum der Vernunft, in dem sie sich als autonome Macht konsolidiert. Dabei findet eine Klärung und Veredelung statt, die auf der letzten Stufe das Zeitalter der Liebe hervorbringt. Immer ist dieser Fortschritt auch mit einem Wissen ermöglicht, der die Erhellung des eigenen Selbst genetisch voranbringt. Nur so können Vernunfteinsichten eine höhere Wertigkeit bekommen als bloße Einsichten in Fakten und ihre Ordnungszusammenhänge. Selbst die Einsichten der Sittlichkeit und Religion vermitteln noch nicht diese letzte Gewissheit, die durch die genetische Einsicht in den Zusammenhang aller Einsichten gewährleistet ist und erst darin zur Liebe führt.

Insofern ist die Liebe auch nicht die bloße Folge einer religiösen Erkenntnis, geschweige denn, dass sie sich aus der Sittlichkeit ergäbe. Der "genetische" Standpunkt, wie ihn die *Wissenschaftslehre* allein ermöglichen kann, ist für die Liebe ausschlaggebend: "Für die Wissenschaft wird genetisch, was für die Religion nur Factum ist," sagt Fichte und gibt damit zu erkennen, dass ein lebendiger Zusammenhang des Glaubens von der Religion allein nicht vermittelt werden kann.[1] Die Religion als Wahrheit, die von der Vernunft anerkannt und damit nicht dem Aberglauben zu überantworten ist, gibt ihren inneren Zusammenhang mit der Entwicklung der Vernunft zu erkennen. So ist auch das religiöse Geschehen der Erscheinung Jesu als historische Tatsache nicht durch das bloße Faktum bezeugt, sondern wird erst durch das Moment, im Faktum die Selbstoffenbarung der Vernunft mitzuerleben, zum Zeugnis für die Lehre, welche die christliche Religion ausmacht.

---

1. Johann Gottlieb Fichte, *Anweisung zum seligen Leben, oder auch die Religionslehre* (1806), in *Fichtes Werke*, Bd. 5, 399–580 (hrsg. von Immanuel Hermann Fichte; Berlin: Veit & Comp., 1845–1846 [8 Bde.] und Bonn: Adolph Marcus, 1834–1835 [3 Bde.]; Nachdruck in 11 Bde., Berlin: de Gruyter, 1971), 472.

2. Offenbarung als Wiedererkennung der Vernunft

Schon in der *Kritik aller Offenbarung* (1792) formuliert Fichte die Kriterien, die eine Religion glaubhaft machen und sie sich vom Aberglauben unterscheiden lässt. Danach ist das allgemeine Gesetz, "ein Princip zu suchen, aus welchem Gott als moralischer Gesetzgeber erkannt werde; oder es wird gefragt: hat sich Gott uns als moralischer Gesetzgeber angekündigt, und wie hat ers."[2] Zu einer solchen Frage der Offenbarung gehört beispielsweise, dass ein "moralisches Bedürfnis" danach zu erkennen ist.[3] Die Offenbarung kann nicht unvermittelt oder als Oktroy vorstellbar sein, da der "Endzweck jeder Offenbarung" die "reine Moralität" ist, die nur durch "Freiheit" möglich ist und sich also "nicht erzwingen" lässt:[4] "Keine göttliche Religion muss durch Zwang oder Verfolgung sich angekündigt oder ausgebreitet haben."[5]

Das Prinzip einer moralischen Religion oder der Übereinstimmung von Moralität und Religion wird Fichte dann in seiner Verteidigung gegen die Anklage des Atheismus vorbringen. Mit seiner Aussage: "Religion ohne Moralität ist Aberglaube"[6] meint er, den gegen ihn gerichteten Spieß umdrehen zu können. In seiner *Appellation an das Publicum gegen die Anklage des Atheismus* (1799) wird die Gegenständlichkeit Gottes und seine Faktizität zum Beweis des Atheismus und zur Grundlage für die Verrichtung eines heillosen Götzendienstes.[7] Die Vergegenständlichung ist aber die unterste Form der Vernunfteinsicht, die weit davon entfernt ist, eine moralische genannt zu werden. So kann Fichte zu seiner Verteidigung sagen: "Was sie Gott nennen, ist mir ein Götze. Mir ist Gott ein von aller Sinnlichkeit und allem sinnlichen Zusatz befreites Wesen, welchem ich daher nicht einmal den mir allein möglichen sinnlichen Begriff der Existenz zuschreiben kann."[8]

Wenn Fichte in seiner Schrift *Anweisung zum seligen Leben* von 1806 das Evangelium des Johannes als Vernunftwahrheit herausstellt, dann scheint dies deshalb in mehrfacher Hinsicht keine Überraschung zu sein. Allem voran ist es die Geistgeburt der Schöpfung aus dem Wort, die seiner Vorstellung von der unsinnlichen Gegenwart Gottes näher steht als die Genesis des Alten Testaments. Dieser philosophischen Begründung für die Priorität dieses Evangeliums stand aber zu Fichtes Zeiten

---

2. Johann Gottlieb Fichte, *Kritik aller Offenbarung* (1792), in *Fichtes Werke*, Bd. 5, 11–174 (hrsg. von Immanuel Hermann Fichte; Berlin: Veit & Comp., 1845–1846 [8 Bde.] und Bonn: Adolph Marcus, 1834–1835 [3 Bde.]; Nachdruck in 11 Bde., Berlin: de Gruyter, 1971), 60.
3. A.a.O., 5:113.
4. A.a.O., 5:114.
5. A.a.O., 5:115.
6. Johann Gottlieb Fichte, *Appellation an das Publicum gegen die Anklage des Atheismus* (1799), in *Fichtes Werke*, Bd. 5, 193–238 (hrsg. von Immanuel Hermann Fichte; Berlin: Veit & Comp., 1845–1846 [8 Bde.] und Bonn: Adolph Marcus, 1834–1835 [3 Bde.]; Nachdruck in 11 Bde., Berlin: de Gruyter, 1971), 209.
7. A.a.O., 5:219–20.
8. A.a.O., 5:220.

noch die theologische zur Seite, galt dieses Evangelium in der Leben-Jesu-Forschung seit Johann Gottfried Herder doch als die authentische christliche Quelle, weil sie Jesus nicht nur als jüdischen Messias herausstellte, sondern, mit ihrem Bezug zum griechischen Geistesleben, als Heiland der Welt. Jesus fällt in dieser griechischen Bezeugung die Bedeutung des Gründers einer neuen Religion zu. Erst David Friedrich Strauss sollte mit seinem revolutionären Buch über das *Leben Jesu* dem vierten Evangelium diese Bedeutung aberkennen, indem er gerade in dem Hintergrund des griechischen Geistesleben mit seinen metaphysischen und gnostischen Tendenzen genau jene Gefahren sah, die mit ihrer Weltverneinung die eigentliche Bedrohung für die christliche Religion darstellen. Als Schüler von Ferdinand Christian Baur war Strauss mit der Thematik der Gnosis sehr wohl vertraut und hatte damit eine Perspektive, die weder Herder noch gar Fichte einzunehmen in der Lage gewesen wären. Insofern klingen die von Fichte vorgetragenen Thesen weder originell noch bezeugen sie einen großen Gelehrten, sie gehört zu der in der Zeit typischen Einschätzungen und Bewertungen der historischen Quellenlage der Evangelien.

So sind seine Ausführungen in der 6. Vorlesung der *Anweisung* theologisch eher wertlos. Eine Bedeutung haben sie allein dadurch, dass sie in einer Schrift auftauchen, die Fichte zu dem populären Teil seiner Arbeiten zählt. Die populären Schriften Fichtes, neben der *Anweisung* vor allem die *Grundzüge des gegenwärtigen Zeitalters*, sollen Fichtes Konzeption der *Wissenschaftslehre* einem breiteren Publikum verständlich machen. Da schon die verschiedenen Fassungen der *Wissenschaftslehre* von großem, fast missionarischem Eifer für die Vernunft und ihre Selbsteinsicht getragen sind, stellen diese sogenannten populären Schriften den Kern seiner durchaus als Vernunftreligion zu bezeichnenden Gedanken dar. Dabei ist es wiederum, wie Fichte im Vorwort bemerkt, die *Anweisung*, die den "hellsten Lichtpunct"[9] bildet. In diesem Zusammenhang seines philosophischen Konzepts muss die 6. Vorlesung gesehen werden. Das Evangelium des Johannes wird damit zum Evangelium der kritischen Philosophie, insbesondere der Philosophie Fichtes selbst.

3. Das Johannesevangelium als Vernunftoffenbarung

Unter diesem Aspekt ist auch sein "Princip der Auslegung" zu verstehen, das nicht nur für Johannes, sondern generell für alle christlichen Schriftsteller zu gelten hat. Danach ist die Auslegung "zu verstehen, als ob sie wirklich hätten etwas sagen wollen, und, so weit ihre Worte das erlauben, das rechte und wahre gesagt hätten."[10] Die Angemessenheit zur Vernunft selbst und ihrem Anspruch nach Selbsterkenntnis wird in diesem Prinzip deutlich. Diesem Verfahren einer vernunftgemäßen

---

9. A.a.O., 5:399 (*Anweisung zum seligen Leben*).
10. A.a.O., 5:477.

Auslegung stellt Fichte das Unangemessene eines "hermeneutischen Princips" gegenüber, das die Äußerungen dieser Schriftsteller für "blosse Bilder und Metaphern" hält.[11] Das Wirkliche und Wahre ist die Vernunft selbst und damit weder eine jenseitige Welt über noch eine sinnliche Welt vor der Vernunft. Die Äußerungen der christlichen Schriftsteller und hier vor allem von Johannes sind reine Wahrheit, insofern sie das Sichwissen der Vernunft zum Ausdruck bringen. Dennoch ist die Religion in den Zeugnissen der Evangelien und des Johannesevangeliums nicht die höchste Stufe der Vernunft. Es fehlt noch die kritische Einsicht in die Genese des Wissens vom bloß sinnlichen Wissen bis hin zu der Selbsterkenntnis der Vernunft in den christlichen Wahrheiten.

Für Fichte steht die kritische Philosophie also am Ende der geistigen und kulturellen Entwicklung und bietet die genetische Einsicht in das Faktum der Offenbarung und seinen Zusammenhang mit der Sinnlichkeit. Die Offenbarung ist damit von sich aus nicht auch schon für die Vernunft einsichtig und wird es erst dann, wenn wie in der *Kritik aller Offenbarung* die angesprochenen vernünftigen Kriterien und Bedingungen erfüllt sind. Diesem Anspruch genügt das Johannesevangelium vor allen anderen Zeugnissen, weil es das Leben Jesu zur anschaulichen Umsetzung des Selbstwissens der Vernunft werden lässt.

Es ist also weniger die theologische Bedeutung, die Fichtes Auslegung des Johannesevangeliums auch heute noch interessant erscheinen lässt, als vielmehr die philosophische, die seine Stellung innerhalb einer Schrift von Fichte einnimmt, die nicht nur die vielleicht wichtigste seines gesamten Werkes darstellt, sondern die von ihrer Wirkungsgeschichte her gar nicht überschätzt werden kann. Dies gilt nicht für sein zeitlich nahes Umfeld und die Philosophie Hegels, dies gilt vor allem für Heidegger und dessen "Daseinsanalytik" in *Sein und Zeit*, wobei eine explizite Nennung jeweils unterdrückt bleibt. Die Einheit von Sein und Bewusstsein, die Fichte mit der *Wissenschaftslehre* von 1804 glaubte gezeigt zu haben, wird in den populären Schriften von 1806 und den *Tatsachen des Bewusstseins* zu einer Erscheinungslehre der Vernunft von ihrem genetischen Faktor her beleuchtet. Damit war auch der philosophische Boden für Identitätsthesen bereitet, die den ideologischen Hintergrund auch für politische Vorstellungen verschiedener Couleurs im 19. und 20. Jahrhundert bildeten, eine Entwicklung, die Fichte in dieser Form weder beabsichtigte noch gut geheißen hätte. Seine Einheit von Sein und Bewusstsein zeigte sich erst am Ende des kritischen Verfahrens und seiner genetischen Einsicht. Diesen Standpunkt vermag noch nicht einmal die christliche Heilslehre selbst zu vermitteln, die im Faktischen bleibt, die aber nicht den imperativen Charakter dieses Faktischen aufzuzeigen vermag.

In diesem zentralen Wendepunkt der Philosophie Fichtes insbesondere und darüber hinaus der ideologischen Entwicklung der letzten 200 Jahre im Allgemeinen steht für ihn das Johannesevangelium als höchstes Zeugnis davon, was die Vernunft

---

11. Ebd.

faktisch und anschaulich an Wahrheit zu verkünden hat. Das Evangelium veranschaulicht, wie Sein und Bewusstsein, Dasein und Wissen übereinkommen und sich materialisieren. Das Sein, das sich dem menschlichen Erkennen im Ist zeigt, ist das göttliche Dasein, ist Gott. Im Aussprechen des Ist nennen wir das göttliche Sein, allerdings unbewusst. Die Aufgabe der Philosophie ist es, dieses unbewusste Wissen in ein bewusstes zu überführen.

Diese Überführung des unbewussten Wissens vom Sein in ein bewusstes und offenbar gewordenes Seinsbewusstsein ist nun nicht nur das zentrale Anliegen Fichtes und seiner—wie man sagen könnte—philosophischen Mission, es ist auch die Botschaft insbesondere des Evangeliums des Johannes, welches das Wort an den Anfang setzt und nicht die Schöpfungstat ins Nichts hinein: "Aus Unkunde der im bisherigen von uns aufgestellten Lehre entsteht die Annahme einer Schöpfung, als der absolute Grundirrthum aller falschen Metaphysik und Religionslehre und insbesondere, als das Urprincip des Juden- und Heidenthums."[12] Der Gedanke der Schöpfung bringt das Problem der "Willkür" eines Handelns hinein, das zusammen mit dem Anfang für Fichte nicht denkbar ist. Es bedurfte für ihn keiner Schöpfung, denn am Anfang war schon das Wort, "und durch dieses erst sind alle Dinge gemacht."[13] Das Dasein, als welche die Dinge auch als geschaffen erscheinen, ist nur die faktische Seite des "inneren und in sich verborgenen Seyns," das Gott immer schon ist und war. Außer diesem inneren und verborgenen "Seyn" ist er "auch noch überdies da."[14] Dieses Dasein erfassen wir für Fichte faktisch. Insofern besteht für uns immer schon ein Unterschied zwischen Sein und Dasein, der sich aber als Folge des Verstehens oder Reflexion erweist. Die Reflexion spaltet sich nämlich in das Bewusstsein des Seins, das sie unmittelbar ist, und die Vorstellung dieses unmittelbaren Seins in den Formen des "Als" oder der Analogien, als die dieses unmittelbare göttliche und innerliche Sein da ist.

Diese Doppeltheit von Innerlichkeit und Äußerlichkeit des Seins ist für Fichte nur darin fasslich, dass das "Als" sein "soll."[15] Sein ist nicht einfach nur, Sein soll auch da sein, und in diesem *Soll* manifestiert sich der Daseinswille Gottes, der allem Dasein zugrunde liegt und das Sein ins Dasein überführt. Dies ist aber keine Schöpfung im herkömmlichen Sinn, es ist die Verwandlung von Sein in Dasein. Dasein ist gesollt, es soll sein. Im Soll liegt die Begründung und Legitimation des äußerlichen und faktischen Seins neben dem innerlichen und verborgen. Die Faktizität des Seins ist Ausdruck eines Soll. Im Dasein ist das "göttliche Leben" zwar in eine "stehende Welt" verwandelt,[16] in der Reflexion erkennt sich aber das Bewusstsein des Daseins als "Bild" des Seins. Das Ist der Fakten ist die Manifestation des göttlichen Willens, dass Sein da sein soll.

---

12. A.a.O, 5:479.
13. A.a.O., 5:480.
14. Ebd.
15. A.a.O., 5:455.
16. A.a.O., 5:457.

Die Faktizität der Welt verleitet damit einerseits zum "todten Begriff" durch die "ertöthenden Blicke des tothen Beschauers,"[17] der das Faktum nicht als Erscheinung zu denken vermag. Das Faktum offenbart aber in gleicher Weise das unendliche Leben des Seins, wenn es als gesolltes Faktum erkannt wird. "Dasein ist Pflicht" wird Goethe diesen Gedanken dann später aussprechen. Diese Einsicht in das Soll will Fichte vermitteln und dazu ist ihm das Evangelium des Johannes die "reinste Urkunde."[18]

Über dieses Einsicht in das Erkennen von Sein hinaus entwirft das Johannesevangelium aber auch eine Perspektive der Versöhnung, Heilung oder Wiederherstellung des durch die Faktizität verleiteten Bewusstseins. So ist die Sinnlichkeit mit ihrer Orientierung an den Fakten zwar an der Quelle des reinsten Wissens, sie sieht in ihnen aber nicht den Willen zum Sein. Die Fakten sind insofern nur Fakten und ihre bloß sinnliche Erfassung toter Begriffe. Erst indem die Fakten in ihrem Bildsein erscheinen, als das sie für den lebendigen Willen zum Sein stehen, werden sie selbst zur Offenbarung. Der Kern der Offenbarung ist damit die Verwandlung der toten Faktizität in eine gewollte. Orientierung dafür ist das Dasein als Soll. Die Trennung von Sein und Soll, in der eigentlich die Bewahrung vor einem "naturalistischen Fehlschluss" liegen soll, ist für Fichte geradezu die Ur- oder Erbsünde, da sie die Sinnlichkeit an die Fakten als bloße Fakten kettet.

4. Erweckung der Sinnlichkeit von der toten Faktizität

Die Offenbarung leistet damit auch eine Befreiung der Sinnlichkeit, indem sie die Fakten zum Bildsein befreit und damit das unter dem toten Begriff begrabene Leben spürbar macht. Da wir nur faktisch erkennen können, ist das Faktische als Quelle des Wissens zu behandeln. Das Faktische ist aber zur verstehen als Bild des Seins. Dieses Verstehen gelingt im wahren Verstehen des faktischen Ist. Hier liegt deshalb das Ziel der Offenbarung. Da für Fichte das göttliche Sein nicht nur die innerliche und absolute Seite hat, sondern "auch noch überdies *da ist*," wird die Klärung des Verhältnisses von Sein und Dasein zur primären philosophischen Aufgabe, zu der nun von religiöser Seite nur der Evangelist Johannes etwas beitragen kann, "denn nur dieser allein hat Achtung für die Vernunft."[19] Damit fallen Wunder und andere der Sinnlichkeit widersprechende Ereignisse als mögliche Wege zur Offenbarung weg.[20] Wunder können nicht veranschaulichen, wie das Sein zum Dasein kommt, da sie nur einen Zufall oder bestenfalls eine Willkür widerspiegeln, nicht aber den Soll-Charakter, der im Sein liegt und durch das Dasein des Seins zum Ausdruck gebracht wird. Nicht übernatürliche Ereignisse, wohl aber die Fleischwer-

---

17. A.a.O., 5:404.
18. A.a.O., 5:476.
19. A.a.O., 5:476.
20. A.a.O., 5:477.

dung des Wortes zeigt dagegen, wie das Sein zum Dasein kommt und wie umgekehrt das Dasein das *Da* des Seins *ist*. Jesus ist damit "schlechthin in und durch sich, durch sein blosses Daseyn, Natur, Instinct, ohne besondere Kunst, ohne Anweisung, die vollkommene sinnliche Darstellung des ewigen Wortes."[21] Fichte lehnt mit dieser Einsicht nicht nur grundsätzlich alle möglichen Emanationslehren ab, er wendet sich auch gegen die "jüdischen Träume von einem Sohne Davids und einem Aufheber eines alten Bundes, und Abschliesser eines neuen, bei Paulus und den übrigen."[22] Dieser christlich-theologischen Überheblichkeit stellt er eine zunächst demütig scheinende philosophische Haltung zur Seite, nach der diese Einsicht in die Einheit von Sein und Dasein in der Fleischwerdung des Wortes die "tiefste Erkenntnis" bedeutet, der ein Mensch teilhaftig werden kann und die vor Jesus niemand hatte, die aber auch nach Jesus "ausgerottet und verloren" war.[23]

Hier zeigt sich nun die Aufgabe der philosophischen Einsicht in die Einheit von Sein und Bewusstsein, zu zeigen und zu erklären, wie Jesus selbst diese tiefste Erkenntnis überhaupt hatte und zu ihr gelangte. Die Möglichkeit dazu liegt in der Transsubstanziation, die sich zunächst in der Fleischwerdung des Wortes vollzieht und die im Sakrament des Abendmahles wiederholt wird: "Sein Fleisch essen und sein Blut trinken, heisst: ganz und durchaus er selbst werden und in seine Person, ohne Abbruch oder Rückhalt, sich verwandeln,—ihn in seiner Persönlichkeit nur wiederholen,—transsubstantiiert werden mit ihm—so wie er das zu Fleisch und Blut gewordene ewige Wort ist, ebenso zu seinem Fleische und Blute, und, was nun daraus folgt und dasselbe ist, zu dem zu Fleisch und Blut gewordenen ewigen Worte selbst werden: denken durchaus und ganz wie er, und so, als ob er selber dächte und nicht wir; leben durchaus und ganz wie er, und so, als ob er selber lebte in unserer Stelle."[24]

Die Verbundenheit mit Jesu vollzieht sich in der Fleischlichkeit. Indem wir sein Fleisch essen, vereinigen wir uns leiblich mit Jesu. Dadurch vollzieht sich für uns die tiefste Erkenntnis, die sich auch für Jesum selbst vollzog, das Fleischwerden des Wortes. *Im Fleischwerden des Wortes vollzieht sich das Da des Seins.* Die Verleiblichung ist die Materialisierung und Vergegenständlichung des innerlichen Seins. Wie es sich im Ist seiner daseienden Gegenstände ausspricht, aber als verborgenes Sein, so offenbart es sich im Fleischwerden des Wortes. Indem sich Jesus in dieser Sohnschaft des Wortes erkannte, stellte er den Zusammenhang zwischen Sein und Dasein her, der von nun an im Gedächtnismahl wiederholt werden kann.

Mit dieser Offenbarung des Seins im Dasein fällt aber auch die Vereinzelung weg, die das faktische Ding an sich hat. Zwar *ist* das Faktische als je solches, die Offenbarung bringt das Ist aber in den Zusammenhang des Seins, aus dessen

---

21. A.a.O., 5:483.
22. Ebd.
23. A.a.O., 5:483–84.
24. A.a.O., 5:488.

Unendlichkeit und Ewigkeit heraus es ist. Dieses Herstellen des Zusammenhanges, das durch die tiefe Erkenntnis Jesu vollzogen wurde, bringt aber nicht nur einen Erkenntnisfortschritt für alle, die am Gedächtnismahl teilnehmen, es erweitert den verschlossenen Selbstbezug des Ich zu einem umfassenden Liebesbezug. Damit wird das Leben als Liebe offenbar, die Einheit, von der aus Fichte seine Überlegungen in der ersten Vorlesung begonnen hat.[25]

5. Fichtes Seligkeitslehre als Allversöhnung

Das Leben als Liebe und aus der Liebe heraus zu zeigen, ist Anfangs- und Zielpunkt von Fichtes "Seligkeitslehre." In diesen "tiefsten Sätzen der Erkenntnis,"[26] welche die Seligkeitslehre ausspricht, werden alle Gräben und Differenzen überwunden und alles in den lebendigen Blick aufgenommen: das scheinbar tote Faktum als Gegensatz zum Lebewesen, das geteilte und abgespaltene Ich als Gegensatz zum denkenden und setzenden und der Tod überhaupt als Gegensatz zum Leben. Fichte kündigt schon zu Beginn seiner Vorlesung die Apokatastasis an, die durch die Offenbarung der Liebe vollbracht wird: "Es kann keinen reinen Tod geben, noch eine reine Unseligkeit."[27] Die Versöhnung des Geistes mit dem toten Faktum geschieht in der Sinnlichkeit, die durch Vernunft belehrt wird. Von der Sinnlichkeit geht die Vernunft aus und zu ihr kehrt sie wieder zurück. Deshalb ist das Fleischwerden des Wortes die Lehre, die die Sinnlichkeit mit der Vernunft versöhnt. Das Fleisch geht mit der Schöpfung vom Wort aus und kehrt im Gedächtnismahl zum Wort zurück. Die Einsetzungsworte "dies ist mein Fleisch" und "dies ist mein Blut" können daher für Fichte nur vom Johannesevangelium her als Liebeszeichen verstehbar werden. Sie lassen in der Einheit von Wort und Fleisch, die der Prolog gestiftet hat, Jesum in uns, "in unserer Stelle"[28] erscheinen, sie geben damit aber das Prinzip für die Wiedererkennung des Seins im Dasein, der Vernunft in der Sinnlichkeit. Wenn Leben Liebe ist, dann muss die Vernunft im Gegen-stand das Für-einanderstehen erkennen. Die Offenbarung im Leben und Sterben von Jesu befreit die Erkenntnis zu dieser tiefsten Einsicht und verwandelt damit alles Leben in Liebe.

Abstract

The philosophical question with which Fichte and other Absolute Idealists wrestled was the metaphysical question concerning the relation between being (*Sein*) and existence (*Dasein*). How can it be explained that existence is free from its ground-in-being yet embedded within it? For post-Kantian philosophers, the answer to this question could not be obtained on the basis of reason alone, as was the case with Kant. Rather, history was consti-

---

25. A.a.O., 5:401.
26. Ebd.
27. Ebd.
28. A.a.O., 5:489.

tutive for philosophical conceptions concerning the way reason cognizes the truth of existence through the genesis of self-consciousness. In his works, particularly the *Kritik aller Offenbarung* (1792) and the later *Anweisung zum seligen Leben* (1806), Fichte offers his respective answer to the question by presupposing an integral relation between historical religion and philosophy and by using John's Gospel, particularly its Prologue, as his exegetical basis.

This philosophical question concerning reality has two dimensions in Fichte's post-Kantian context. The metaphysical question can only be answered in view of epistemological parameters. For Fichte, knowledge begins with sensation (*Sinnlichkeit*). Cognition grasps the data of sense perception through a concept that is "dead" because it does not show up the dynamic interrelations of entities within the matrix of a living whole. In order to arrive at knowledge of the living whole in relation to its ground, reason must use sense perception as the point of departure for grasping the essence of that entity to be related to its ground in a relation of freedom and dependence. The metaphysical question includes the theological question of creation in its purview. This creation, however, is not a *creatio ex nihilo*. Rather, Fichte sees the transition from being to existence to be constituted by an imperative (*Sollen*); existence is the necessary externalization of God as its ground and its "inner" side.

It is in view of Fichte's metaphysics that the category of *revelation* is given a decisive determination. Revelation is not a miracle, but is epistemologically necessary, although it must be criticized according to reason's criteria. Religious revelation contains particular truths, yet it is philosophy's task to determine the criteria according to which religious truths can be accepted and believed as authentic witnesses to truth. Fichte offers such criteria in his own work (*Kritik aller Offenbarung*). In the *Anweisung zum seligen Leben*, Fichte turns to John's Gospel as the "purest source of revelation." Fichte's exegetical choice reflects a common nineteenth-century privileging of John's Gospel for metaphysical insights. Fichte differs from other treatments by focusing explicitly on the incarnation as the historical fact of revelation that reveals reason's knowledge concerning the relations between both being and existence, and existence and knowledge. Knowledge of metaphysical truth begins with the revelation of the word in the flesh: in Jesus' life and in his eucharistic presence in bread and wine. The particular unity between word and flesh reveals universal reconciliation between these two aspects. Ultimately Fichte's doctrine of blessedness (*Seligkeitslehre*) incorporates the theological doctrines of creation and reconciliation into the metaphysical insight that reality is based on and is oriented to love.

The Consummation of Reality: Soteriological Metaphysics in Schleiermacher's Interpretation of Colossians 1:15–20

Christine Helmer

Contentions concerning the relationship between past and present continue to press upon discussions of method, particularly if exegesis and systematic theology are brought into the ring. The study of the past, mainly by exegetical scholars, and the construction of the present-day constellation of self, world, and God, primarily by systematic theologians, remind, at best, that past and present cannot be naively brought into relation with each other. The difficulty of fit is partially due to the semantic difference between past and present, established by eighteenth-century criticism against Protestant Orthodoxy's semantic equivocation between the two. Difference, not sameness, qualifies the relation between biblical studies and systematic theology, with bridge disciplines, such as biblical theology, sometimes sent in to mediate the two.[1]

One source of the contention seems to be its dual epistemological presupposition. If, on the one hand, historical reason is seen to be discontinuous with speculative reason, as in the Kantian paradigm, then a judgment arises that the study of the historical past by empirical reason cannot serve theological claims made by appealing to speculative reason. This dualist view can be challenged for the reason that it seems to insulate the study of history from any motivation by present concerns, whether as a hermeneutical pre-judgment or for the purpose of informing those concerns. History is for sheer, and mere, history's sake. If, on the other hand, historical reason is seen to be epistemologically continuous with speculative reason, then another criticism rears its head: speculative thinking is imposed onto past history. On this view, it seems as if the introduction of the speculative thinking required for systematic theology necessarily *distorts* the historical objectivity required for a "true" reading of the biblical text. To err on one side seems inevitable; which side is left to one's choosing.

---

1. On the bridge-building function of biblical theology, set with its origins in Johann Philipp Gabler's famous inaugural speech delivered at the University of Altdorf on March 30, 1787, see Christine Helmer, "Biblical Theology: Bridge Over Many Waters," *CurBS* 3 (April 2005): 169–96.

It is precisely the unresolved suspicion haunting systematic theology that I address in view of a theologian, philosopher, and New Testament scholar who continued to protest against accusations of the sort, but to no avail. My intention is to point out a way beyond the presupposed epistemological impasse by offering a new construal of the relation between exegesis and theology in view of the topic of this book, the question of reality. In this essay, I study Friedrich Schleiermacher's 1832 interpretation of one of the New Testament's christological hymns, Colossians 1:15–20.[2] I argue two points. By negative argument, I show that Schleiermacher's alleged dogmatic bias is not the result of his imposing theological doctrines onto the literal text. Rather, Schleiermacher takes great care to analyze the biblical passage's Greek terms and syntax. By positive argument, I show that Schleiermacher's exegetical work presupposes an idiosyncratic understanding of the relationship between the reality of the past and the reality of the present. This distinct understanding plays into his theological method that is applied in such a way as to collapse the historical distance between text and interpreter into a metaphysically construed temporal simultaneity between past and present. What Schleiermacher does is to take the historical feature of the text and transpose this into a transhistorical feature, thereby turning a historical claim into a speculative claim. The christological bias is not a result of dogmatic imposition, but is, in fact, a function of a soteriological metaphysics concerning the redemptive goal of creation. By rehabilitating Schleiermacher's philological precision, I hope to show that his hermeneutical insights can be appreciated, while also demonstrating that his operating metaphysic is open to criticism.

The first section, "Text and Context," summarizes the standard criticism directed against Schleiermacher's "christological bias." I point out that such a criticism does not take seriously enough Schleiermacher's own defense concerning his hermeneutical innocence and the historical privileging of both his exegetical theol-

---

2. "Ueber Kolosser 1, 15–20" was first published in *Theologische Studien und Kritiken: Eine Zeitschrift für das gesammte Gebiet der Theologie* 3 (1832): 497–537. It was subsequently reprinted in Friedrich Schleiermacher, *Sämmtliche Werke*, vol. I/2 (Berlin: G. Reimer, 1836), 321–59. (Hereafter referred to as SW.) The text has been recently reprinted in the *Kritische Gesamtausgabe*, vol. I/8, *Exegetische Schriften* (ed. Hermann Patsch and Dirk Schmid; Berlin: de Gruyter, 2001), 195–226. (Hereafter referred to as KGA.) The English translation is by Esther D. Reed and Alan Braley, "On Colossians 1:15–20 (1832)," *New Athenaeum/Neues Athenaeum* 5 (1998): 48–80. (Hereafter referred to as NANA.) Esther Reed's detailed introduction to this text is in NANA, 33–47. In addition to publishing his commentary on Col 1:15–20, Schleiermacher also lectured five times on this book together with other shorter letters of the New Testament at the University of Berlin, during the winter semesters of 1811–1812, 1815–1816, 1818–1819, 1824–1825, and in the summer semester of 1832 (see Patsch and Schmid, "Einleitung der Bandherausgeber," KGA I/8, xlii and n. 130). He also preached two sermons on this text in 1830: the first sermon on Col 1:13–18 on July 25 and the second sermon on Col 1:18–23 on August 8. These two sermons are part of a sermon series on Colossians that Schleiermacher delivered from June 13, 1830, to July 17, 1831 (ibid., xliv and n. 143). For a record of the sermon, see SW II/6 (ed. Friedrich Zabel; Berlin: Verlag von Friedrich Aug. Herbig, 1835), 232–43 and 244–55.

ogy and his dogmatic theology. The difficulty lies elsewhere. The second section, "Text and Interpretation," thematizes Schleiermacher's interpretation of the christological hymn in Col 1:15–20. I focus on analyzing Schleiermacher's hermeneutical results in relation to his soteriological determination of the realities reconciled by God in Christ. It is an underlying power/appearance metaphysic that determines the interpretation. The third section, "Text and Reality," summarizes my thesis regarding the metaphysics underpinning the exegetical method that Schleiermacher applies to Col 1:15–20. It is my contention that the soteriological metaphysics Schleiermacher uses to connect creation (stanza one in verses 15–16b) to redemption (stanza two in verses 18b–20b) is not a function of his hermeneutical insights, but is a result of his theological method that reads into the past what is probably best left in Schleiermacher's present.

1. Text and Context

It is practically a platitude that a text is interpreted in a specific context. In this section, I take this platitude to show that Schleiermacher's own exegetical works tend to be interpreted in a context that presupposes an epistemological dualism between historical and speculative reason. By sketching his presupposed epistemological continuity between the two types of reason, I pave the way for explaining the "christological bias" in the Col 1:15–20 commentary as a function of his operating metaphysics.

Schleiermacher is considered to be one of the eminent New Testament scholars of his time.[3] His exegetical work on the four Gospels and the deuteropauline corpus broke new ground, and his commentary on Col 1:15–20 is no exception. Until the present day, scholars acknowledge their own point of exegetical departure to begin with Schleiermacher's identification of the passage's parallel literary structure.[4] In his study, Schleiermacher points out the "two unmistakable" literary parallels structuring the text "if one confines oneself simply to the text as the sole consideration."[5] Verses 15–16b are parallel to verses 18b–20b by the repetition of ὅς and ὅτι in both parts: "'He (ὅς) is the image . . . for (ὅτι) in him all things were created.' . . . 'He (ὅς) is the beginning. . . . For (ὅτι) in him all the fullness of God was pleased to dwell.'"[6] Schleiermacher contrasts his literary observation with Chrysostom's interpretation that allocates Christ's dignity to three sites: "the first above, the first in the

---

3. For a detailed discussion of Schleiermacher's exegetical achievements, see Christine Helmer, "Schleiermacher's Exegetical Theology and the New Testament," in *Cambridge Companion to Schleiermacher* (ed. Jacqueline Mariña; Cambridge: Cambridge University Press, forthcoming).
4. Christian Stettler, *Der Kolosserhymnus: Untersuchungen zu Form, traditionsgeschichtlichem Hintergrund und Aussage von Kol 1,15–20* (WUNT 2/131; Tübingen: Mohr Siebeck, 2000), 1.
5. NANA, 52.
6. Ibid. Schleiermacher cites the following Greek: "ὅς ἐστιν εἰκών . . . ὅτι ἐν αὐτῷ ἐκτίσθη τὰ πάντα . . . ὅς ἐστιν ἀρχη . . . ὅτι ἐν αὐτῷ εὐδόκησε" (ibid.).

church, and the first in the resurrection."⁷ In spite of his respect for the Greek acumen of this church parent, Schleiermacher writes that he can find no literary evidence for this triple eminence of Christ.⁸ By dismissing Chrysostom's theology on philological grounds, the burden is on Schleiermacher to interpret the literary parallel to make a theological claim concerning the relation between Christ in creation (verses 15–16b) and Christ in redemption (verses 18b–20b). In his commentary, Schleiermacher begins by criticizing a christological imposition onto the text. But will he himself be found guilty of the same exegetical crime?

Scholarship seems to answer the question in the affirmative. From its earliest reception, criticism was directed specifically against what Schleiermacher insisted on in the opening paragraphs. Schleiermacher assures readers of his intention to proceed on the basis of hermeneutical rules alone, rather than out of dogmatic interest.⁹ In spite of the praiseworthy rhetoric, scholarship deemed that Schleiermacher did not carry through with his intention and, instead, tainted his hermeneutical inquiry with dogmatic claims. In his reminiscences of Schleiermacher published one year after the latter's death, Friedrich Lücke writes that Schleiermacher "belongs to the class of those who are far more strongly inclined towards a distinctive individuality of apprehension than to self-surrender; who rather draw over the author to their own position, then allow themselves to be drawn by him."¹⁰ Rather than "understanding particularly the written discourse" of the Apostle Paul "correctly," as was the objective Schleiermacher prescribed in his *Hermeneutics*,¹¹ Schleiermacher transformed the apostle into his own image.¹² In their introduction to Schleiermacher's commentary on Col 1:15–20, Patsch and Schmid write of reviews published immediately after Schleiermacher's death, which reiterate a similar criticism.¹³ In spite of some uncontained awe for the sensitive reading that Schleiermacher offers, reviewers raise the claim that Schleiermacher imposes his dogmatic opinion onto the text. In her informed introduction to her English translation, Reed too raises the question of a dogmatic bias, yet attempts to defend Schleiermacher on his statements

---

7. Ibid., 53. In this and in other exegetical works, Schleiermacher engages the Greek fathers, such as Chrysostom and Theodoret, as dialogue partners because of their philological superiority in reading and writing Greek texts (ibid.).

8. "Yet, for our part we cannot find three equipollent sentences for these three members" (ibid.).

9. "It is so much concerned with the much discussed and disputed question concerning the higher nature and dignity of Christ, and concerning his relationship to God and the world that I think it is pertinent to state here and now my belief that this endeavor proceeds, not from any dogmatic interest at all but from a purely hermeneutical interest" (ibid., 51).

10. Friedrich Lücke, "Reminiscences of Schleiermacher," in Friedrich Schleiermacher, *Brief Outline of the Study of Theology* (trans. William Farrer; Edinburgh: T & T Clark, 1850), 33. Cited in Reed, "Introduction," 34 and n. 6.

11. Friedrich Schleiermacher, *Hermeneutics and Criticism and Other Writings* (trans. Andrew Bowie; Cambridge Studies in the History of Philosophy; Cambridge: Cambridge University Press, 1998), 3.

12. Lücke, "Reminiscences," 34. Cited in Reed, "Introduction," 47 and n. 59.

13. Patsch and Schmid, "Einleitung der Bandherausgeber," KGA I/8, xlvi–l.

concerning the importance of grammatical interpretation.[14] Yet Reed acknowledges that Schleiermacher is less defensible on the one charge that his possible unfamiliarity with early-nineteenth-century research on the gnostic, or λόγος, theological backdrop to Paul (who Schleiermacher supposes is the author of Colossians) led him to downplay possible Essene and gnostic influences on the apostle,[15] and on the other charge that his exegetical portrayal of Jesus looks remarkably like the Redeemer of *The Christian Faith*.[16] Could it be that Schleiermacher was so naive as to dismiss any possibility of a dogmatic equivocation with his exegesis?

In the face of insidious suspicion and recurrent criticism, the charge of dogmatic imposition cannot be easily dismissed. Nevertheless, it is the bias of the charge itself that demands a second look. The epistemological continuity between historical and speculative reason that Schleiermacher advocates in his *Dialektik* seems to preclude the charge of imposition.[17] As he argues, a concept acquires its predicates solely by historical investigation, not by speculative fantasy. Furthermore, no bifurcation between history and speculation is admissible in view of his theological systematicity. In fact, Schleiermacher sees exegetical and dogmatic theology as two of three subdisciplines of historical theology, distinguished solely by virtue of the historical epoch under consideration. Exegetical theology considers the origins of Christianity, dogmatic theology its present state.[18] Given Schleiermacher's own defense of hermeneutical innocence, his epistemological continuum, and his subsumption of both exegetical and dogmatic theology under historical theology, could it be that Schleiermacher is meriting the attack of dogmatic imposition on different grounds? In the following section, I argue that there is nothing inherently dogmatic about the application of Schleiermacher's hermeneutical rules. It is, rather, his soteriological metaphysics that should be the object of contention, not the christological reading of the Colossians passage.

2. Text and Interpretation

Since Manfred Frank's edition of Schleiermacher's *Hermeneutik und Kritik* was published in 1977, it has been an established thesis that Schleiermacher privileged

---

14. Reed, "Introduction," 34–40.
15. Ibid., 40–44. Reed argues that Schleiermacher's dismissal of sources "renders him vulnerable to the charge of prejudice in interpreting Paul's Christology in terms of ecclesiology and ethics" (ibid., 41).
16. Ibid., 44–46.
17. Friedrich Schleiermacher, *Vorlesungen über die Dialektik*, in KGA II/10,2 (ed. Andreas Arndt; Berlin: de Gruyter, 2002), 541 (1822; 43rd lecture).
18. Friedrich Schleiermacher, *Brief Outline of Theology as a Field of Study* (trans. Terrence N. Tice; Schleiermacher Studies and Translations 1; Lewiston, N.Y.: Mellen, 1990), § 85 (48–49). (Page numbers are indicated in parentheses.)

the grammatical side of the interpretative task for arriving at a text's meaning.[19] This commitment to the text's formal elements is explicitly reiterated in the Col 1:15–20 commentary.[20] In this section, I restrict myself to a few examples of Schleiermacher's literary-linguistic analysis of the Colossians commentary in order to show that he must be taken at his intended word. Nevertheless, a difficulty seeps into the interpretation as I suggest in this section and analyze in the next section.

According to Schleiermacher's hermeneutical rules, determining a text's authorship is integral to interpreting the text correctly. Produced by an author—or school—a text is a record of that respective author's experience of reality as it is shaped by a particular authorial intention. In his work on Colossians, Schleiermacher makes some claims about the text's author that, although not any more agreed upon by contemporary scholars, must be mentioned in order to understand how these claims structure his interpretation. Unlike twentieth-century commentators on Colossians, Schleiermacher assumes Pauline authorship for the entire letter, including its christological hymn (Col 1:15–20).[21] By assuming Paul to be the author for the entire work, Schleiermacher also reads the passage as a literary integrity.[22] These assumptions are key because they explain why Schleiermacher determines the passage in the context of Paul's theology as a whole, and especially in view of passages that he deems to refer to a similar content: Eph 2:12–16 and Rom 11:36.[23] Paul's authorial intention is read by Schleiermacher to constitute the simi-

---

19. Friedrich Schleiermacher, *Hermeneutik und Kritik* (ed. Manfred Frank; STW 211; Frankfurt: Suhrkamp, 1977). Frank's edition has recently been translated into English by Andrew Bowie (see n. 11).

20. "Now, undeniably this is the case here to such a degree that one cannot evade the demand to probe into the extent to which the meaning of the formal elements can be detected from the logical and grammatical relationships among the sentences in which they occur; and this is the task I have set myself here" (NANA, 51).

21. For an example, see Stettler, *Kolosserhymnus,* 43. Also unlike contemporary interpreters, Schleiermacher does not determine the passage's genre to be a hymn. Contemporary consensus claims that the letter's author reworked an already existing hymn into the text. See ibid., 79, 100–103. The Pauline authorship of Colossians was first called into question by Ernst Theodor Mayerhoff, *Der Brief an die Colosser mit vornehmlicher Berücksichtigung der drei Pastoralbriefe* (Berlin: H. Schulze, 1838), as Reed notes in her "Introduction," 37 and n. 19.

22. Hofius rejects Käsemann's claim that the passage includes two interpolations: the *genitivus appositivus* in verse 18a (τῆς ἐκκλησίας), and verse 20b (διὰ τοῦ αἵματος τοῦ σταυροῦ αὐτοῦ). On the other hand, Hofius notes two other interpolations: the four powers in verse 16 and the δι' αὐτοῦ in verse 20. See Otfried Hofius, "'Erstgeborener vor aller Schöpfung'—'Erstgeborener aus den Toten': Erwägungen zu Struktur und Aussage des Christushymnus Kol 1,15–20," in *Paulusstudien II* (WUNT 143; Tübingen: Mohr Siebeck, 2002), 217–19.

23. Schleiermacher explicitly appeals to both these passages in the Colossians commentary. For example, Schleiermacher asks the classic question of whether Colossians should be cross-referenced with Ephesians (NANA, 51 n. 67). He argues for the chronological priority of Colossians because of its more systematic arrangement and sustained argument. "That is why I am puzzled whenever I hear it conjectured that this letter was based on the letter to the Ephesians; that would have to imply that in the present letter Paul was trying to produce an improved version of the other one" (ibid.). For reference to

larity between the passages. For Schleiermacher, all of Paul's works are stamped with a particular construal of reality, given decisive shaping in Paul's conversion. In his works, Paul's authorial intention is the explication of a dramatic transition from one kingdom to another that is effected by Christ.[24] Thus the subject matter thematized by all New Testament authors, "the higher nature and dignity of Christ, and concerning his relationship to God and the world,"[25] is idiosyncratically articulated by Paul as a transition.

Schleiermacher demonstrates this transition in the Colossians text by analyzing the textual milieu of verses 15–20 and finds the interpretative clue in verse 13: "He has delivered us from the dominion of darkness and transferred us to the kingdom of his beloved Son, in whom we have redemption, the forgiveness of sins."[26] The transition is itself evident in the text's syntax. Schleiermacher acknowledges that the opening passage of Col 1 is divided into two full sentences: verses 3–8 and verses 9–23.[27] In the second sentence, two transitions indicate two subjects of activity. The first articulates a shift from God as the subject of the main text (verses 9–23) to the subject of Christ in verse 15, and the second describes the transition from Christ back to God in verse 16 and then in verse 19 of the main text.[28] From this textual analysis, Schleiermacher concludes that the main point in the hymn is the transference of "us" (καὶ ὑμᾶς in verse 21) into the kingdom of the Son. Thus Schleiermacher sees Paul's particular authorial intention in the syntactical structure of the entire passage that has as its content "our" transition from darkness into the kingdom of Christ. Conversion is a transition from one reality to another.

The soteriological determination cannot be judged an alien imposition. According to Schleiermacher, the New Testament as a whole grounds the entire Christian tradition by relating "everything in" Christianity to the "redemption accomplished by Jesus of Nazareth."[29] A basic agreement attributing the work of redemption to Jesus of Nazareth qualifies the central perspective of both the New Testament and the subsequent history of the Christian church.[30] In view of this attri-

---

Eph 2:12–16, see ibid., 73; for Eph 2:16, see ibid., 75–77. For reference to Rom 11:36, see ibid., 64–65, n. 88, and ibid., 68.

24. See SW I/8, 147 (*Einleitung ins neue Testament*), in which Schleiermacher argues for the key significance of Paul's conversion in determining his *Tendenz*.

25. NANA, 51.

26. Ibid.

27. In this paragraph, I am summarizing Schleiermacher's argument in ibid., 50–51.

28. Ibid., 72.

29. This understanding of reality is the concept of the essence of Christianity given in Friedrich Schleiermacher, *The Christian Faith* (ed. H. R. Mackintosh and J. S. Stewart; trans. D. M. Baillie et al.; Edinburgh: T & T Clark, 1999), § 11, proposition (52): "Christianity is . . . essentially distinguished from other such faiths by the fact that in it everything is related to the redemption accomplished by Jesus of Nazareth." (Hereafter referred to as CF. Page numbers are given in parentheses.)

30. A religion's determining characteristic is an original intuition of the deity, as Schleiermacher describes it in the fifth speech. Friedrich Schleiermacher, *On Religion: Speeches to Its Cultured Despisers*

bution, Paul's distinctive understanding of that reality is in agreement with the soteriological claim of Christianity as grounded in the texts of the New Testament.

Attention, however, must be drawn to the way Schleiermacher attributes work to person. In his Colossians commentary, Schleiermacher follows his own dogmatic theological logic by relating soteriology to Christology: only as much as is experienced as Christ's effect can be attributed to the dignity of Christ's person.[31] By this rule, Schleiermacher avoids the speculative tendency to attribute docetic predicates to Christ that are not warranted by the redemptive effect of his person. Schleiermacher follows this same rule when determining Paul's Christology in the Colossians passage. In order to do this, however, Schleiermacher must solve an interpretative difficulty presented by the literary parallel that appears to distinguish between Christ as mediator of creation in the first stanza and Christ as mediator of redemption in the second stanza. If the passage is read according to the classic two-natures dogma of Christ, then the first stanza must be predicated of a preexistent λόγος, at least according to classic theological consensus.[32] Schleiermacher disagrees with this consensus, denies the referent to be the second person of the Trinity, and reads the subject of the entire passage as "the whole Christ."[33] With this designation, the passage's two stanzas cannot refer to a metaphysical division in Christ according to his two natures: stanza one as attributed to the divine nature, stanza two to the human nature. Rather, both stanzas are referred to the "whole Christ."

The question, however, as to what is meant by "the whole Christ" is the controversial matter. At this point, Schleiermacher's exegetical-theological results differ from the traditional doctrinal interpretation regarding the preexistent Christ. In order to understand what is meant by the unity of Christ's person in two works, Schleiermacher focuses on the literary connection between the parallels. As Schleiermacher argues, the literary parallels must refer to the same subject.[34] Christ's relation to creation is determined solely from creation's redemptive *telos*, which is already indicated by the transfer idea in verse 13. On the basis of this soteriological restriction, Schleiermacher prohibits any cosmological speculation regarding τὰ πάντα (verses 16 and 20), preferring to read this term in view of the καὶ ὑμᾶς (verse 21).[35] All aspects of the passage refer to Paul's message concerning the universal

---

(trans. Richard Crouter; Cambridge Texts in the History of Philosophy; Cambridge: Cambridge University Press, 2000), 107.

31. "If the peculiar dignity of the Redeemer can be measured only by His total activity as resting upon that dignity . . . then the dignity of the Redeemer must be thought of in such a way that He is capable of achieving this" (CF § 93, 1 [377]).

32. Hofius interprets the first stanza to refer to the preexistent Christ. See Hofius, "Christushymnus," 223.

33. "[R]ather Paul can have been thinking only of the whole Christ, and we must therefore also be content to interpret the sentence in a way that can be applied to the whole Christ" (NANA, 55).

34. Ibid.

35. Ibid., 54.

redemptive outcome of creation in Christ.[36] The reality of universal reconciliation is precisely the metaphysical question inherent in the soteriological claim.

The metaphysical question concerns how Schleiermacher understands Christ's person in relation to his activity in creation. Given his soteriological determination of the whole Christ as the historical Jesus of Nazareth, Schleiermacher cannot attribute this activity to a preexistent and nonembodied Christ as the second person of the Trinity. Rather, he conceives the role of the historical Jesus in creation in a way that avoids claiming Jesus' preexistence. By analyzing the Colossians passage in view of this question, Schleiermacher addresses a question not investigated in Part I of *The Christian Faith*.[37] If soteriology is the lens through which Christ is viewed, then the Colossians passage explicitly raises the unavoidable question concerning Christ's relation to creation.

In order to answer this question, Schleiermacher turns to the verb "to create." In his Colossians commentary, Schleiermacher reads the phrase "ἐκτίσθη τὰ πάντα" (Col 1:16a) to refer "only to the founding and establishing of something that will continue to exist and develop in the future."[38] On philological grounds, Schleiermacher argues that the verb κτίζειν does not denote the creation of something not previously existing. For this meaning, both Paul (Acts 17:24) and the LXX use the term ποιῆσαι. According to Schleiermacher, κτίζειν refers to the incorporation of disparate elements into one reality. From the verb's meaning, there is no requirement to posit a temporal priority of a *creatio ex nihilo* over which a second person of the Trinity presided.[39]

If the text is read without reference to a *creatio ex nihilo*, then the question arises regarding the relationship between past and present. Schleiermacher begins to answer this question by advancing a claim concerning the metaphysical continuity of entities from past to present by noting the literary parallel between κτίζω (verse 16a) and συνίστημι (verse 17b).[40] Both verbs are embedded in clauses containing

---

36. Schleiermacher mentions Paul's idea concerning the universality of Christianity in SW I/8, 147.

37. In this first part of his dogmatic theology, Schleiermacher thematizes the doctrines of creation and providence as statements derived from religious self-consciousness as abstracted from the consciousness of sin and the consciousness of grace. The entire section is ordered to divine causality, without reference to Christ. Explicit soteriological claims are only made when Christ is discussed in section 2 of part II under the consciousness of grace. See CF §§ 92–105 (374–475).

38. NANA, 57. See the entire philological argument in ibid., 57–61.

39. This philological point dovetails with Schleiermacher's well-known thesis in the CF concerning the absorption of creation into preservation (cf. CF § 38, 1 [146]). Creation is a doctrine of divine activity only to the extent that the essences which endure through time are explained as having their origin and their preservation in divine activity. If reason attempts to conceptualize a *creatio ex nihilo* as a moment distinct from preservation, then it risks capturing God in the antithesis characterizing finite thinking. See CF § 41 (152–56), which tries to avoid making God's creation from nothing part of finite activity in time and also the *Dialektik* that rejects the *creatio ex nihilo* altogether on philosophical grounds because a rational conception cannot extricate God from the antitheses marking finite thinking. See KGA I/10,2, 535–37 (1822; 42nd lecture).

40. This paragraph summarizes the argument found in NANA, 59–61.

ἐν αὐτῷ and τὰ πάντα. The difference between them lies in the different verb tenses. Schleiermacher resolves the discrepancy by arguing that what is contained in the perfect συνέστηκεν is also contained in the aorist passive ἐκτίσθη. The aorist past is absorbed into the perfect tense, thereby emphasizing continuity along a historical trajectory. Schleiermacher notes a further connection between past and present by the literary parallels in verses 17a and 18a. Both phrases are formulated in the present tense (καὶ αὐτός ἐστιν πρὸ πάντων and καὶ αὐτός ἐστιν ἡ κεφαλή). First, Schleiermacher claims an analogy between the absorption motif of the aorist and perfect verbs and the two phrases in the present tense. The phrase "before all things" is also to be absorbed into "he is the head" by virtue of the analogy that one reality is brought into another reality. Second, Schleiermacher determines the object of the verbs in light of the intransitive συνέστηκεν. He appeals to a rule stipulating that the intransitive must be read in conjunction with its transitive form.[41] The application of this rule results in determining the object as that which is brought together with another. What is brought together is not the "continuation of existence" but the "becoming established, the being consolidated of conditions and institutional arrangements."[42] Third, Schleiermacher determines the reality in which all "conditions and institutional arrangements" are brought together. That one reality is given in verse 18: "Christ is the head of the body, of the church." Through this soteriological determination, τὰ πάντα are determined to have their foundation in him.[43] All is dependent on Christ, not as the mediator of creation, but as its consummation. Creation has its purpose to be related to Christ in such a way that it "further[s] his kingdom in one way or another."[44] If all things are to be transferred into the kingdom of the Son, then even the metaphysical question concerning the absorption of past into present can be determined soteriologically.

After Schleiermacher soteriologically determines Christ's relation to creation, he then turns to the more specific metaphysical question concerning the nature of the realities dependent on Christ. Schleiermacher's word study of the terms in verse 16 designating heavenly and earthly realities (τὰ πάντα ἐν τοῖς οὐρανοῖς καὶ ἐπὶ τῆς γῆς), unseen and seen realities (τὰ ὁρατὰ καὶ τὰ ἀόρατα), and the four Greek terms in verse 16c (εἴτε θρόνοι εἴτε κυριότητες εἴτε ἀρχαὶ εἴτε ἐξουσίαι)—as well as his general determination of τὰ πάντα—yields a decisively embodied metaphysical picture. Schleiermacher rejects not only any spiritually disembodied entities

---

41. Ibid., 60.
42. Ibid.
43. "Paul is not saying something inappropriate but is saying exactly what we would have had to wish him to say, namely that conditions on earth for human beings are related to Christ and how they are so related" (ibid., 64). Cf., "That is to say, he [Paul] could have affirmed this providing that redemption through Christ, and one can also just as correctly say Christ himself, is the key to all the divine institutions that refer to humankind, and consequently that he is the one foundation of all" (ibid., 65).
44. Ibid., 66.

as denotations of these terms,[45] but any links Paul might have had with gnostic, speculative, or wisdom teaching in which those spiritual realities play a metaphysical role.[46] Although Schleiermacher's rejection of the spiritual realities denoted by these terms seems to be discredited by scholarship,[47] his results are grounded in philological observations. Schleiermacher documents his scholarly opinion with arguments about the text's historical continuity with Judaism, as well as with considerations of syntax and literary parallelism. In verse 16, Schleiermacher determines τὰ πάντα by first arguing against correlating the invisible with heaven and the visible with earth. Rather than taking Paul's contrasts as equal parallels,[48] Schleiermacher takes "heaven" in the "wider messianic sense" of the "kingdom of heaven," together with the "narrower" Pauline sense of the "kingdom of the Son."[49] "Heaven" refers to the *telos* of creation, its redemption. Furthermore, the pair "invisible/visible" are referred to the proximate term earth, not heaven, as its precise specification.[50] Schleiermacher construes the distinction between the invisible and the visible pertaining to earthly things in terms of Paul's soteriological *Tendenz*. Earthly conditions, whether invisible or visible, have as their end and goal the heavenly realm of Christ's kingdom.[51] These earthly conditions are referred to by the four terms in verse 16: thrones, dominions, principalities, and authorities.[52] The exegetical result of this philological study is a soteriological designation of the heavenly as the goal of the earthly.

It is at this exegetical juncture that Schleiermacher's operating metaphysics makes its entrance. The ontology operating in his exegesis is not that of an ontological dualism between heaven as an invisible reality and earth as a visible reality. Rather, the location of the invisible/visible distinction within earthly reality is characteristic of a monistic ontology. The language is explicitly Leibnizian. Schleiermacher refers to the terminology of power (*Kraft*) and appearance (*Erscheinung*) in order to make his point.[53] Earthly reality has both an inner invisible reality and an external manifestation. The inner is the power which comes to appearance

---

45. Ibid., 61–67.
46. For example: "how little we can assert that the expressions . . . regarded as designations for superhuman existence, would have been known and in current use" (ibid., 61). See also CF §§ 42–45 (156–70) on Schleiermacher's agnosticism concerning the existence of angels and devils.
47. Reed, "Introduction," 42.
48. Schleiermacher appreciates Paul's "penchant for contrasts" (NANA, 63), but claims that the *Tendenz* determines the meaning, not the contrast (ibid., 64).
49. On this point, Schleiermacher refers to continuity with Jewish thought (ibid., 63).
50. Ibid., 64.
51. ". . . [N]amely that conditions on earth for human beings are related to Christ and how they are so related" (ibid.).
52. Ibid., 62, 64. According to Schleiermacher, both the invisible/visible earthly realities and the four terms in verse 16 are earthly conditions related to Christ (ibid., 64).
53. "Indeed, even anywhere on earth only external things are visible, effects and deeds, whereas what is internal, the movement of the will, power, is invisible" (ibid., 63).

in physical, external reality, and which drives that visible reality to its heavenly consummation. The invisible dimension is the power that becomes visible as physical reality is infused with it; the spiritual is embodied in the physical, and infuses it with eternal life. It is precisely a metaphysical picture of a spirit/body or heaven/earth unity informed by a power/appearance metaphysic that Schleiermacher uses to interpret the text's grammar. Schleiermacher's soteriological metaphysics points forward from the power of invisible reality to its visible consummation in Christ.

At this point in the commentary, it seems as if Schleiermacher is viewing the salvific *telos* of Christ's work from the perspective of a power/appearance metaphysics. The "inner" redemptive power established in Christ on the Earth is permeating the "outer" heavenly realm through its expansion. This heavenly realm, however, is not geographically separate from the earth. Rather, it is understood as the earth's *telos* according to the metaphysics implicit in Schleiermacher's idea of soteriological expansion.

The questions that remain concern the determination of the precise reality that is reconciled and the agent of that reconciliation. Schleiermacher's exegetical move seems to be a look at the position of the subordinate clauses in relation to the main clauses to arrive at the meaning of the entire passage (verses 18b–20b).[54] The main clause in verse 18 (Christ is the head of the church, the firstborn from the dead) is related to the two subordinate clauses in verse 19 (fullness dwells in Christ) and verse 20b and c (the two elements, things on earth and in heaven, are reconciled). Schleiermacher relates the parity he detects in the subject of the subordinate clauses to God, the subject of the verbs in these clauses (to dwell, to reconcile, to make peace).[55] According to a common predication in the New Testament, God is pleased to dwell, to reconcile, to make peace.[56] This observation dovetails with an earlier insight indicating God as the subject of the transference theme in verse 13. God is the agent of salvation.

The next issue concerns the object of reconciliation. Schleiermacher first clarifies the meaning of the verbs by syntactical association. According to the argument, "making peace" has no apposition and is absorbed into "to reconcile."[57] Schleiermacher then handles their object, the referent of τὰ πάντα. From contextual information, verse 21 gives one warrant for associating τὰ πάντα with the Colossians as the referent of καὶ ὑμᾶς ("you who were once set at enmity having been

---

54. I am attempting to reconstruct the argument found in ibid., 72–73. In his *Hermeneutics*, Schleiermacher gives the following interpretative rule: "If we pursue the canon that has been established further we must, in order to proceed organically, *first and foremost distinguish main and secondary thoughts* in relation to the elements of an utterance which can be controversial." Schleiermacher, *Hermeneutics and Criticism*, 64 (italics in original).

55. Ibid., 73.

56. Ibid. Schleiermacher argues that fullness (πλήρωμα) cannot be the subject of indwelling, of reconciling, or of making peace (ibid., 72).

57. This is the main point of a complex argument on ibid., 73.

reconciled").[58] The next warrant is given with the literary parallel between the first "good pleasure," the fullness dwelling in Christ (verse 19), and the second "good pleasure," reconciling all things (verse 20). According to Schleiermacher's interpretation, the parallel indicates an equality of meaning, which gives the reconciliation in Christ of two elements as the content of the fullness.[59] Schleiermacher then finds the second element reconciled to the ὑμᾶς (verse 21) in the analogical passages of Rom 11:12 and 25: "the uniting of Jews and gentiles in the kingdom of the Son and under his lordship" is the resulting interpretation.[60] The elements joined in Christ are neither heaven and earth, nor cosmic powers, but two personal realities: Jews and Gentiles.[61]

The final question concerns the divine agency in view of the soteriological goal of reconciliation. Here Schleiermacher concentrates on the two divine pleasures (verses 19 and 20) in order to determine how these pleasures are related to the one reconciliation in Christ. From syntactical association, Schleiermacher deems that God's second pleasure (verse 20) is the reconciling work that is accomplished in Christ's cross.[62] Although he glosses over the impact of his claim, Schleiermacher states that the cross is the means by which the two realities at enmity with each other are reconciled with each other in relation to it.[63] The type of relation between the two pleasures accomplished by the cross is one of a "mutual conditioning."[64] The condition of reconciliation, which is the first pleasure, is the indwelling of the fullness in Christ, yet the unification of Jews and Gentiles in Christ, the second pleasure, precedes and determines this condition. Conversely, the fullness in Christ, the first pleasure, presupposes peace between the two factions, the second pleasure.[65] Reconciliation in Christ refers back to the subject of both pleasures, and reveals the

---

58. Ibid., 74.

59. This is the summary of the argument found in ibid., 75–76. Schleiermacher rejects Chrysostom's interpretation of fullness as standing for deity, and opts for Theodoret's interpretation for the term as the church (ibid., 74).

60. Ibid., 75. According to Schleiermacher, the difference between the Colossians hymn and the Romans passages is the universalistic outlook of the former. Colossians 1 describes the uniting of Jews and Gentiles in the "totality of Israel." See also ibid., 75–77, on Eph 2:6.

61. Schleiermacher asserts this point on grammatical grounds. Although τὰ πάντα is a neuter noun, Schleiermacher argues against a literal interpretation on the grounds of the passage's context. The context of enmity and reconciliation implies a personalist interpretation (ibid., 77).

62. Ibid., 79.

63. Although he asks, "Again, how were we supposed to imagine that such a reconciliation is conditioned by an establishment of peace by virtue of the cross?" Schleiermacher does not dwell on an analysis of the cross and the blood (ibid., 77). In the CF, Schleiermacher argues for a correlation between the person and work of the Redeemer, rather than for a theory of vicarious satisfaction. On Schleiermacher's understanding of Christ's priestly office, the classical locus of the theory of atonement, see CF § 104 (451–66).

64. NANA, 75.

65. "This is obvious, for the dwelling of this totality in Christ is the definitive, constant condition; it is the complete unification that must necessarily precede that condition and that determines it; yet, in

glory of the one who initiated and accomplished creation's goal. The universalistic reconciliation of personal entities is a result of the divine pleasure in ordaining creation toward its goal of consummation in Christ.

Schleiermacher's careful philological work permits, at the very least, a defense against the charge of a christological imposition onto the text. It is in view of his soteriological metaphysics, however, that the verdict might be another one. It seems that Schleiermacher is reading the literary parallel in Col 1:15–20 with a soteriological restriction in mind that opens up the question regarding Christ's relation to creation. It is this relation that is determined as the consummation of creation. And from this perspective, the divine agency in view of creation is seen in analogical proportion to Christ's consummating function. When analyzing the parallel terms εἰκών and πρωτότοκος in verses 15 and 18, Schleiermacher concludes that as God takes precedence over the world in creation, so too does Christ take precedence over the world in his soteriological function of consummating creation.[66] Schleiermacher implies that with Christ's consummation of creation, reality is to be determined soteriologically. Schleiermacher summarizes his explanation concerning the equivalence of εἰκών and πρωτότοκος: "Thus, this explanation appears fully to satisfy the requirement indicated above, that the whole passage must refer to the progress of Christianity, and to the arrangement for gathering the gentiles into it."[67]

To his readers, Schleiermacher's interpretation might seem suspect. In order to guard against a hasty rejection of his exegesis, I have shown in the above section that Schleiermacher's primary determination of the passage's central concern is fleshed out in view of careful grammatical work. Given this analysis of Schleiermacher's exegetical praxis, the question remains. Is he overdetermining the concept by importing more into the text than is permitted by the predicates? I conclude this essay by briefly arguing that Schleiermacher's overdetermination results from his soteriological metaphysics.

3. Text and Reality

It was Schleiermacher who posed the question of reality from the literary parallel in Col 1:15–20. Rather than allocating the parallel to two distinct spheres of

---

the same way this unification is conditioned by the fact that both parts must have become peaceable" (ibid., 75).

66. "Furthermore, as the 'because' (ὅτι) shows, Christ is here so named because his relationship to this microcosm is exactly the same as God's relationship to the whole world; on this account, he takes precedence over everything in the world; he is the head of the community whereby everything else is first established in its true value, and through him the human spirit attains its full stature" (ibid., 71). "Christ is 'the firstborn image of God' . . . because God has created all things in relation to him; and Christ is 'the beginning, the firstborn from the dead' . . . because God has willed that the 'fullness' . . . should dwell in him" (ibid., 72).

67. Ibid., 71.

reality, Schleiermacher interprets the passage in view of the same reality. Reality has an inner power manifesting itself gradually in appearance. The entrance of redemptive power into human history begins with the appearance of Jesus of Nazareth, and the consummation of creation is accomplished in Christ. This divine goal for creation is achieved when all personal entities are transferred into the kingdom of the Son.

Nevertheless, consensus is still critical of Schleiermacher's reading. The problem, however, that I raise is not one of dogmatic imposition; the Colossians text's soteriological imprint is clear. Rather, Schleiermacher's soteriological metaphysics seems to overdetermine the text by applying a particular conception of reality to it. How might Schleiermacher have methodologically arrived at this exegetical result?

A close look at Schleiermacher's exegetical praxis reveals that his interpretative method is characteristic of his theological method in general. On the basis of reason's capacity for concept formation, concepts are formed by making judgments concerning the respective concept's predicates.[68] Predicates glean concepts from experience that are then attributed to a concept that stands for a subject. By oscillating between a "speculative" grasp of the concept and an "empirical" determination of the predicates, the concept is saturated with predicates; the essence of that concept is gradually approximated by concept and judgment formation operating simultaneously. Schleiermacher's trademark oscillation method between conceptual and empirical reason is itself founded on a nondualist epistemology; speculation and empirical reason are joined to each other as two ends of a minimum/maximum continuum. What is predicated of the concept by empirical reason is also determined by the product of speculative reason. In his exegesis of Col 1, Schleiermacher follows the methodological procedure that he stipulates in the *Dialektik*. The text's concept is soteriological, determined from the passage's context and Paul's theology as a whole; its predicates are gleaned from the text's syntax, grammar, and terms. Nevertheless, a specific predicate seems to be attributed to Paul's concept that seems not to belong there.

The soteriological concept Schleiermacher selects for Paul is one that has a christological justification. It is here that Schleiermacher makes a metaphysical claim of sameness with respect to the "whole Christ." The Christ as agent of redemption is the one who makes an experiential impact on Christian self-consciousness in such a way as to free it from the inhibitions of sensible self-consciousness. For Schleiermacher, this whole Christ is the one experienced as a bodily presence in the first century and then as a spiritual presence in the church. Experienced in terms of "simultaneous contemporaneity,"[69] it is the same Christ who continues to impart

---

68. I summarize the mechanism of concept and judgment formation that Schleiermacher gives in Part I of the *Dialektik*. My argument is to take the epistemology of the *Dialektik* and to apply it to the theological method that Schleiermacher uses in the CF.

69. On this concept, see CF § 14, 1 (69): "But the impression which all later believers received in this way from the influence of Christ, *i.e.* from the common Spirit communicated by Him and from the

redemption to those coming into his proximity by virtue of his continuous personhood. The biblical merit of Schleiermacher's Christology consists of his selecting the christological criterion as the sole experiential center of the New Testament. The doctrinal merit of Schleiermacher's Christology consists of the attribution of redemption to Christ whose person is the vehicle of redemption, whether as bodily or as spiritual presence.

Nevertheless, the problem rests on Schleiermacher's determination of what belongs essentially to Christ's simultaneous contemporaneity. For Schleiermacher, what belongs to this concept is Christ's historical personhood. The christological concept is informed by the sameness of Christ's person from his historical appearance onward. Here, Schleiermacher elevates the self-identity of person to the concept that corresponds to the self-sameness of Christ's historical personhood through time. When Schleiermacher's soteriological metaphysics is linked to this Christology, it prohibits an alternative, speculative reading of Christ's preexistence before his historical appearance in time. On Schleiermacher's historically determined soteriological ground, the speculative determination cannot belong to the self-identity of the person of Christ. The result is that Schleiermacher's conceptual grasp of the essence of Christ's person renders him unable to entertain that concept of self-sameness as itself a historically situated predicate. The conceptual grasp claims the historical predicate so that it is rendered integral to the concept. Rather than allowing his own understanding of reality to enter into the dialogue with Paul as a historically situated predicate, Schleiermacher's soteriological metaphysics reads a predicate of Christ's person as belonging essentially to the christological concept.

The application of the oscillation method to attribute a predicate to the conceptual grasp of reality results in an overdetermination of the text. By determining the concept as essentially stable between Paul and his own Christology, Schleiermacher is prevented from seeing historical difference between biblical authors and his own perspective. He does not reckon with the possibility of a λόγος theology or a theory of speculative wisdom in Paul because he cannot include a speculative, nonpersonalist dimension in his transhistorical soteriological metaphysics. Schleiermacher's own construal of reality, necessary to his soteriological understanding, ends up claiming transhistorical stability, when, in fact, difference between past and present should have been posited. As the conceptual parameter for interpreting the text, Schleiermacher's soteriological metaphysics of sameness misses an appreciation for the historical difference between Paul's theology and his own.

---

whole communion of Christians, supported by the historical representation of His life and character, was just the same impression which His contemporaries received from Him directly."

4. Conclusion

In this essay, I have addressed the classic criticism hurled at dogmatic theologians by their biblical colleagues in my analysis of the exegetical work of a theologian who is representative of such a controversy. By studying Friedrich Schleiermacher's commentary on Col 1:15–20, I have shown that the classic criticism does not hold water, at least in Schleiermacher's case, for a number of reasons. A nondualist epistemology funds Schleiermacher's scientific method oscillating between conceptual and empirical reasoning. On this basis, the New Testament texts are to be viewed according to a christological criterion that has warranted their production in the first place. This hermeneutical key is not an importation into the text, but a teasing out of the christological impulse behind the texts. Furthermore, Schleiermacher's own adherence to the grammatical side of interpretation confirms his own conviction that the empirical study of literature's formal elements does yield textual meaning. Meaning is gleaned from the text; it is not a random transfer of subjective opinion to authorial intention. These reasons expose the initial criticisms against Schleiermacher in particular, and dogmatic theology in general, to be one-sided.

Nevertheless, if conceived correctly, the criticism does serve to tease out a factor in Schleiermacher's exegetical practice that results in an overdetermination of the text. I have studied this difficulty as one of a conceptual overdetermination, not of a flawed hermeneutical application or of an uncritical dogmatic imposition. The conceptual overdetermination results from, although is not necessarily a function of, speculative reason that grasps the essential determination of the concept in a way that overrides historical predicates. This grasp predicates of the past Schleiermacher's own soteriological restriction that determines his Christology along with a power/appearance dynamic of soteriological expansion emanating from Christ's person from the point of his historical appearance onward. Grasped in the concept as its transhistorical determination, Schleiermacher's soteriological metaphysics blurs the possibility of conceiving Paul's predicates of reality on their own. The soteriological metaphysics that Schleiermacher attributes to Paul functions as his transhistorically stable concept, when, in fact, it is a feature of Schleiermacher's own temporally located understanding of reality.

In spite of a reading of Paul that goes against the grain of scholarly consensus, Schleiermacher's exegetical practice discloses the merit of conceiving exegetical work in close connection to the concepts derived from dogmatic theology and philosophy. By considering the philosophical question of reality as determined theologically, Schleiermacher shows the significance of posing precisely these questions of the biblical text. The unique theological perspective of reality is not one that should be monopolized by the metaphysicians. Rather, theologians too make claims about reality that commit them to a particular vision of creation's *telos*, the hope that redemption will be actualized for all. In order to argue for the truth of this claim, interdisciplinary work is required to flesh out its different facets. It is the integrity of this commitment that Schleiermacher embodies as a biblical scholar, theologian, and philosopher in his own right and one who, in spite of the results, studies scripture with the purpose of deepening his own understanding about the truth of universal redemption. As he preached in his own sermon on Col 1, in the study of scripture, "[W]e only study it in the right way . . . in order that the study leads to edification, that we make clear for ourselves the blessedness to which we are called, that we are taught concerning who we are in the body, the head of which is Christ, and what we are and what we should do in the body. This is the aim of all study of the Holy Scriptures."[70]

ZUSAMMENFASSUNG

Dieser Essay über Schleiermachers Auslegung von Kol 1,15–20 ist der Frage nach der Beziehung zwischen einem Wirklichkeitsbegriff und einem biblischen Text gewidmet. Von den ersten Rezensenten seiner exegetischen Arbeit bis heute wird Schleiermacher derselbe Vorwurf gemacht: Schleiermacher trage sein christologisches Vorverständnis in die biblischen Texte ein. Dieser Vorwurf wird hier bestritten, indem 1. Beispiele für eine sorgfältige grammatische Auslegung des christologischen Hymnus' im Kolosserbrief gegeben werden, und indem eine präzise Analyse einiger Wörter im Text des Hymnus und eine Deutung seiner Syntax durch Schleichermacher dokumentiert werden, und indem 2. gezeigt wird, wie Schleiermacher seine theologische Interpretation von dieser grammatischen Analyse her zu gewinnen versucht. Auf diese Weise bestätigt die vorgelegte Untersuchung die These, daß Schleiermacher—der Vater der modernen Hermeneutik!—den Sinngehalt des Textes aus dem Text selbst erschließt.

Wenn dieser Vorwurf gegen Schleiermacher aus philologischer Sicht nicht korrekt ist, dann muß er von einer anderen Seite her analysiert werden. Die Anwendung der theologischen Methode Schleiermachers, nämlich der Oszillation zwischen empirischer und spekulativer Vernunft, projiziert seine soteriologische Metaphysik in den Begriff. Dabei wird Schleiermachers eigener Begriff als transhistorischer Wirklichkeitsbegriff gesetzt.

In einem ersten Schritt "Text und Kontext" möchte ich zeigen, daß Schleiermacher in den neutestamentlichen Fragen seiner Zeit ein führender Exeget war. Seine Forschung über die Synoptiker und Johannes, wenn auch bestritten, trug im 19. Jahrhundert zur Diskussion über die Entstehung der Evangelien bei. Mit seinem Kommentar über den 1. Timotheusbrief hat Schleiermacher die deuteropaulinische Forschung begründet und mit seiner Entdeckung eines literarischen Parallelismus in Kol 1 (Verse 15–16b und 18b–20b) hat er der Auslegung dieses Briefs eine neue Richtung gegeben. Vom Parallelismus ausgehend interpretiert Schleiermacher den Text im Blick einerseits auf seinen Zusammenhang mit der paulinischen Theologie—Schleiermacher hält den Kolosserbrief für paulinisch—und andererseits im Blick auf die theologische Frage nach der Beziehung von Schöpfung und Erlösung. Das Verhältnis zwischen einem soteriologisch bestimmten, historischen Jesus und seiner Beteiligung an der Schöpfung wird dadurch problematisiert, daß Schleiermacher in Kol 1,15–16b keine *creatio*

---

[70]. "[D]aß wir es nur auf die rechte Weise thun mögen . . . daß es gereiche zur Erbauung, daß wir uns die Seligkeit, zu der wir berufen sind, klar machen, daß wir uns belehren über das, was wir sind an dem Leibe, dessen Haupt Christus ist, was wir an diesem sein und thun sollen. Das ist der Zweck alles Forschens in der heiligen Schrift" (SW II/6, 240 [on Col 1:13–18; July 25, 1830; trans. Helmer]).

ex nihilo findet und gegen einen präexistenten Christus als zweite Person der Trinität argumentiert.

In einem zweiten Schritt "Text und Interpretation" gehe ich einigen exegetischen Beobachtungen Schleiermachers im Detail nach, um zu zeigen, wie er seine soteriologische Metaphysik im Blick auf das Verhältnis Christi zur Erlösung und zur Schöpfung versteht. Von einer Kraft/Erscheinung-Dynamik her konzipiert Schleiermacher eine soteriologische Ausbreitung, die von Christus ausgeht und sich über Juden und Heiden bis zur Allversöhnung erstreckt. Dabei erklärt er, daß der Bezug des "ganzen Christus" zur Schöpfung darin besteht, daß Christus der Vollender der Schöpfung sei.

In einem dritten Schritt "Text und Wirklichkeit" beschreibe ich das hermeneutische Problem: Schleiermacher versteht seine soteriologische Metaphysik als eine, die wesentlich zur Begrifflichkeit des Paulus gehört. Dabei benutzt Schleiermacher seine eigene Begrifflichkeit, um weitere Prädikate darein zu setzen. Diese Methode ist an sich nicht problematisch. Sie setzt ein Kontinuum zwischen empirischer und spekulativer Vernunft voraus. Und ein solches Kontinuum wird auf die Begriffsbestimmung angewendet. Indem aber Schleiermacher den Begriff spekulativ nach seiner eigenen soteriologischen Metaphysik vorstellt, stellt er eine historischen Nähe zu Paulus her. Statt einer durch die kritische Methode gewonnene Wirklichkeitsdistanz wird eine Wirklichkeitsnähe zwischen Schleiermacher und Paulus methodologisch hergestellt. Eine angemessene Distanz hätte sich ergeben, wenn Schleiermacher seinen eigenen Wirklichkeitsbegriff für seine eigene Gegenwartsdeutung gebraucht hätte, und den Wirklichkeitsbegriff des Paulus aus dem Kontext des 1. Jahrhunderts herausgearbeitet hätte. Was aber an dieser Auslegung wertvoll ist, ist Schleiermachers theologisches Ergebnis, eine universale und individuelle Deutung der Allerlösung in Christus.

Die Dialektik von Freiheit und Sünde: Hegels Interpretation von Genesis 3

Joachim Ringleben

Für Kant ist die Freiheitsidee entscheidende Voraussetzung und hauptsächliches Gedankeninstrument, um das Böse zu begreifen und die Erzählung vom Sündenfall zu rekonstruieren. Der für sich schon feststehende Freiheitsbegriff wird sekundär eingesetzt und bloß angewendet, um die Sündenthematik angemessen zu behandeln. Das bedeutet: der Notwendigkeit des Freiheitsgedankens entspricht die Zufälligkeit des Bösen. Diese erscheint bei Kant als die Unerforschlichkeit seines Ursprungs. Die Allgemeinheit des Bösen ist selber nur zufälliges Faktum.

Hegels wesentlicher Schritt über Kant hinaus besteht nun m. E. in der Einsicht, daß die Genesis subjektiver Freiheit selber schon das Thema des Bösen einschließt bzw. daß der Sündenfall und das dadurch heraufgeführte Wissen von Gut und Böse gerade auch die Entstehungsgeschichte von Freiheit selber ursprünglich betrifft. "Der Ursprung des Bösen überhaupt liegt in dem... Mysterium... der Freiheit."[1] Für Hegel wird also das Böse zu einem Moment im Zusichkommen von Subjektivität, und der Sündenfall bezeichnet ein Werdemoment in der Freiheitsgeschichte des Menschen.

1. Genesis 3 als Mythus

Nach Hegel verobjektiviert sich in Gen 3 die Genesis menschlicher Freiheit; er liest die Erzählung als die "Geschichte des menschlichen Geistes."[2] Das vorstellende religiöse Bewußtsein hat hier den "ewigen Mythus der Menschwerdung" vor sich, das Wesen des Menschen als Geist wird in der Form einer historischen Geschichte erzählt.[3] Adam ist der Mensch überhaupt.[4] Die Interpretationsvoraussetzungen sind insofern nahezu dieselben wie bei Kant. Von Hegel wird aber die Verzeitlichung der

---

1. Georg Wilhelm Friedrich Hegel, *Werke: Auf der Grundlage der Werke von 1832–1845* (hrsg. von Eva Moldenhauer und Karl Markus Michel; 20 Bde.; Theorie-Werkausgabe; Frankfurt: Suhrkamp, 1969–1971), 7:261, Anm.
2. A.a.O., 8:88–91.
3. Vgl. A.a.O., 12:79 u. 389–90.
4. A.a.O., 8:88.

Vorstellung nicht nur als unangemessen aufgefaßt; indem für Hegel der Geist wesentlich Selbsttätigkeit ist, also nur ist, wozu er sich selber macht, ist es ihm gerade wesentlich, in einer Genesis zu sich zu kommen. Es ist dem Geist adäquat, daß sein Wesen geschichtlich ist. In Gen 3 läuft aber diese Verzeitlichung gleichsam in die falsche Richtung: was Ziel der Werdegeschichte ist (die ihrer selbst im Absoluten gewisse Freiheit), das wird als Ursprung vorgestellt. Der Mythus läßt als Verlassen eines anfänglich-heilen Zustandes vorstellen, was gerade der erste Schritt auf die Selbstverwirklichung des Geistes hin ist. Insofern muß Gen 3 in der Gegenrichtung gelesen werden: "Daß das Paradies verloren ist, zeigt uns, daß es nicht absolut als Zustand wesentlich ist."[5] Die Wahrheit des Geistes liegt vor ihm als das Ganze, zu dem er sich erst entwickelt. Für Hegel kann, was überwunden (verlassen) wird, nicht das Wahre sein.

2. ENDLICHE SUBJEKTIVITÄT ALS WIDERSPRUCH: UNSCHULD UND FALL

Hegels Deutung des Sündenfalls ist konzentriert auf die beiden Momente von "Unschuld" und "Fall." Sie werden begriffen als wesentliche Momente in der Genesis von Subjektivität.

a. In der Vorstellung der "Unschuld" ist die substantielle Einheit der Subjektivität mit ihrem göttlichen Grund, mit der Natur und mit sich selbst gemeint. Die Unmittelbarkeit dieser Einheit widerspricht aber dem Wesen des Geistes, Einheit nur zu sein in selbsttätiger Überwindung seiner Entzweiung. In dem ursprünglichen "Gutsein" paradiesischer Unschuld ist der Mensch vom Tier nicht unterschieden, weil seine Freiheit noch nicht aktuell ist bzw. weil er, in jene substantielle Einheit versenkt und eingebunden, noch gar kein Selbst ist.

b. Weil der Mythus das wesentliche Ziel der Einheit als unmittelbare Gegebenheit vorstellt, muß dieser anfängliche Zustand eines unschuldig-unfreien Seins verlassen werden. Die Widersprüchlichkeit der Unschuldsvorstellung treibt über ihre Unmittelbarkeit hinaus. Im "Fall" entfaltet der Geist notwendig diese Widersprüchlichkeit der Unschuld.

In der Vorstellung vom "Fall" ist demnach zunächst das Zu-sich-selbst-Kommen der Subjektivität zu erkennen. Indem das Selbst reflexiv wird, "in sich geht," wie Hegel sagt,[6] entzweit es sich von jener ursprünglichen Einheit und ist im Sichlosreißen von seinem Ursprung überhaupt erst selbsthaft. Nur in der Selbstentzweiung von ihrem substantiellen Grund ist subjektive Freiheit wirklich. Subjektivität als solche konstituiert sich in Entzweiung. *Für sich* ist das freie Selbst nur in

---

5. A.a.O., 12:267.
6. A.a.O., 3:562.

der Selbstunterscheidung von der vorausgesetzten Ganzheit (Gott, Natur) und von sich selbst *als* unmittelbarem Moment des Ganzen (seinem An-sich-sein). Als diese selbsthafte Verwirklichung der für sich seienden Freiheit bezeichnet der "Fall" bei Hegel ein "ewiges Moment des Geistes,"[7] denn er realisiert den Begriff des Menschen. Insofern ist der Fall notwendig. Zugleich ist der Sündenfall, wie auch die konkreten Einzelzüge von Gen 3 zeigen, ein tief zweideutiger Schritt. Die konstitutive Entzweiung der Subjektivität von ihrem Ursprung setzt mit der Freiheit zugleich die Möglichkeit ihrer Verfehlung, d. h. des Bösen. Das hängt damit zusammen, daß auch die Entzweiung noch auf die Einheit des Geistes bezogen bleibt. Entzweiung kann im Geist nur Durchgangsmoment sein; sie ist konstitutive Bedingung, aber nicht selber und nicht allein das Telos der Subjektivität. Weil die Emanzipation vom Ursprung doch auf seine Einheit bezogen bleibt, kann die entzweite Subjektivität nur als Widerspruch existieren; das heißt sie ist endlich, indem sie zugleich von ihrer eigenen Ganzheit entzweit und in sich selber von sich entzweit ist. Als dieser existierende Widerspruch steht die endliche Subjektivität in der Antinomie von Besonderheit und Allgemeinheit, Naturhaftigkeit und Willkür, Ansich und Fürsich, Ich und Nichtich, Freiheit und Substanzlosigkeit (Leere), Getrenntheit von Gott und Bezogenheit auf Gott.

    c. Vor allem aber manifestiert sich die widersprüchliche Verfassung der durch Entzweiung zu sich kommenden Subjektivität am Verhältnis zum Guten und Bösen. Hierin erreicht die an sich notwendige Genesis der Freiheit ihre kritische Zuspitzung, und genau an diesem Punkt wird der Ursprung des Bösen thematisch.

    Ein explizites Verhältnis zu gut und böse ist nämlich die spezifische Folge der Entzweiung, in der sich die Subjektivität antinomisch konstituiert. 1. Das Gute kann als solches dem Selbst nur gegenwärtig werden, wenn dies selbst schon davon unterschieden ist bzw. sich davon unterschieden weiß. Erst in der bewußten Unterscheidung davon gibt es für die Freiheit das Gute als ihre an sich seiende Einheit mit dem göttlichen Grund. Der Fall etabliert eine Distanz zum Guten, die gerade Bedingung seiner Erkenntnis *als* des Guten, d. h. eines freien Verhältnisses dazu ist.

    Mit dem Guten in seiner Bestimmtheit erscheint zugleich notwendig auch dessen Anderes. 2. Ein ausdrückliches Wissen vom Guten gibt es nur als Wissen um das Böse als das Nichtgute. Wer sich frei zum Guten verhält, verhält sich notwendig auch zum Bösen. Denn nach dem Fall erscheinen Gut und Böse der davon unterschiedenen Freiheit als Gegenstände ihrer Wahl. D. h. das eigene Erkennen von Gut und Böse impliziert eine Absonderung vom Guten, die schon Verlust der Unschuld ist. 3. Der Fall konstituiert das Wissen um Gut und Böse, und dieses Wissen ist Bedingung menschlicher Sittlichkeit, d. h.: eines freien Verhältnisses zu Gut und Böse. Indem das Selbst frei *von* Gut und Böse ist, ist es erst frei *zu* Gut und Böse. Die Zweideutigkeit des Falles liegt im Gewahrwerden des Bösen als solchen. Die

---

7. A.a.O., 17:79.

Freiheit ist nach Hegel ein "gefährliches Geschenk,"[8] weil sie nicht sein kann ohne die Möglichkeit ihres Selbstverlustes, und die höchste Bestimmung des Menschen, das Gute zu wissen, ist verknüpft mit der Möglichkeit, sein Wesen schuldhaft zu verfehlen. Selbstbewußtsein ist als freie Negativität die gemeinsame Wurzel des Bösen und der Moralität.

d. Daß die endliche Subjektivität als Widerspruch existiert, ist daher in spezifischer Weise an ihrem Verhältnis zu Gut und Böse ablesbar. Diese Widersprüchlichkeit, die das entzweite Selbst selber ist, in der es sein Dasein hat, stellt sich in folgender Weise dar: 1. Das Selbst hat selber am Gegensatz von Gut und Böse teil, weil beides Seinsweisen seiner Freiheit sind. 2. Es ist substantiell auf das Gute bezogen und erfährt sich darin faktisch als davon getrennt. 3. Das Gute (als Gehalt der Freiheit) erscheint zugleich als das Aufgegebene (Gesetz, Soll), weil die Freiheit von ihrer wesentlichen Einheit entfremdet ist. 4. Dieser Widerspruch (3.) ist selber Bedingung von Freiheit. 5. Das Selbst *ist* selber die Existenz dieser Widersprüchlichkeit und steht doch, indem sie davon weiß, auch über ihr; sie ist der Widerspruch und ist zugleich frei davon als unendliche Beziehung auf sich. In diesem fünffachen Sinne beschreibt Hegel das Selbst als Austragen seiner Entzweiungsnatur, als Kampf: "Ich bin in mir selbst als unendlich gegen mich als endlich. Ich bin der Kampf."[9]

3. Der Widerspruch der Sünde

a. Darin, daß Entzweiung auf Einheit bezogen bleibt, gründet der Widerspruch, als der sich endliche Subjektivität vollzieht. Die im "Fall" eröffnete Freiheit ist damit an die doppelte Möglichkeit verwiesen, sich in absoluter Einheit zu vollenden (Versöhnung) oder aber Einheit aus sich selber herzustellen (Sünde). Findet die versöhnte Subjektivität ihr Telos im Absoluten, so daß die kritische Bewegung des Falles sich zu einem Moment im Geist aufheben läßt, so ist dagegen das Böse zu begreifen als der Versuch, Einheit dadurch selber herzustellen, daß die Genesis des Geistes aus der Freiheit gleichsam angehalten wird. Was nur als übergehendes Moment Wahrheit hat, wird fixiert und zur ohnmächtigen Usurpation des Ganzen. Sünde ist Freiheit, die sich selber festhält und so sich ins Böse verkehrt. Böse ist die Subjektivität, die nicht nur "in sich geht," sondern darin sich in sich verschließt als fixierte Einzelheit gegen die allgemeine Bewegung, die ihre Wahrheit wäre: "Es ist die Freiheit, die sich so vergreift, ihr Wesen in diese Abstraktion zu setzen und in diesem Beisichsein sich schmeichelt, sich rein zu gewinnen."[10] Bei diesem Versuch, exklusiv in sich selber Halt zu finden, schlägt die einseitig in sich reflektierte Frei-

---

8. A.a.O., 17:76.
9. A.a.O., 16:69.
10. A.a.O., 5:192.

heit um in pure Natürlichkeit, als böse Willkür nimmt das Subjekt seinen Gehalt aus sich in seiner Unmittelbarkeit, und Freiheit wird zum bloßen Instrument von Sinnlichkeit.

Die "Abstraktion" des Bösen liegt in der potenzierten Formalität des Freiheitsvollzugs, der sein eigener Inhalt wird. In der bösen Selbstaffirmation der Freiheit verkehrt sich ihre Negativität durch ausschließliche Beziehung auf sich zu etwas Positivem; insofern lautet Hegels Formulierung des Bösen: "positive Negativität."[11] Als Streben, die Einheit des Geistes aus sich und in sich selber zu produzieren, ist die Sünde der vergebliche Versuch, den Widerspruch der Subjektivität so zu lösen, daß eines seiner Momente für das Ganze genommen wird: das Besondere, das sich an die Stelle des Allgemeinen setzt. Damit aber wird der Widerspruch nur gesteigert. Das Böse ist der potenzierte Widerspruch, einseitige Lösung des Grundwiderspruchs von Subjektivität und zugleich seine extreme Stabilisierung zu sein. Die undialektische Einseitigkeit dieser Lösung (Eigenmächtigkeit) verschärft nur die Entzweiung des "Falles" zur definitiven Entfremdung von "Sünde." Die nur angemaßte, einseitige Einheit fixiert sich gerade in der Trennung von der wahren. Insofern ist Sünde der überhaupt denkbar höchste Widerspruch im Geiste gegen den Geist: sich dem zu verdanken, gegen das sie gerichtet ist. Sie sondert sich nur in Kraft absoluter Einheit von dieser ab. Sünde ist Versöhnung aus eigener Kraft, Selbstsein gegen den Gott, in dem allein es wahres Selbstsein gibt. "Diese Selbständigkeit ist . . . der Irrtum, das als negativ anzusehen und sich gegen das als negativ zu verhalten, was ihr eigenes Wesen ist. Sie ist so das negative Verhalten gegen sich selbst, welches, indem es sein eigenes Sein gewinnen will, dasselbe zerstört, und dies sein Tun ist nur die Manifestation der Nichtigkeit seines Tuns."[12]

b. Das Böse ist also für Hegel das sich selbst Widersprechende: es ist die willkürlich-zufällige Verkehrung eines Momentes (Fall) zu dem scheinhaften Habitus, aus sich selber das Ganze sein zu wollen (Sünde). Die Notwendigkeit der Freiheit tritt im Bösen in der zufälligen Gestalt eines unberechtigten Faktums auf. Insofern ist das Böse der nur faktisch-zufällig existierende Widerspruch, und Hegel kann sagen: "Mit dieser Seite der Notwendigkeit des Bösen ist ebenso absolut vereinigt, daß dies Böse bestimmt ist als das, was notwendig nicht sein soll."[13] Das Böse ist nur als das Aufzuhebende: das Faktum von etwas Notwendigem, das so zugleich nicht sein soll. Die Entzweiung im Fall ist notwendig, weil nur so menschliche Freiheit sich gewinnt und das Selbst wirklich Gut und Böse erkennt; aber das Stehenbleiben in diesem Übergang und das isolierende Festhalten der Trennung macht die Sünde aus: "Sünde ist Erkennen des Guten und Bösen, als Trennung."[14]

---

11. A.a.O., 6:72.
12. A.a.O., 5:192.
13. A.a.O., 7:262.
14. A.a.O., 12:391.

c. Insofern diese Trennung "noch nicht" in der Versöhnung mit Gott aufgehoben und zugleich die Entzweiung "nicht mehr" bloßes Moment ist, ist der Mensch "von Natur aus," d. h. immer schon böse. Sein Bleiben in der an sich notwendigen Entzweiung ist tatsächlich ein Festhalten der eigenen Unversöhntheit, worin er sich so vorfindet, daß er dies "Natürliche" stets schon selber übernommen hat. So eignet sich Hegel kritisch die Vorstellung von der Erbsünde an: "Der Mensch erscheint in ihr als böse von Haus aus, ist also in seinem Innersten ein Negatives mit sich selbst, und der Geist, wie er in sich zurückgetrieben ist, findet sich gegen das unendliche, absolute Wesen entzweit."[15] Mit diesem Gedanken sind weder die Natur als solche noch die in sich gehende Reflexion als böse qualifiziert; vielmehr ist das Böse gerade ihre dialektische Koinzidenz. Nicht die Endlichkeit selber schon ist böse, sondern sie als verabsolutierte; das Böse ist "gewollte und beabsichtigte Endlichkeit."[16] Derart hält die Erbsündenvorstellung daran fest, daß der Mensch *selbst* Sünder ist; das Böse ist sein innerster Seinswiderspruch. Darum hat gerade die Religion der Freiheit, das Christentum, nach Hegel diese Lehre ausgebildet.[17]

d. Das Böse ist der Schatten der Freiheit. Wie die Möglichkeit des Bösen Bedingung wirklicher Freiheit ist, so ist seine faktische Wirklichkeit die schuldhafte Verkehrung von deren Notwendigkeit. In der Selbstunterscheidung von diesem zufälligen, aber tatsächlichen Mißbrauch identifiziert sich erst die wahrhafte Freiheit, denn der Geist "findet seine Wahrheit nur, indem er in der absoluten Zerrissenheit sich selbst findet."[18] Die wahre Auflösung des Selbstwiderspruchs, den die Existenz des Bösen darstellt, ist die Versöhnung im Absoluten (Gott) als der absoluten Einheit des Geistes: "Die Versöhnung ist die Anerkennung dessen, gegen welches das negative Verhalten geht, vielmehr als seines Wesens, und ist nur als Ablassen von der Negativität seines Fürsichseins, statt an ihm festzuhalten."[19] Indem die Sünde in der Versöhnung aufgehoben wird, vollendet sich die Werdegeschichte der Freiheit, die nach Hegel ohne das anstößige Faktum des Bösen nicht zu begreifen ist.

Abstract

Thematized in this essay is Hegel's understanding of freedom in view of the myth of Gen 3. Hegel presupposes Kant who relates freedom to the universality of evil as an accidental fact. Yet Hegel moves beyond Kant by defining evil as a moment in subjectivity's quest for consciousness and the fall as a generating moment in the history of human freedom. Gene-

---

15. A.a.O., 16:25–26.
16. A.a.O., 13:485.
17. Vgl. A.a.O., 7:69.
18. A.a.O., 3:36.
19. A.a.O., 5:192–93.

sis 3 becomes the paradigmatic text for Hegel's explication of the genesis of subjective freedom in the context of evil and the fall.

This genesis of freedom begins at a point of origin. For Hegel, the myth of Gen 3 represents, in the form of historical narrative, the essence of Adam or the human in general. The myth recounts Adam's fall from an original state of integrity as the first step in the self-realization of spirit. Hegel focuses his interpretation of the fall on the two moments of "innocence" and "fall," viewing them as essential moments in the genesis of subjectivity. In the original state of "innocence," the self is not free because it is constituted by an immediate unity between self and ground that has not yet achieved division; this unity without division contradicts the essence of spirit that strives for division and the overcoming of division in a higher unity. In the "fall," the self tears itself away from its ground and becomes a self for the first time. It is this separation that gives evidence for the self's quest for freedom that coincides with its quest for consciousness.

As a necessary step to freedom, however, the fall is steeped in ambiguity. The constitutive disunion of subjectivity from its ground results in both freedom and the possibility of its failure, that is, evil. In this transitional state, the self exists in the various contradictions characterizing finite subjectivity; both good and evil appear as flip sides of the same relation of the self to its ground. The fall establishes a distance to the good, which is the connection to the ground. The self can either establish a free relation to this ground, which is the very condition for its knowledge *as* the good, or the self can choose in freedom to remain distant from its ground, which is the choice for evil. Freedom is, as Hegel writes, a dangerous "gift."

Sin is the self's attempt to achieve unity out of itself. It is the abstract and estranged self-affirmation of formal freedom vis-à-vis God; it is "positive negativity." Sin becomes evil by "turning in upon itself," becoming rigidly fixed against the spirit's movement to its natural goal of reconciliation with its ground. Evil is one-sided in its rigidity, the finite existing for-itself over and against the universality of spirit. In spite of sin and evil, the subject's goal of freedom is its reconciliation with the ground, or the Absolute, in a unity. When sin is sublated into reconciliation, the genesis of freedom is complete, a development that, nevertheless, cannot be understood without the offensive fact of evil.

ANERKANNTE KONTINGENZ: SCHELLINGS EXISTENTIALE INTERPRETATION DES JOHANNESPROLOGS IN DER *PHILOSOPHIE DER OFFENBARUNG*

Wilhelm Gräb

1. Schelling in Berlin

Im Wintersemester 1841–1842 hielt Schelling seine erste Vorlesung als Nachfolger auf Hegels Lehrstuhl in Berlin. Die Vorlesung über "Philosophie der Offenbarung"[1] geriet zu einem kulturellen Großereignis. Kierkegaard, Friedrich Engels, Jakob Burckhardt, Bakunin, Savigny und Ranke befanden sich unter den Hörern. Friedrich Engels schrieb in der Dezembernummer des "Telegraph für Deutschland": "Wenn ihr jetzt hier in Berlin irgendeinem Menschen, der auch nur eine Ahnung von der Macht des Geistes über die Welt hat, nach dem Kampfplatze fraget, auf dem um die Herrschaft über die öffentliche Meinung Deutschlands in Politik und Religion, also über Deutschland selbst, gestritten wird, so wird er euch antworten, dieser

---

1. Eine Nachschrift der Berliner Vorlesung vom Wintersemester 1841–1842 ist von dem rationalistischen Theologen H. E. G. Paulus gegen den Willen Schellings 1843 unter dem Titel "Die endlich offenbar gewordene positive Philosophie der Offenbarung" veröffentlicht worden. Manfred Frank hat diese Edition zusammen mit Auszügen aus anderen Vorlesungsnachschriften, Dokumenten zu den historischen Hintergründen und Auszügen aus Hörerberichten neu herausgegeben. Vgl. Friedrich Wilhelm Joseph von Schelling, *Philosophie der Offenbarung 1841/42* (hrsg. und eingl. von Manfred Frank; 3. neu durchgesehene und korrigierte Aufl.; STW 181; Frankfurt: Suhrkamp, 1995). Im Folgenden zitiert als Schelling, *Philosophie der Offenbarung*, hrsg. Frank. Schelling hatte die "Philosophie der Offenbarung" freilich mehrfach schon während seiner Münchner Zeit gelesen. Nachschriften aus den Münchner Vorlesungen sind in die Ausgabe von 1858 eingegangen, wieder abgedruckt in Friedrich Wilhelm Joseph von Schelling, "Philosophie der Offenbarung," in *Ausgewählte Werke* (Bde. 1–2; Darmstadt: Wissenschaftliche Buchgesellschaft, 1973–1974). Im Folgenden zitiert als Schelling, AW. Zu vgl. ist außerdem Friedrich Wilhelm Joseph von Schelling, *Urfassung der Philosophie der Offenbarung* (Teilbde. 1–2; PhB 445a/b; Hamburg: Felix Meiner, 1995). Da es anlässlich des International Meeting der Biblical Theology Group der SBL um die großen Berliner Philosophen und ihre Bibelinterpretation gehen sollte und der Berliner Schelling mit seiner ersten großen Vorlesung über die "Philosophie der Offenbarung" in der Ausgabe des Dr. Paulus am deutlichsten zu greifen ist, versucht vorliegende Abhandlung weitgehend mit der Paulus-Nachschrift zu arbeiten.

Kampfplatz sei in der Universität, und zwar das Auditorium Nr. 6, wo Schelling seine 'Vorlesung über Philosophie der Offenbarung' hält."² Auch Kierkegaard war anfangs begeistert, weil von der "Wirklichkeit" die Rede schien, dann aber zunehmend enttäuscht, um sich gegen Ende des Semesters ganz von Schelling wieder abzuwenden.³

Man hatte insbesondere von Seiten des preußischen Hofes Schelling in Berlin haben wollen. Es wurde von ihm eine Verteidigung des Christentums als Entgegnung auf die religionskritischen Stimmen aus dem Lager der Junghegelianer erwartet. Die Linkshegelianer hatten denn auch Grund, in der Berufung Schellings, der bei seinem Dienstantritt vier Jahre älter war als Hegel in seinem Todesjahr, den Auftakt einer christlichen Restauration zu sehen. Bekannt waren schließlich die Worte des Königs Friedrich Wilhelm IV., er bezwecke die Ausrottung der "Drachensaat des Hegelschen Pantheismus, der flachen Vielwisserei und der gesetzlichen Auflösung häuslicher Zucht."⁴ Der Applaus von theologischer Seite mußte den Argwohn der Junghegelianer bezüglich des Betreiben des Königs, Schelling von München nach Berlin zu holen, noch verstärken. Theologen sahen in Schellings Philosophie der Offenbarung—wie ein Zeitgenosse sagte—"das notwendige Korrektiv für die neueren Entdeckungen der Kritik, vor der kein Buch des Neuen Testaments mehr sicher ist, und für die Verwüstung der gesamten theologischen Wissenschaft."⁵ Im Berlin des Jahres 1841, da man sich, wie Gustav Mayer in seiner Engels-Biographie schreibt "die Bibel und den Hegel an den Kopf zu werfen" pflegte,⁶ wurde Schellings Berufung jedenfalls als kulturkämpferische und politische Herausforderung an die Adresse der Religionskritik interpretiert. Und diese war eben keine fachinterne Angelegenheit, sondern es galt "die Kritik der Religion" wie Karl Marx in seiner "Kritik der Hegelschen Rechtsphilosophie" schrieb, "als die Voraussetzung aller Kritik."⁷

---

2. Schelling, *Philosophie der Offenbarung*, hrsg. Frank, 535.
3. Kierkegaard äußerte sich zu Beginn des Semesters geradezu euphorisch. So schrieb er am 22. November 1841 in seine Tagebücher: "Ich bin so froh, Schellings zweite Stunde gehört zu haben—unbeschreiblich. So habe ich denn lange genug geseufzt und haben die Gedanken in mir geseufzt; als er das Wort 'Wirklichkeit' nannte, vom Verhältnis der Philosophie zur Wirklichkeit, da hüpfte die Frucht des Gedankens in mir vor Freude wie in Elisabeth. Ich erinnere mich fast an jedes Wort, das er von dem Augenblick an sagte. Hier kann vielleicht Klarheit kommen. Dies ein Wort, das mich an all meine philosophischen Leiden erinnert" (Schelling, *Philosophie der Offenbarung*, hrsg. Frank, Anhang III, 530). Gegen Ende des Semesters, am 27. Februar 1842 teilt Kierkegaard hingegen seine Enttäuschung mit: "Schelling salbadert grenzenlos, sowohl in extensivem wie in intensivem Sinne. Ich verlasse Berlin und eile nach Kopenhagen . . . " Schelling, *Philosophie der Offenbarung*, hsrg. Frank, 533.
4. So gab Bunsen in seinem Berufungsschreiben an Schelling eine Äußerung des Königs wieder. Vgl. in Schelling, *Philosophie der Offenbarung*, hrsg. Frank, Anhang II, 486.
5. Vgl. G. Bacherer, zit. nach Helmut Pölcher, "Schellings Auftreten in Berlin (1841) nach Hörerberichten," *ZRGG* 6,3 (1954): 197.
6. Vgl. Gustav Mayer, *Friedrich Engels: Eine Biographie* (Berlin: J. Springer, 1920), 62.
7. Vgl. Karl Marx, "Zur Kritik der Hegelschen Rechtsphilosophie," in *Marx-Engels-Werke* (4e Aufl.; Berlin: Dietz, 1982), 1:378.

2. Die Verteidigung des Christentums

Schelling gibt mit seiner ersten Berliner Vorlesung zur "Philosophie der Offenbarung," die er freilich mehrfach in München schon gelesen hatte, tatsächlich eine Verteidigung des Christentums. Er warnt allerdings zu Beginn auch vor dem Missverständnis, als mache diese Verteidigung Anleihen bei außerphilosophischen Autoritäten, etwa der der Bibel. Schelling insistiert darauf, daß mit der von ihm sogenannten Philosophie der Offenbarung gerade nicht "eine durch die Auktorität der Offenbarung vorhandene Philosophie gemeint"[8] ist. Es geht ihm um das Christentum als Religion der Offenbarung. Zum Christentum gehört die Bibel, aber es geht in ihr nicht auf. Die Religion der Offenbarung, das ist für Schelling das Christentum, so wie es mit dem biblischen Symbolsystem und der auf ihm aufbauenden dogmatisch-theologischen Lehrbildung gegeben ist.

Das Christentum hat eine vollständige Realisierung der religiösen Idee heraufgeführt, eine letzte Bestimmung dessen, was wir Menschen von Gott und seinem Verhältnis zu Mensch und Welt wissen können. Deshalb ist das Christentum die Religion der Offenbarung, wegen des geschichtlichen Faktum der Person Jesu, dieser ebenso freien wie in Gott gegründeten Persönlichkeit. Dieses geschichtliche Geschehen ist in der Bibel bezeugt, vom Alten Testament vorausgedeutet, vom Neuen Testament kund gemacht, dann in der altkirchlichen Christologie und Trinitätslehre auf den Begriff gebracht. Erst in Verbindung mit dieser seiner über die Bibel hinausgehenden, auch die kirchliche Lehrbildung, das altkirchliche Dogma und mit der eigenen Philosophie auch noch die neuzeitliche Gegenwart in sich einbeziehenden Geschichte des Christentum ist dieses die Religion der Offenbarung. Das Neue Testament, so Schelling, erzählt vom "geschichtliche(n) Hervortreten in der Offenbarung."[9] Dabei ist das historisch Faktische des Auftretens Jesu für Schelling wichtig, daß ein Ereignis in der Zeit das *wirkliche Geschehen* der Offenbarung ist.

Fragt man nach Schellings Verständnis der Offenbarung, reicht der biblische Bezug denn auch noch sehr viel tiefer. Die Bibel ist schließlich nicht nur Urkunde des historischen Offenbarungsgeschehens. Es zeigt sich, daß Schelling sein Verständnis von der Offenbarung selber in der Auslegung der Bibel gewonnen hat. Was das Christentum zur Religion der Offenbarung macht, findet Schelling insbesondere in der Entfaltung des Johannesprologs (Joh 1,1–18), dann noch im Hymnus des Briefes des Apostel Paulus an die Philipper (Phil 2,5–11). So gesehen kann die Philosophie der Offenbarung vielleicht doch eine biblische Philosophie der Offenbarung genannt werden, nicht in dem Sinne, daß sie sich unter die Autorität der Bibel stellt, wohl aber, daß sie den Gedanken der Offenbarung in der Auslegung des Johannesprologs entfaltet. Der johanneische Christus ist die Offenbarung Gottes

---

8. Schelling, "Paulusnachschrift," in *Philosophie der Offenbarung*, hrsg. Frank, 98.
9. A.a.O., 277.

und die historischen Gestalt des Offenbarers. Offenbar geworden ist durch Christus eine handelnde Persönlichkeit, die sich ebenso frei im Verhältnis zur Welt wie in Gott gebunden weiß. Die Vernunft, der Logos, so der Johannesprolog, war schon im Anfang der Schöpfung bei Gott (Joh 1,1). Die Entstehung, d. h. die Erkenntnis und Gestaltung der Welt ist durch den Logos, die theoretische und praktische Vernunft, vermittelt. Sie steht unter der Bedingung, gewusst zu werden. Die Vernunft jedoch gründet in Gott. Gott ist der Grund der die Welt hervorbringenden und gestaltenden menschlichen Freiheit. Das hat Christus gezeigt, indem er es faktisch vorgelebt hat. Christus, so Schellings Argumentation, ist der Offenbarer, weil er die Freiheit der in Gott gebundenen individuellen Persönlichkeit faktisch realisiert hat, also in die Wirklichkeit eingeführt hat. Christus ist der Mensch, aus Gott geboren. Er weiß sich in Gott gegründet, dem Vater untertan und zugleich zum Herrn über alle Dinge gesetzt.

Im Prolog des Johannesevangeliums, mit Seitenblicken auch noch auf den Philipperhymnus, findet Schelling die Grundzüge dieser Christologie. Das Christentum steht zentral für die Lehre von der Fleischwerdung des Logos (Joh 1,14). Und die Fleischwerdung des Logos meint im Christentum ein geschichtliches Faktum. Es ist damit eine Tatsache bezeichnet. Die Fleischwerdung des Logos, die Inkarnation der weltschöpferischen Vernunft ist im Christentum eine erfahrbare Wirklichkeit, aber zugleich auch ein metaphysischer Tatbestand. Der Logos ist der Schöpfungsmittler (Joh 1,2). Der Logos, die menschliche Vernunfttätigkeit, ist die Vermittlung Gottes zur freien, vernünftigen Hervorbringung alles dessen, was ist. Dieser Logos ist präexistent, d. h. er geht als der präexistente Logos der Gegebenheit einer Welt voraus. Dieses wiederum meint, daß er die bedingende Möglichkeit, die Potenz ist, vermöge deren Gott ursprünglich, schon vor der Schöpfung einer Welt, aus der Transzendenz (dem anderen, dem Jenseits des Wissens und der Vernunft) in die Immanenz der menschlichen Erkenntnis und der Gestaltung der Wirklichkeit übergeht. Darin liegt dann wiederum als letzte Konsequenz, daß dieser Logos so bei Gott ist, daß er Gottes Hervorbringung einer Welt durch die menschliche Vernunft und deren Freiheit vermittelt. Der Logos ist im Fleisch erschienen als der Sohn Gottes, der Christus, so daß seine Herrlichkeit, sein Einssein mit dem Vater, am historischen Faktum des Auftretens der Person Jesu zu erkennen war.[10] In diesem Sinne ist das Christentum das historische Faktum des Auftretens eines ebenso freien wie in

---

10. Vgl. ebd; Schelling, "Paulusnachschrift," in *Philosophie der Offenbarung*, hrsg. Frank, 277: "Nur das letzte Faktum: das Subjekt, das mit all den Prädikaten ausgestattet ist, ward Fleisch und wohnte unter uns; wir *sahen*, da sie vorher verborgen war, seine Herrlichkeit, die sich von seiner ursprünglichen Gottheit, seinem Einssein mit dem Vater herschreibt, wir sahen ihn, der wahrhaft mit dem Vater Eins ist: es ist ein Wille nicht bloß der Potenz, sondern des Sohnes, der sich als vom Himmel gekommen offenbart im Menschgewordenen. Wer den Sohn sieht, sieht den wahren Sohn und in ihm den Vater. Diese Geschichte des Johannes enthält das wahre Wissen, wodurch unserem Bewußtsein etwas wahrhaft Positives, Erweiterndes zu Teil wird."

Gott sich gegründet wissenden individuellen Subjekts, die Person des Christus. Deshalb ist das Christentum die Religion der Offenbarung.

Die zentralen biblischen Bezüge lagen für Schelling dabei im Prolog des Johannesevangeliums (Joh 1,1–18) sowie des Philipperhymnus (Phil 2,5–11). In beiden Texten des Neuen Testament fand Schelling zum einen den Gedanken der Einheit Gottes mit dem Logos, der die Beziehung der Welt auf Gott als ihren schöpferischen Grund vermittelt, zum anderen die Lehre vom historisch-wirklichen Vorkommen des Logos in der Gestalt eines von Gott unabhängigen, selbständigen, aber gleichwohl mit Gott sich verbundenen wissenden Menschen, dem Christus.

Der Logos, die Vernunft, ist das Prinzip aller Wirklichkeitserkenntnis. Diese Vernunft kann sich aber aus sich selbst und durch sich selbst nicht begründen. Sobald sie ihr eigenes, Welt erschließendes und hervorbringendes Tun zu erkennen versucht, wird sie sich selbst zum Gegenstand der Erkenntnis. Sie erfaßt sich nicht an der Stelle ihres Tätigseins, ihres Leistens. Alles, was sie erkennt, rückt ein in die Welt des gegenständlich Seienden, des Erkannten. Das Sein des Seienden und der Vollzug seiner Erkenntnis entzieht sich dem alles vergegenständlichenden Erkennen. Das Erkennen vollzieht sich aus einem Grund heraus, der im erkennenden Subjekt gegeben sein muss, den es aber nicht erkennend vor sich zu bringen vermag. Die Vernunft erkennt nur das durch sie selbst Bedingte. Im Blick auf sich selbst steht sie vor einem Unbedingten, das sie gerade nicht wissend zu ihrem Objekt machen kann. Sie muss die Unbedingtheit ihres eigenen Vollzugs sich voraus und aus sich heraussetzen, ein Absolutes, aus dem sie lebt, in dem sie ihr Leben hat, aber nicht auf gegenständliche Weise, nicht im Bewußtsein. Wo sich der menschlichen Vernunft eine Welt auftut, die Wirklichkeit erschließt, ist sie immer schon aus der Einheit ihres Grundes herausgefallen. Sie ist eine von ihrem göttlichen Grund abgefallene Vernunft, deshalb auf Vermittlung angewiesen.

Schelling verteidigt das Christentum, weil er in seiner biblischen Erzählung von der Fleischwerdung des präexistenten Logos in dem geschichtlichen Christus, in dem Mensch gewordenen Gottessohn, das Prinzip der Freiheit, des Hervorbringens und Erkennens einer Welt zur Vorstellung gebracht findet und dies so, daß es in der Erfahrung des geschichtlichen Faktums der Person Jesu als historische Wirklichkeit begegnet.

Das Johannesevangelium beschreibt das geschichtliche Faktum des Christus als die Offenbarung des Gottessohnes. Der Gottessohn ist die Inkarnation des Prinzips der Freiheit, durch das Gott, der Schöpfer, die Welt der Gegenstände hervorbringt. Er ist das Leben und das Licht, in dem zu sehen ist, was ist. Das Johannesevangelium erzählt von Christus als dem Offenbarer so, daß das geschichtliche Faktum eines Menschen erkennbar wird, der sich selbst durchsichtig macht auf das metaphysische Prinzip hin, das uns Menschen zu Wesen der Freiheit macht. Er ist selbständig, frei und im Vollzug der Freiheit, wahrer Selbstbestimmung, macht er zugleich seine Gründung im weltlich Unbedingten, in Gott erkennbar.

3. Vernunft und Offenbarung

Schelling verteidigt das Christentum, weil es mit seiner Botschaft vom historischen Auftreten des Gottessohns das philosophische Problem der Begründung der Einheit der die Welt auf freie Weise erschließenden und gestaltenden Vernunft lösen kann. Die Vernunft kann nämlich aus und durch sich selbst ihren Seingrund nicht wissend in sich einholen. Sie kann ihn nur als sich gegeben sich voraussetzen, in den Bedingungen ihrer eigenen Ermöglichung sich voraus denken. Immer nimmt sie sich selbst, ihr Tätigsein als denkende Vernunft bereits in Anspruch, wenn sie in den unbedingten Grund von dessen Ermöglichung einzukehren versucht. Auch das Unbedingte ist insofern durch das menschliche Wissen von ihm bedingt, es sei denn, es tritt selbst in einer historischen Gestalt hervor, die sich auf diesen ihren unbedingten Daseinsgrund hin durchsichtig macht. Das ist im historisch kontingenten Auftreten des Gottessohnes der Fall. Deshalb ist er die Offenbarung.

Die Offenbarung wird uns, weil sie ein kontingentes historisches Faktum ist, durch Erfahrung zuteil: "Die Offenbarung aber ist ein nur durch Erfahrung uns zu Teil werdendes Wissen."[11] Schelling besteht darauf, daß "durch die Offenbarung Wahrheiten gegeben sein *müssen*, die ohne sie nicht nur nicht gewußt wurden, sondern gar nicht gewußt werden konnten . . . Denn *wozu gäbe es sonst eine Offenbarung*."[12] Er wehrt die rationalistische Auffassung ab, daß sich "die Offenbarungswahrheiten auf bloße Vernunftwahrheiten zurückbringen"[13] ließen. Schelling insistiert auf dem erfahrbaren, faktischen Ereignis der Offenbarung durch den Offenbarer. Das ist der johanneische Christus. Nur durch das Faktum und nur durch die Erfahrung desselben wird erkannt, was die Vernunft aus und durch sich selbst, im bloßen Denken, nicht erkennen kann. "Entweder hat also der Begriff der Offenbarung gar keinen Sinn, oder man muß einräumen: der Inhalt der Offenbarung kann ohne sie nicht gewußt werden. Hier also wird die Offenbarung zu einer eigenen Erkenntnisquelle."[14]

Schelling braucht die Offenbarung, so könnte man auch sagen, weil sie der Vernunft zur Selbsttranszendierung auf den ihr eigenen unvordenklichen Grund verhilft. Die Offenbarung und damit indirekt auch die Bibel, die von ihr als einem historischen Ereignis erzählt, eröffnet der menschlichen Vernunft die Möglichkeit eines Sich-Verhaltens zu den ihr eigenen Voraussetzungen. Sie vermittelt ihr die Erkenntnis dessen, was sie sonst nicht erkennen könnte: Den kontingenten Ursprung ihres eigenen Vollzugs, ihres eigenen Seins, das ein unbedingtes Tätigsein ist, den Seinsgrund der Freiheit, das Prinzip des Erkennens und Gestaltens der Wirklichkeit.

---

11. Schelling, "Paulusnachschrift," in *Philosophie der Offenbarung*, hrsg. Frank, 251.
12. A.a.O., 250.
13. Ebd.
14. A.a.O., 251.

Das Christentum ist die Religion der Offenbarung, wobei im Christentum die Vollendung dessen liegt, was im Alten Testament bzw. im Judentum vorbereitet worden ist. "Der eigentliche Inhalt des A. T. ist eine Religion der Zukunft."[15] Diese "Religion der Zukunft" ist das Christentum, das für Schelling das Ende der Offenbarung ist, da in Christus diejenige in Gott gegründete Person geschichtlich wirklich geworden ist, die zugleich in Freiheit sich zur Welt verhält, Welt hervorbringt, über sie Herr ist.

Die Offenbarung durch den Christus, den inkarnierten Logos, vermittelt die Erfahrung mit dem Faktum des ins Wissen nicht einholbaren Prinzips der Vernunft. Offenbarung fängt mit Erfahrung an, der Begegnung mit dem Christus als dem Offenbarer. Sie muss dann aber auch denkend in ihrem Sinngehalt nachvollzogen werden. Deshalb grenzt Schelling sich sowohl von den Exegeten und—wie er sagt—ihrer Flachheit in der Auslegung der biblischen Texte ab wie von der rationalistischen Dogmatik der "halb-Orthodoxen."[16] "Die Philosophie der Offenbarung schließt weit eigentlicher den Sinn der Schrift auf."[17] Die Philosophie kommt in dieses tiefere Verstehen, weil sie sich in der Auslegung der Schrift an den letzten Fragen abarbeitet, der Selbstbegründung der Vernunft. Letzte Fragen, vor die das Denken gerät, führen die Philosophie zur Religion, bringen die Vernunft vor die biblische Offenbarung.

Der Religion der Offenbarung ist die Religion der Mythologie vorgeordnet.[18] Schelling findet sie pauschal im Heidentum, womit er des näheren die griechisch-römische Religionswelt verbindet. "Religion der Offenbarung" und "Religion der Mythologie" sind begriffliche Unterscheidungen, die nicht am Material der religionsgeschichtlichen und biblischen Überlieferungen gewonnen sind, sondern einer idealistischen Konstruktion der Religionsgeschichte entspringen. Auch dies macht deutlich, daß Schelling zu seinen Aufstellungen über die Religion, dann auch zur Offenbarung und der Bibel, als dem Buch der Offenbarung, nicht von Aufstellungen der Christlichen Dogmatik, der kirchlichen Lehre her kommt, sondern weil er sie für die Lösung von gedanklichen Problemen braucht, die sich der Philosophie stellen. Sie stellen sich ihr, wenn sie die Fragen der Letztbegründung der menschlichen Vernunft als dem einheitlichen Vermögen der Erkenntnis und der freien Tat aufnimmt.

Schellings Spätphilosophie arbeitet sich dabei freilich an Grundproblemen, die sich dem transzendentalen Idealismus durchgängig, auf der Linie von Kant zu Fichte

---

15. A.a.O., 281.
16. A.a.O., 268.
17. Ebd.
18. In Berlin hat Schelling in seinem zweiten Semester, im Sommersemester 1842, dann auch noch einmal 1845, "Philosophie der Mythologie" gelesen. Vgl. Friedrich Wilhelm Joseph von Schelling, *Philosophie der Mythologie. In drei Vorlesungsnachschriften 1837/1842* (Jena-Sophia I/1,1; Nachdruck, München: Fink, 1996). Vgl. auch die aus dem handschriftlichen Nachlass der Münchner und Berliner Vorlesungen herausgegebene Ausgabe von 1856, wiederabgedruckt in Schelling, AW 2.

und Hegel, gestellt haben. Es geht ihm um eine Auslegung der menschlichen Vernunft, ihres Vermögens und ihrer Grenzen. Die philosophische Frage ist die nach den Konstitutionsbedingungen der Vernunft, durch die alle Erkenntnis und praktische Gestaltung der Wirklichkeit in Natur, Geschichte und Kultur bedingt ist. Die Vernunft ist das Prinzip aller Wirklichkeit, sofern sie eine für uns Menschen ist. Aber kann sie sich auch selbst im Blick auf den Grund und die Grenze ihres Vermögens recht erkennen? Sie kann es gerade nicht, sofern sie tätige, sich vollziehende, die Welt erkennende und gestaltende Vernunft ist. In der Auslegung der Vernunft, die nur ihre Selbstauslegung sein kann, stößt die Vernunft auf die Struktur der Subjektivität. Diese macht die ihr eigene Verfassung aus. Und d. h., daß sie sich selbst, ihren Vollzug, ihr Tätigsein immer schon voraussetzen und in Anspruch nehmen muss, wenn sie sich selbst erkennen will. Also kann die Vernunft ihre Selbstvoraussetzung gar nicht zum Inhalt ihrer rationalen Erkenntnis machen. Was die Vernunft erkennt, wird ihr zum Gegenstand des Wissens und des Handelns. Sie erfasst sich in den Gegenständen, die sie hervorbringt, aber nicht in der Subjektivität ihres Vollzugs, damit auch nicht im Grunde ihrer Freiheit, ihres nicht von anderwärts, sondern allein aus und durch sich selbst Bestimmtseins, des durch und mit sich selbst Anfangenkönnens. In der Struktur ihrer Verfassung als Subjektivität kann die Vernunft sich selbst nur als kontingentes Faktum, in ihrem Sich-Gegebensein, hinnehmen, aber nicht rational rekonstruieren.

Das Faktum ihres freien, von selbst anhebendes Vollzugs kann die Vernunft sich nur blind voraussetzen. Sie kann dieses Faktum nicht wissend vor sich bringen. Wie kommt die Vernunft dann überhaupt zu sich im letzten Grunde ihres Sich-Vollziehens, ihres Tätigseins?

Die Antwort, die Schelling auf diese Frage entwickelt, führt ihn zur Einsicht in die Dunkelheit, die der Vernunft, insofern sie die strukturelle Verfassung der humanen Subjektivität hat, hinsichtlich ihres eigenen, freien, die Welt erschließenden und gestaltenden Tuns innewohnt. Die Vernunft muß sich selbst transzendieren bzw. negieren, um ins Verhältnis zu ihrem transzendenten Grund zu kommen. Auf dem Wege ihrer Selbsttranszendierung gelangt die Vernunft aber eben nicht zu einem bestimmten Wissen von ihrem transzendenten Grund. Sie erkennt nur, daß ihr Tätigsein dem Wissen von diesem Tun—dieses ermöglichend—vorausliegen muß. Schelling spricht von einem "unvordenklichen Sein" bzw. "unvordenklichen Actus,"[19] einem Sein bzw. Tätigsein der Vernunft, dem "nichts voraus zu denken" ist, sondern das "ein unmittelbar wirkliches" ist.[20] Dieses unvordenkliche Sein der Vernunft ist kein sich selbst bestimmtes, somit gegenständlich Wissendes. Es ist "unmittelbar" gegeben, weshalb Schelling auch von einem "Blindseienden" spricht. Es ist die unmittelbar vorauszusetzende, reine Tätigkeit des Vollzugs der Vernunft. Sie

---

19. Schelling, "Paulusnachschrift," in *Philosophie der Offenbarung*, hrsg. Frank, 171.
20. Ebd.

bringt Wissen und Gewusstes hervor, die Welt der Gegenstände, die Geschichte und die Kultur.

So erzählt Schellings Philosophie von der Praxis der Vernunft im Aufbau von Natur und Geschichte, einer Praxis, die sich selbst bezüglich ihrer Herkunft dunkel, ein Geheimnis bleibt. Weil es Schelling von früh an um diese geheimnisvolle Seinsgeschichte der Vernunft ging, hat er der Philosophie der Freiheit die der Natur zugeordnet. Die Philosophie der Natur thematisiert die Vorgeschichte der Freiheit, die ihr voraus liegende Seinsgeschichte, in der sie aber noch nicht einmal auf der Suche nach sich gewesen ist.

Die Selbsttranszendierung der Vernunft, ihre Selbstnegation, wie Schelling auch sagen kann, auf ihr unvordenkliches Sein hin, ist derjenige Schritt, zu dem die sich in der Struktur der Subjektivität erfassende Vernunft auf dem Wege ihrer philosophischen Letztbegründung sich gedrängt sieht. Die Religion jedoch führt auf diesen Weg, der sich in der negativen und positiven Philosophie vollendet. Die Religion öffnet, mitten in Kultur und Geschichte der Menschheit, den Weg für ein bewußtes Sich-Verhalten der Vernunft zu ihrem unvordenklichen Seinsgrund. In der Geschichte der Religion bzw. der Religionen, in Gestalt der Mythologie und der Offenbarung, wird nach Schellings Auffassung gewissermaßen das philosophische Problem der Beantwortung der Frage bearbeitet, wie die menschliche Vernunft in eine Kultur des Verhaltens zum unvordenklichen, nicht machbaren und eben auch nicht erkennbaren, kontingenten Grund ihres eigenen Seins bzw. Tuns kommen kann.

Die Religion der Mythologie und die Religion der Offenbarung haben gemeinsam, daß sie "beide—Religionen sind,"[21] geschichtliche, symbolische Formen des Bewusstseins vom Unbedingten. Beide Religionsformen stellen Weisen des Sich-Verhaltens der Vernunft zum unverfügbar Gegebenen, zum unvordenklichen Grund ihres eigenen Tätigseins, wie damit auch der Gegebenheit und Erschlossenheit einer Welt, dar.

Der Unterschied zwischen der Religion der Mythologie und der Religion der Offenbarung ist nur der, daß die Mythologie in den Vorstellungen jenseitiger Mächte aufgeht, einer alles bestimmenden Wirklichkeit, der sich die menschliche Vernunft blind unterworfen weiss, geheimnisvollen Kräften und Mächten, die die Dinge des Lebens über alles menschliche Lenken und Verstehen hinaus steuern. Die Offenbarung hingegen ist das Faktum des Auftretens, des geschichtlichen Erscheinens vernünftigen Lebens, das sich auf den Grund seines Vollzugs hin durchsichtig macht. Die Offenbarung ist die geschichtliche Existenz eines Menschen, der für Gott spricht, die Inkarnation des Logos.

Die Einsicht in die Dunkelheit, vor die die Vernunft in ihrer Selbstbegründung gerät, bringt Schellings Philosophie zur Religion, als dem menschlichen, kulturell geformten Verhalten zum Transzendenten. Auf dem Weg über die Religion kommt

---

21. A.a.O., 250.

die Philosophie dann auf Gott und seine Offenbarung, durch den für Gott sprechenden Gottmenschen. Die Religion deutet den unvordenklichen Seinsgrund der Vernunft auf Gott hin. Ihr wird der Gott zum Grund des Seins und im Auftreten des Offenbarers, der für Gott spricht, zum Grund des Wissens von der in Gott gründenden Freiheit.

Schellings Philosophie arbeitet sich an den Grenzen des Wissens, der menschlichen Vernunft ab. So schafft sie den Raum, in dem die Religion, das Glauben, seinen Platz hat. Weil das Glauben an den Grenzen der Vernunft, im Scheitern ihrer absoluten Selbstbegründung entsteht, ist dann aber auch das Glauben auf das Vorgegebensein seines Inhalts verwiesen. Der religiöse Glaube beginnt nicht erst dort, wo die Vernunft mit ihren Möglichkeiten ans Ende kommt. Er steht an ihrem Anfang. Der Offenbarungsglaube setzt auf den freien, schöpferischen Anfang allen Anfangs dessen, was ist. Die vernünftige Einsicht in die Wahrheit des an ein absolutes Faktum (der geschichtlichen Offenbarung) sich haltenden und seine Kontingenz anerkennenden Glaubens folgt diesem Glauben nach.

4. Negative und Positive Philosophie

Schellings Religionsphilosophie baut sich des näheren über die Unterscheidung von negativer und positiver Philosophie auf. Die Vernunft, die das Prinzip und Vermögen aller Wirklichkeitserkenntnis ist, kann sich nicht aus sich selbst begründen, da sie sich dabei schon in ihrem Vollzug in Anspruch nehmen muss. Das hat auch Hegel gesehen. Aber Hegels Weg zur Lösung der Selbstbegründungsproblematik der Vernunft konnte und wollte Schelling nicht gehen. Hegels Lösung bestand darin, daß die Vernunft sich in der Vermittlung über ihre Inhalte fortschreitend ins absolute Wissen, ins Wissen des Absoluten, bringt. Die Selbstbegründung der Vernunft verläuft über das, was sie leistet im Aufbau des Ganzen der geschichtlichen Welt, die sie zugleich in ihrem Sinn erschließt. Hegels Dialektik ist ein Weg, auf dem sich die Vernunft mit der Unmittelbarkeit ihres eigenen Vollzugs über die Inhalte, die er hervorbringt, vermittelt.

Schelling wollte den Weg Hegels nicht gehen, weil er darin die Ursprünglichkeit, das anfängliche, freie Hervorbringen der Vernunft in ihrem Tätigsein nicht anerkannt gefunden hat. Hegels Dialektik findet ins Absolute erst am Ende, kommt zu einem Gott mit dem "nichts anzufangen"[22] ist, der selber keinen

---

22. A.a.O., 110; Schelling über Hegel: "Es ist wichtig, *die Grenze dieser Wissenschaft* genau einzusehen. Man könnte das System dieser Wissenschaft etwa ein Emanationssystem nennen; aber man hüte sich wohl, als Prinzip derselben **Gott** zu denken. Man müsste vielmehr sagen: *Gott ist selbst nur die letzte (d. h. bloß logische) Emanation dieses Systems. Gott* kann in dieser Wissenschaft nur Ende sein, und so sehr Ende, daß er nie in ihr Anfang werden kann. *Er ist die Endursache*, wozu Alles in diesem System hinstrebt, *nicht aber bewirkende Ursache*. Er ist ein Begriff von regulativer Bedeutung, der nie zum Prinzip (konstitutiv) gemacht werden kann." A.a.O., 109. (Fettdruck und kursiv im Original.)

Anfang setzen kann, der die menschliche Freiheit des Anfangenkönnens und des kontingenten Anderswerdens, die offene Zukunft, gerade nicht vorsieht. Einen solchen Gott, der in Freiheit, aus und durch sich selbst den Anfang macht, einen freien, schöpferischen Gott wollte Schelling haben—selbstverständlich um die menschliche Freiheit, das neu Anfangenkönnen, die Selbstbestimmung aus metaphysischen, empirisch nicht Vorgegebenen Gründen zu retten.

Der Weg dahin führt über die Selbstnegation der Vernunft, die Transzendierung auf ihren reinen Vollzug hin, ein reines Tätigsein, ohne Wissen von sich. Das macht die negative Philosophie. Die positive Philosophie geht dann vom reinen Sein, Tätigsein, dem Unvordenklichen eines actus purus aus. Dieser actus purus ist noch nicht Gott, weil er kein Wissen von sich hat. In Gott gelangt das reine Tätigsein der Vernunft in ein Wissen von sich selbst. Die Vernunft wird zum Subjekt, zum Herrn über das Sein. Gott ist der Gott von Menschen, die sich im Stadium ihres magisch-mythischen Bewußtseins dunklen Mächten unterworfen wissen. Gott wird schließlich—durch die Offenbarung—zum Menschen, der sich, in Gott und durch ihn, selber zur persönlichen Freiheit berufen weiß. Diese Geschichte ist der Inhalt der Philosophie der Mythologie und dann der Offenbarung.

5. Mythische, religiöse und geistige Existenz: Die existentiale Interpretation des Johannesprologs

Die Philosophie der Mythologie und der Offenbarung bilden zusammen die Philosophie der Religion und der Religionsgeschichte. Die Religion und die Religionsgeschichte gewinnen in Schellings positiver Philosophie deshalb diesen zentralen Ort, weil die Philosophie vermittels der Religion in das wirkliche, geschichtliche, kulturelle Leben der Menschen kommt und zugleich vor jene Phänomene, die zeigen, daß Menschen Wesen der Grenzüberschreitung sind, daß sie auch eine Kultur des Sich-Verhaltens zum unverfügbaren Gegebensein des eigenen vernünftigen Daseins ausbilden. In der Religion verhalten die mit Vernunft begabten Menschen sich immer auch zu dem Sein, das sie sind, längst bevor sie dieses wissend vor sich bringen können. In der Religion transzendieren sie sich auf das unvordenkliche Sein, den transzendenten Grund ihrer Freiheit hin. Sie tun dies konkret in Gestalt der geschichtlichen Religionen, ihrer Symbole und Rituale.

Schelling unterteilt die Religionsgeschichte schlicht in die Religion der Mythologie und der Offenbarung. Die Mythologie, die Schelling in der ganzen Welt des Heidentums vorherrschen sieht, bildet Vorstellungen aus vom Ursprung der Welt und des Lebens. Die göttlichen Mächte werden als Wirkungen eines unbedingt Verfügenden erfahren. Das Christentum ist dem gegenüber die Religion der Offenbarung und das Judentum eine Vorausdeutung auf das Christentum als Offenbarungsreligion. Religion der Offenbarung ist das Christentum, weil es die Erfahrung mit dem geschichtlichen Auftreten des Offenbarers, der geschichtlichen Person Jesu, der zugleich der Gottessohn ist, machen läßt. Der Sohn Gottes weiß sich nicht mehr göttlichen Mächten blind unterworfen, sondern ist eins mit Gott, dem Vater, eine menschliche Person, die sich in freiem menschlichen Handeln auf Gott, als den Grund der Freiheit hin, durchsichtig gemacht hat.

In der Auslegung des Johannesprologs[23] expliziert Schelling diese Auffassung des Christentums als der Religion der Offenbarung. In Abgrenzung zu Fichte hebt er hervor, daß man die Offenbarung nicht auf solch rationalistische Weise verstehen dürfe wie dieser. Die bestimmte, historische Person des Jesus von Nazareth hat nicht nur, wie Fichte meint, zur Einsicht gebracht, was die Vernunft früher oder später auch durch sich selbst hätte erkennen können.[24] Schelling arbeitet in seiner Auslegung von Joh 1,1–18 heraus, daß es das kontingente, historische Auftreten der Person Jesu war, wodurch es zur Wiederherstellung der Einheit der Vernunft als dem Weltprinzip mit ihrem göttlichen Seinsgrund auf reale Weise gekommen ist. Die historische Erscheinung Jesu in der Welt ist nicht deshalb die Offenbarung, weil sie ein theoretisches Wissen von Gott ermöglicht hätte, das anders nicht oder nur auf Umwegen zu gewinnen gewesen wäre, sondern weil sie die Aneignung und Übernahme, somit die Verwirklichung einer neuen Existenzform, der in Gott sich gegründet wissenden menschlichen Freiheit, bewirkt hat. Das Erscheinen Jesu ist die Offenbarung, weil mit ihm, "jetzt, da er als Person erscheint . . . die Zeit des Begreifens und also auch des freien Annehmens" gekommen war.[25] Mit dem historischen Auftreten Jesu kam es zur Verwirklichung einer neuen, mit ihrem göttlichen Ursprung wieder vereinten, menschlichen Daseinsgestalt. Die Person Jesu führte für alle, die ihn annahmen, die in ihm die Herrlichkeit des Vaters erkannten, den Sohn Gottes, ein menschliches Leben herauf, daß sich zugleich ganz in seinem transzendenten, göttlichen Grund erschlossen weiß. "Die ihn aber annahmen (fährt der Apostel fort, der jetzt ganz ins Persönliche übergeht), die ihn annahmen, denen gab er Macht (Möglichkeit) Kinder Gottes zu werden, d. h. die durch den Fall unterbrochene göttliche Geburt in sich wiederherzustellen. Das Ende offenbart, was im Anfang war."[26]

Das ist die Pointe in Schellings Auslegung des Johannesprologs. Das, was im Anfang war, der Logos, der bei Gott war, steht auch am Ende, nur ist er sich dort auch dessen bewußt, in und aus Gott zu sein. Das reine Tätigsein der Vernunft kommt im Gottessohn in seinem unbedingten Gegebensein zum Wissen von sich.

Was im Anfang war, findet Schelling in den ersten drei Versen des Johannesprologs entfaltet, Schritt für Schritt. Es ist die Beschreibung dessen, daß uns die Welt immer schon erschlossen ist, wir Menschen ein Seiendes von der Art sind, das im wissenden Verhältnis zu sich und der gegebenen Welt steht. Im Anfang war diese

---

23. A.a.O., 271–7; Schelling, AW 2, 89–118.
24. Vgl. die ausführliche Auseinandersetzung mit Fichte und dessen Auslegung des Johannesprologs: A.a.O., 101–3.
25. A.a.O., 117.
26. Ebd.

Bewegung eines zu Gott gehörenden und zugleich die geschaffenen Welt erschließenden Seins, der Logos, der bei Gott war und durch den zugleich alle Dinge dieser Welt gemacht sind. Dieser Anfang ist auch das Ende. Aber am Ende erkennen wir auch, was am Anfang war. Wir erkennen es durch die Offenbarung des Offenbarers, das geschichtlich kontingente Auftreten des Gottessohnes, dieser geschichtlichen Person des sich auf Gott hin auslegenden und andere für diese religiöse Selbstauslegung gewinnenden Menschen. Durch ihn ist uns die humane Vernunft in der Einheit ihres göttlichen Grundes auf bewußte Weise erschlossen, stehen die Dinge dieser Welt im Lichte der Deutung des Sinnes, den sie für uns haben. Der Logos ist das Licht der Menschen. Er war das Leben zwar schon vor seinem Auftreten in der Person Jesu. Aber erst mit diesem Auftreten kommt es zu entsprechendem Selbstverstehen menschlichen Lebens, zu mit Gott versöhntem Dasein. Jesus ist die Symbolisierung unseres Verhältnisses zum Unverfügbaren, wie das kontingente Faktum der geschichtlichen Realisierung dieses Verhältnisses: Anerkannte Kontingenz.

Schellings Philosophie der Offenbarung ist die Lehre davon, wie der absolute Grund der Vernunft, ihr reiner Vollzug zur Vorstellung und Erkenntnis der Vernunft selber werden kann. Die Vernunft weiß sich im Mythos den Seinsmächten unterworfen. Sie findet in der Offenbarung des mit Gott, dem Vater, sich eins wissenden Gottessohns zur Erkenntnis des kontingenten Grundes der Freiheit. Sie realisiert diese Freiheit als Allgemeine im Zeitalter des Geistes. Dieses sah Schelling mit der von ihm gefundenen Philosophie der Offenbarung eröffnet. Auch das Zeitalter des Geistes bleibt an die biblische Offenbarung gebunden, macht jedoch deren mit dem geschichtlichen Auftreten der Person Jesu verknüpfte Besonderheit als allgemein gültige Wahrheit einsichtig.

Abstract

The question of reality is treated in this paper from the speculative philosophical perspective of Friedrich Wilhelm Joseph von Schelling (1775–1854). In his late work from 1841–42, the *Philosophy of Revelation*, Schelling focuses primarily on two New Testament texts, John's Prologue (John 1:1–18) and the christological hymn of Paul's letter to the Philippians (Phil 2:5–11), in order to unfold his understanding of the Christian religion as a religion of revelation. The author aims to show that Schelling gained his understanding of revelation from his interpretation of the Bible. Thus, Schelling's *Philosophy of Revelation* can aptly be called a biblical philosophy of revelation.

In his interpretation of John's Prologue, Schelling shows that the Christ portrayed in John's Gospel is God's revelation; Christ is the historical form of the Revealer (John 1:14). What Christ reveals is a historical person who acts and who knows himself to be, on the one hand, free in his relation to the world and, on the other hand, to be essentially related to God. Furthermore, Christ reveals the *logos* of God who was with God (John 1:1–3). According to Schelling, this *logos* is both theoretical and practical reason and therefore grounded in God, and as reason, the *logos* mediates the actualization of the world in history. In bringing forth the world, God remains the world's ground, particularly the ground of human freedom. The world also exists under the condition that it be known, and it is the *logos* that mediates this knowledge. As the religion of revelation, Christianity discloses the transcendence of God as the world's ground, the immanence of the *logos* in human reason, and the principle of freedom incarnate in a historical individual.

The main philosophical question of nineteenth-century transcendental Idealism concerned the ground, the capacity, and the limits of reason. By answering this question in view of his biblical interpretation, Schelling claims that philosophy, rather than biblical studies, glimpses into the deeper meaning of the Bible's account of revelation. It is through Christ's revelation that reason is made aware of its incapacity to conceptualize its own ground. Revealed through a contingent historical fact as an instance of human subjectivity, is the knowledge and experience that reason's relation to its ground is one not within human control, but one that is given to it. What is given is the possibility for self-transcendence. Reason transcends itself when it is placed in relation to its ground. This self-transcendence is not mediated by objective knowledge. Rather, it is given immediately to reason as "being prior to thinking that itself cannot be thought" (*unvordenkliches Sein*). As such, it inspires religion that has the function to mediate reason's self-transcendence to its ground. On the basis of the revelation in the Christian religion, philosophy can make claims concerning this relation. With this "negative philosophy" denying reason's possibility to conceptually exhaust its own ground, Schelling distinguishes his philosophy from both Fichte's and Hegel's "positive philosophy" that affirms this possibility. And in his recovery of biblical sources for his own philosophy, Schelling, quite possibly, captures the truth of biblical insights into the transcendent ground's creation of the world in freedom, to be experienced and never to be entirely determined by reason.

Feuerbach and the Hermeneutics of Imagination
Garrett Green

> *. . . the name of Feuerbach has become a thorn in the flesh of modern theology, and perhaps will continue to be so: so long as the relation to God is not unconditionally inconvertible for us, and does not remain so under all circumstances, we shall have no rest in this matter.*
> —Karl Barth[1]

A good way to highlight Feuerbach's position on theological hermeneutics and reality is to pose the apparently straightforward question: Is Feuerbach an atheist? If the answer seems obvious to most people—is he not, after all, the most infamous denier of God in the nineteenth century, at least after his rebellious intellectual son, Karl Marx?—they should first ponder Feuerbach's own answer to the question. For he was convinced that the true atheists were the modern theologians, who were falling all over themselves to protect the reality of God by appealing to his infinity and his mystery, separating the true concept of the absolute God from the qualities commonly attributed to him by popular piety and premodern tradition. But what is real is not the abstract subject but rather the concrete qualities, and those, Feuerbach protests, are precisely what he affirms and the theologians deny: "Hence he alone is the true atheist to whom the predicates of the Divine Being,—for example, love, wisdom, justice,—are nothing; not he to whom merely the subject of these predicates is nothing."[2] As one who wants to rescue the real attributes of "God" by reclaiming them for humanity, Feuerbach rejects the label "atheist" and attributes it instead to his theological opponents: "The negation of the subject is held to be irreligion, nay, atheism; . . . [but] to deny all the qualities of a being is equivalent to denying the being himself."[3] Thus Feuerbach denies "God" in order to save reli-

---

1. Karl Barth, "An Introductory Essay," trans. James Luther Adams, in Ludwig Feuerbach, *The Essence of Christianity* (trans. George Eliot; New York: Harper & Row, 1957), xxiv. Barth's essay was originally part of a lecture he delivered in Münster in 1926.
2. Ludwig Feuerbach, *The Essence of Christianity* (trans. George Eliot; New York: Harper & Row, 1957), 21. (Hereafter referred to as EC. I have generally followed Eliot's elegant and reliable English translation, departing from it only for the sake of greater clarity.)
3. EC 14.

gion—the true religion, that is, of humanity—from those closet atheists, the modern theologians. Like Nietzsche after him, he finds in Christianity itself the seeds of its own dissolution. The history of religion, on his account, is the story of the progressive reappropriation of those essential human qualities that had been "alienated" by projecting them on God. He thus concludes his introduction to *The Essence of Christianity* with this aphorism: "What yesterday was still religion is no longer such to-day; and what to-day is atheism, tomorrow will be religion."[4] If only he could have stayed around long enough to experience the "death-of-God" theology of the 1950s, not to mention the more radical versions of feminist and liberation theology that followed in its wake, he would surely have felt vindicated.

So the question of Feuerbach's atheism turns out to be a complicated and ambiguous one. Hans Frei probably put it best in an early essay in which he identifies two quite different types of modern atheism.[5] We are accustomed to thinking of the atheist on the model of Hume, who thought that theological claims were meaningless if not outright falsehoods. But there is another kind of modern atheist, epitomized by Feuerbach, who poses a much greater threat to theology. This kind of thinker could be called a *theological* atheist, one who begins from within theology but interprets it in such a way that its "real meaning" turns out to be atheistic. Rather than assaulting the fortress of religion from without, the Feuerbachian atheist poses as a friend, taking his point of departure from the theologians themselves in order to expose their "bad faith" (to use the concept developed by Marx, who of course learned to think "theologically" from Feuerbach).

I

Karl Barth had a lifelong fascination with Ludwig Feuerbach that is comparable in its intensity and ambivalence only to Barth's relationship with Friedrich Schleiermacher. And these two definitive relationships to his nineteenth-century forebears are connected, for Barth believed that Feuerbach's reduction of theology to anthropology represented the inevitable fate of the way of doing theology pioneered by Schleiermacher.

It is difficult to locate a characteristically Feuerbachian hermeneutics by searching for a specific teaching about the interpretation of scripture. For what Feuerbach wants to say about the Bible is finally no different from what he wants to say about all religion—about the *essence* of religion, whatever form it may take. As Barth recognized, Feuerbach "wished to say not many things, but one single thing" and he did so "with a tenacity not afraid to risk a thousand repetitions."[6] In his most famous and notorious book, *The Essence of Christianity* (1841), Feuerbach expresses that

---

4. EC 32.
5. Hans W. Frei, "Feuerbach and Theology," *JAAR* 35 (1967): 250–56.
6. Barth, "Introductory Essay," x.

"one thing" in terms of human self-understanding: "Man—this is the mystery of religion—projects his being into objectivity [*vergegenständlicht sein Wesen*], and then again makes himself an object to this projected image of himself thus converted into a subject; he thinks of himself, is an object to himself, but as the object of an object, of another being than himself."[7] Or, reduced to simplest terms, Feuerbach is saying that in religion man projects his own idealized human nature onto an illusory subject called "God," and then imagines himself as an object in relation to that projected divine subject. The "one thing" that Feuerbach wants to say shifts a bit in his later work—exemplified in his *Lectures on the Essence of Religion*,[8] delivered in Heidelberg in 1848—where the imagined divine subject is no longer human self-consciousness but external nature, over against which the contingent self feels vulnerable and dependent. Van Harvey has emphasized the importance of this later Feuerbachian theory of religion, arguing—unconvincingly, in my judgment—that it is superior to the early projection theory of *The Essence of Christianity*.[9] But the hermeneutical consequences are the same in both cases, because the "organ" of religion, the mechanism of religious projection, remains the same: the imagination. Feuerbach is the father of the "hermeneutics of suspicion" because he discovered that the imagination is the heart of religion, and because he assumed that religion is therefore based on illusion.

The hermeneutical implications of this position can be brought out in a number of ways, since, as Barth says, Feuerbach is forever repeating his "one thing"; but it is especially apparent at the point where he mentions scripture explicitly, in the chapter on revelation in *The Essence of Christianity*. In his own way, Feuerbach takes revelation as seriously as Karl Barth. Without revelation, he argues, the existence of God, though objective, remains something in thought only and therefore doubtful. But "this conceptual existence converted into a real existence, a fact [*Tatsache*], is revelation. . . . Faith in revelation is the immediate certainty of the religious mind, that what it believes, wishes, conceives, really is."[10] Revelation plays this role for Feuerbach because he believes that, as a fact, "it makes no appeal to reason."[11] All revelations, on his account, are "self-attesting existences [*sich selbst bezeugende Existenzen*]," not arguments, proofs, or grounds for belief. One cannot doubt a revelation precisely "because it is not an object of theory, but of feeling."[12] The function that produces this "fact" is the imagination—Feuerbach uses the terms *Phantasie*,

---

7. EC 29–30.
8. Ludwig Feuerbach, *Lectures on the Essence of Religion* (trans. Ralph Manheim; New York: Harper & Row, 1967).
9. Van A. Harvey, *Feuerbach and the Interpretation of Religion* (Cambridge: Cambridge University Press, 1995).
10. EC 204.
11. This phrase is George Eliot's attempt to translate Feuerbach's claim, "Tatsache paßt auf die Vernunft, wie die Faust aufs Auge."
12. EC 205.

Vorstellung, Einbildung, and *Einbildungskraft* interchangeably[13]—which he calls "the original organ of religion."[14] In the case of revelation, the imagination operates according to "an inward necessity which impels [man] to present moral and philosophical doctrines in the form of narratives and fables, and an equal necessity to represent that impulse as a revelation."[15] We note here Feuerbach's assumption, so typical of his age, that the content of revelation is "moral and philosophical doctrines" and that imagination distorts them by imposing its own narrative forms upon them. In Feuerbach, imagination is always contrasted with "reality," just as feeling is contrasted with reason; and the two are mutually exclusive. The inevitable outcome, of course (inevitable because it is already presupposed from the outset), is that imagination can only be the medium of distortion and error, never of truth.

Revelation necessarily takes on written form, Feuerbach tells us, because it is always "a particular, temporal revelation: God revealed himself once for all in the year so and so, and did so, not to the universal man, to the man of all times and places, to the reason, to the species, but rather to certain *limited* individuals." It must therefore be "fixed in writing, that its blessings may be transmitted uninjured." But this means that belief in a revelation will become in time "belief in a written revelation, . . . an historical book."[16] At this point, Feuerbach offers his nearest approach to a specifically scriptural hermeneutics: "Faith in a written revelation," he argues, "is a real, true, unfeigned, and so far respectable faith, only where it is believed that *everything* in holy scripture is significant, true, holy, divine." Any book requiring discrimination between truth and falsity, any scripture demanding criticism, "is no longer a divine, certain, infallible book,—it is degraded to the rank of profane books. . . ." The only valid biblical interpretation, Feuerbach is arguing, is literal interpretation; any other approach is already implicitly atheistic. "It is true," he acknowledges, "that such faith is superstition [*Aberglaube*]; but this superstition is alone the true, undisguised, open faith, which is not ashamed of its consequences."[17] But the trap is now set for theology, because the revelation that necessarily takes on written form, which necessarily becomes superstition, likewise leads necessarily to sophistry. For the believer can resolve the contradiction between his own reason and this actual historical revelation only by resorting to "self-deception, only by the silliest subterfuges, only by the most miserable, transparent sophisms." So the consequences of Feuerbach's scriptural hermeneutics are unavoidable: "Christian

---

13. For a discussion of the terminology of imagination in Feuerbach, see Garrett Green, *Theology, Hermeneutics, and Imagination: The Crisis of Interpretation at the End of Modernity* (Cambridge: Cambridge University Press, 2000), 99–100.
14. EC 214.
15. EC 208.
16. EC 209.
17. EC 210.

sophistry is the necessary product of Christian faith, especially of faith in the Bible as a divine revelation."[18]

This scriptural hermeneutics presupposes a metaphysics, for Feuerbach's interpretation of the Bible and Christian doctrine depends on his prior commitment to a specific theory about the nature of reality. And the link between hermeneutics and metaphysics—the hinge that connects scripture to reality—is the imagination. Nowhere is that connection more clearly exhibited than in his treatment of the sacraments. "The identity of the sacraments with the specific essence of religion," he writes, "is at once made evident . . . by the fact that they have for their basis natural materials or things, to which, however, is attributed a significance and effect in contradiction with their nature." The water of baptism, for example, which is something natural and material, has "supernatural effects"; but though the water belongs to material reality, its alleged effects occur "only in idea [*Vorstellung*], only in the imagination [*Einbildung*]."[19] Likewise in the Lord's Supper, the supernatural effects of the material bread and wine depend on the "mental state" (*Gesinnung*) of the participant, which "itself is dependent only on the significance which I give to this bread. . . . In the significance [*Bedeutung*] lies the effect [*Wirkung*]."[20]

The real clincher, however, is Feuerbach's attribution of this transaction to the imagination: "But this supernatural significance exists only in the *imagination* [*Phantasie*]."[21] Not to be overlooked is the powerful effect of the little word "only"; for it encapsulates Feuerbach's metaphysics by highlighting the value judgment that always accompanies it, a judgment rooted in a hierarchical dichotomy between reality (good) and imagination (bad): "The wine and bread are in reality [*Wirklichkeit*] natural, but in imagination [*Einbildung*] divine substances."[22] Religious belief has the unique transformative power to invert reality: "Faith is the power of the imagination, which makes the real unreal, and the unreal real: in direct contradiction with the truth of the senses, with the truth of reason."[23] Again: "A thing which has a special significance for me, is another thing in my imagination than in reality."[24] The imagination is the organ of religion, but it is always a deceiver according to Feuerbach. The sacraments are a vivid example, but finally only one of many, of what Feuerbach calls "the *illusion of the religious imagination*."[25]

---

18. EC 211.
19. EC 236.
20. EC 214; trans. rev.
21. EC 241.
22. EC 242.
23. Ibid.
24. EC 244.
25. EC 244–45.

II

What are we to make of Feuerbach's contribution to biblical hermeneutics a century and a half after he propounded it? Or should we say Feuerbach's deconstruction of biblical hermeneutics, since he exposes an underlying contradiction in the very project of theological interpretation of scripture that renders belief incompatible with understanding? Because of this deconstructive move (to use our contemporary jargon), Feuerbach deserves to be called the father of the hermeneutics of suspicion, that fateful sea change in our understanding of authoritative texts that Paul Ricoeur has identified with reference to Marx, Nietzsche, and Freud.[26] What all four of these thinkers—so different in their viewpoints, including their theories of religion—have in common is the contention that religious faith constitutes a kind of false consciousness (to apply Marx's term to all of them). For all four of them, understanding religion is incompatible with being religious. There is irony in the fact that the hermeneutics of suspicion, developed as a weapon against theology by these notorious nineteenth-century unbelievers, was appropriated by liberation and feminist theologians in the twentieth century, who maintain that the sword of suspicion is not two-edged: it can be wielded against "bad religion" in the service of Christian theology itself.

The way that I propose to come to terms with Feuerbach in the twenty-first century might be thought of as a kind of deconstructive reinterpretation of Feuerbach's own theory of religion. The chief clue (already adumbrated in the foregoing exegesis of Feuerbach) is his concept of imagination as the definitive mechanism of religious consciousness. On this score, he anticipates intellectual developments a century after his own lifetime. In short, I propose that we grant Feuerbach his basic premise: that religion is indeed a form of human imagination. That said, we must turn a critical eye to his concept of imagination, noting (here is the deconstructive move) that it presupposes a hierarchical duality between *reality* and *imagination*, between *fact* and *fiction* that is no longer tenable for us today. In the second half of the twentieth century, a revolution took place in philosophy that fundamentally altered the way in which imagination is understood and evaluated, and if applied to religion yields a different set of assumptions and expectations from those held by Feuerbach in his time. I have in mind, first of all, the revolution in philosophy of science epitomized in the work of Thomas S. Kuhn and others, which has convinced most observers that imagination plays an indispensable role even in the "hardest" natural sciences. After Kuhn's revisionist account of the history of science and its philosophical implications, it will no longer do to treat imagination as the polar opposite of "reality" or to assume (as Feuerbach did) that everything delivered by imagination is imaginary. Similar consequences follow from the nonfoundationalist

---

26. This claim is the thesis of my chapter on Feuerbach in *Theology, Hermeneutics, and Imagination*, ch. 4.

epistemology increasingly accepted by philosophers, theologians, and social theorists. As argued, for example, by Richard Rorty in *Philosophy and the Mirror of Nature*, the deeply held conviction of virtually all the modern philosophers (including Feuerbach) that one's philosophical and religious convictions require a "foundation" of incorrigible truths to be justifiable is an unnecessary and unreasonable criterion that ought to be abandoned.

Against this background it is possible to read in a fresh way Barth's warning about the significance of Feuerbach for theology. When he says, in the epigraph with which we began, that theologians must insure that the human relation to God is "inconvertible," he means that theology must speak about God in ways that are not vulnerable to Feuerbach's reversal of the divine and human predicates. Put in terms of the imagination, theology is possible (according to the Christian gospel) only because Jesus Christ, as the image of God, enables us to imagine God as he truly is. Contrary to what one so often hears from contemporary theologians, the Christian imagination does not "construct" an image of God (which is a virtual definition of idolatry) but rather receives its "content" from the self-revelation of God in Christ. Theology, like the Christian life as such, allows itself to be shaped by that which has been given to it from beyond the horizon of its own possibilities. Such a theological method is "inconvertible," to use Barth's term, because the human imagination is the medium but not the source of its knowledge of God. Scripture is not so much the expression of some prior religious experience or feeling—as both Feuerbach and theological liberals since Schleiermacher have asserted—but rather a lens which focuses our vision of reality, removing the distortion and clutter that otherwise obscures our sight and enabling us to imagine God rightly.

Such a hermeneutics of imagination levels the playing field in the study of religion by resisting every appeal, whether by theologians or by antitheologians like Feuerbach, to a foundational experience outside the brackets of imagination. If scientists in their quest for rational knowledge of the world cannot make an end run around the imagination, neither can philosophers, theologians, or scholars of religion. It remains the great achievement of Ludwig Feuerbach to have identified the imaginative character of human religion. It is our task to develop this insight without falling into his error of assuming that "reason" can operate outside the bounds of imagination. In the end, Feuerbach's biblical hermeneutics is sounder than it might seem, because he—knowing that the language of scripture is imaginative—insists on the *sensus literalis* as the basis for any adequate interpretation of the Bible. Because of his flawed theory of imagination, he thought such interpretation led only to "sophistry." With a more adequate understanding of how the religious imagination really functions, we can hope to do better.

Zusammenfassung

Ludwig Feuerbach verdient es, als der Vater der "Hermeneutik des Verdachts" zu gelten, da er viele der Schlüsselkonzepte vorwegnahm, die späterhin Nietzsche, Marx und Freud entwickelt haben. Feuerbach nimmt einen ungewöhnlichen aber wichtigen Platz in der Geschichte der Bibelauslegung ein, weil seine Religionstheorie an entscheidendem Ort die biblische Exegese beeinflußt hat. Im Licht des Selbstbetrugs der nicht rationalen Elemente der Religion stellt Feuerbach philosophische Fragen zu Offenbarung und Vernunft. Feuerbachs Beitrag zur Religionstheorie hängt mit der Rolle, die die Einbildungskraft in der Entstehung der Religion spielt, zusammen. Für die Einbildungskraft verwendet Feuerbach auch folgenden Begriffe: "Phantasie," "Vorstellung" und "Einbildung." Einerseits nimmt Feuerbachs "Hermeneutik der Einbildung" zeitgenössische philosophische Theorien zur Rolle der Einbildungskraft in der Wirklichkeitswahrnehmung und Wirklichkeitskonstruktion vorweg, wie sie z. B. von Thomas S. Kuhn entwickelt wurden, und antizipiert Positionen, die eine theoriegeladene Wirklichkeitsdeutung vertreten ("anti-foundationalism"). Andererseits versteht Feuerbach den imaginativen Charaker der Religion als eine Selbsttäuschung. Daher läutet Feuerbachs Theorie einer hermeneutischen Wirklichkeitskonstitution sowohl die zeitgenössische kritische Methodik der Wissenschaft als auch den kritischen Blick auf die Religion ein. Was Feuerbach nicht vorhergesehen hat, ist, daß die heutige Philosophie nicht zwischen Wirklichkeit und Einbildung unterscheidet. Feuerbachs Religionskritik aber hängt von dieser Unterscheidung ab. Als ein Produkt der Einbildung ist die Religion in ihre eigene Selbsttäuschung involviert und wird von Feuerbach nicht als subjektive Konstitution von Wirklichkeit gedacht.

Feuerbachs Theorie über das Wesen der Religion hängt eng mit seiner Theorie der biblischen Hermeneutik zusammen. Am Anfang von Feuerbachs Religionstheorie steht seine Projektionstheorie, die das Verhältnis von Einbildungskraft und Religion erläutert. Mit diesem Ansatz befindet sich Feuerbach in einer Linie mit einer Strömung der Religionsphilosophie des 19. Jahrhunderts, die für die Religion nach einer besonderen "Provinz" sucht. Für diese Strömung der Religionsphilosophie kann Religion weder von der Vernunft erklärt, noch bewiesen, noch demonstriert werden. Deshalb ist die "Anlage" zur Religion in einem nicht rationalen Bereich des menschlichen Bewußtseins zu suchen. Feuerbach findet die gesuchte "Provinz" in der Einbildungskraft. Seine Projektionstheorie gründet auf einer Theorie des objektiven Selbstbewußtseins. In einer reflektiven Bewegung des Selbstbewußtseins projiziert das Selbst die idealisierten Attribute des menschlichen Wesens auf eine unendliche und illusionäre Fläche. Gott wird von der Sehnsucht der menschlichen Einbildungskraft gezeugt. Ob Gott oder äußere Natur als Vergegenständlichung der menschlichen Subjektivität—so die Begrifflichkeit der Spätschriften (Vorlesungen über das Wesen der Religion)—die Wirklichkeit, die unendlich anders ist als das Selbst, ist ein Produkt der Illusion der Einbildungskraft.

Feuerbach verbindet die Projektionstheorie mit der Offenbarung und diese mit der Bibel. Feuerbach beruft sich auf die Offenbarung als dasjenige, was weder geprüft, noch mit der Vernunft bewiesen werden kann. Offenbarung ist das Korrelat der Einbildungskraft; sie ist eine historische Gegebenheit, die von der Einbildungskraft geschaffen wurde. Dieser Gedanke Feuerbachs stellt wiederum die Frage nach der Wirklichkeit. Nach Feuerbach verzerrt die Einbildungskraft Wirklichkeit, weil sie der objektiven Welt eine subjektive Fiktion aufzwingt. Die Einbildungskraft ist in eine Selbsttäuschung involviert, indem sie Wirklichkeit mit der Fiktion der biblischen Geschichte durcheinanderbringt. Die Bibel ist eine notwendigerweise verschriftete Form der Offenbarung und ist daher ebenfalls in der List der Einbildungskraft impliziert. Als Glaube haftet die Einbildungskraft der Wahrheit der Schrift an. Doch der Glaube wird ebenfalls als Aberglaube an den buchstäblichen Sinn des biblischen Textes entlarvt.

Select Bibliography

Primary Authors

Ahad Ha-'Am. *Selected Essays*. Translated by Leon Simon. Philadelphia: Jewish Publication Society, 1948.
Feuerbach, Ludwig. *Vorlesungen über das Wesen der Religion: Nebst Zusätzen und Anmerkungen*. Vol. 6 of *Gesammelte Werke*. Edited by Wolfgang Harich. 2nd ed. Berlin: Akademie, 1981. [= *Lectures on the Essence of Religion*. Translated by Ralph Manheim. New York: Harper & Row, 1967.]
―――. *Das Wesen des Christentums*. Vol. 5 of *Gesammelte Werke*. Edited by Werner Schuffenhauer and Wolfgang Harich. Berlin: Akademie, 1984. [= *The Essence of Christianity*. Translated by George Eliot. New York: Harper & Row, 1957.]
Fichte, Johann Gottlieb. *Anweisung zum seligen Leben, oder auch die Religionslehre (1806)*. Pages 399–580 in vol. 5 of *Fichtes Werke*. Edited by Immanuel Hermann Fichte. Berlin: Veit & Comp., 1845–46 [8 vols.], and Bonn: Adolph Marcus, 1834–35 [3 vols.]. Reprint in 11 vols. Berlin: de Gruyter, 1971.
―――. *Appellation an das Publicum gegen die Anklage des Atheismus (1799)*. Pages 193–238 in vol. 5 of *Fichtes Werke*. Edited by Immanuel Hermann Fichte. Berlin: Veit & Comp., 1845–46 [8 vols.], and Bonn: Adolph Marcus, 1834–35 [3 vols.]. Reprint in 11 vols. Berlin: de Gruyter, 1971.
―――. *Kritik aller Offenbarung (1792)*. Pages 11–174 in vol. 5 of *Fichtes Werke*. Edited by Immanuel Hermann Fichte. Berlin: Veit & Comp., 1845–46 [8 vols.] and Bonn: Adolph Marcus, 1834–35 [3 vols.]. Reprint in 11 vols. Berlin: de Gruyter, 1971. [= *Attempt at a Critique of All Revelation*. Translated with an introduction by Garrett Green. Cambridge: Cambridge University Press, 1978.]
Hegel, Georg Wilhelm Friedrich. *Werke: Auf der Grundlage der Werke von 1832–1845*. Edited by Eva Moldenhauer and Karl Markus Michel. 20 vols. Theorie-Werkausgabe. Frankfurt: Suhrkamp, 1969–71.
Josephus. *Josephus in Nine Volumes*. Translated by Henry St. J. Thackeray et al. Cambridge: Harvard University Press, 1966–69.
Josephus ben Mattitahu. *Jewish Antiquities with a Translation from the Greek: Introduction, Commentary, Maps, and Illustrations*. 3 vols. Jerusalem: Bialik Institute, 1944–63.
Mendelssohn, Moses. *Jerusalem, or on Religious Power and Judaism*. Translated by Allan Arkush. Introduction and commentary by Alexander Altmann. Hanover, N.H.: University Press of New England, 1983.
Origen of Alexandria. *On First Principles*. Translated by G. W. Butterworth. Gloucester, Mass.: Peter Smith, 1973.
―――. *Origen, Commentary on the Gospel according to John*. Translated by Ronald Heine. 2 vols. Washington, D.C.: Catholic University of America Press, 1989–93.
―――. *Origène, Commentaire sur Saint Jean*. Translated by Cécile Blanc. 5 vols. Sources chrétiennes 120, 157, 222, 290, 385. Paris: Cerf, 1966–92.
Philo of Alexandria. *Philo of Alexandria: Writings*. Translated (into Hebrew) by Suzanne Daniel-Nataf. 4 vols. Jerusalem: Bialik Institute, 1986–91.
―――. *Philo with an English Translation*. Translated by Francis H. Colson and G. H. Whitaker. 12 vols. Cambridge: Harvard University Press, 1929–62.
―――. *Philonis Alexandrini Opera Quae Supersunt*. Edited by Leopold Cohn and Paul Wendland. 7 vols. Berlin: G. Reimer, 1962–63.

Schelling, Friedrich Wilhelm Joseph von. *Philosophie der Mythologie: In drei Vorlesungsnachschriften 1837/ 1842*. Jena-Sophia I/1,1. Reprint, Munich: Fink, 1996.

———. *Philosophie der Offenbarung*. Vols. 1–2 in *Ausgewählte Werke*. Darmstadt: Wissenschaftliche Buchgesellschaft, 1973–74.

———. *Philosophie der Offenbarung 1841/42*. Edited with an introduction by Manfred Frank. 3rd newly edited and corrected ed. STW 181. Frankfurt: Suhrkamp, 1995.

———. *Urfassung der Philosophie der Offenbarung*. Vols. 1–2. PhB 445a/b. Hamburg: Felix Meiner, 1995.

Schleiermacher, Friedrich. *Der christliche Glaube nach den Grundsätzen der Evangelischen Kirche im Zusammenhange dargestellt (1830/31)*. Edited by Martin Redeker. 7th ed. De-Gruyter Studienbuch. Berlin: de Gruyter, 1999. [= *The Christian Faith*. Edited by H. R. Mackintosh and J. S. Stewart. Translated by D. M. Baillie et al. Edinburgh: T & T Clark, 1999.]

———. *Hermeneutik und Kritik*. Edited by Manfred Frank. STW 211. Frankfurt: Suhrkamp, 1977. [= *Hermeneutics and Criticism and Other Writings*. Translated by Andrew Bowie. Cambridge Studies in the History of Philosophy. Cambridge: Cambridge University Press, 1998.]

———. *Kurze Darstellung des theologischen Studiums zum Behuf einleitender Vorlesungen*. Edited by Heinrich Scholz. Bibliothek klassischer Texte. Darmstadt: Wissenschaftliche Buchgesellschaft, 1993. [= *Brief Outline of Theology as a Field of Study*. Translated by Terrence N. Tice. Schleiermacher Studies and Translations 1. Lewiston, N.Y.: Mellen, 1990.]

———. "Ueber Kolosser 1, 15–20." Pages 195–226 in *Exegetische Schriften*. Vol. I/8 of *Kritische Gesamtausgabe*. Edited by Hermann Patsch and Dirk Schmid. Berlin: de Gruyter, 2001. [= "On Colossians 1:15–20" (1832). Translated by Esther D. Reed and Alan Braley. *New Athenaeum/Neues Athenaeum* 5 (1998): 48–80.]

———. *Vorlesungen über die Dialektik*. Vols. II.10/1–2 in *Kritische Gesamtausgabe*. 2 vols. Edited by Andreas Arndt. Berlin: de Gruyter, 2003.

Modern Authors

Avineri, Shlomo. *The Making of Modern Zionism: The Intellectual Origins of the Jewish State*. New York: Basic Books, 1981.

Barr, James. "Biblische Theologie I." Pages 488–89 in vol. 1 of *EKL*. 3rd ed., 1986.

Barth, Karl. "An Introductory Essay." Translated by James Luther Adams. Pages x–xxxii in Ludwig Feuerbach, *The Essence of Christianity*. Translated by George Eliot. New York: Harper & Row, 1957.

Clarke, Elizabeth. *The Origenist Controversy: The Cultural Construction of an Early Christian Debate*. Princeton: Princeton University Press, 1992.

Ebeling, Gerhard. "Was heißt 'Biblische Theologie?'" (1955). Pages 69–89 in vol. 1 of *Wort und Glaube*. 3d ed. Tübingen: Mohr Siebeck, 1967.

Frank, Manfred. *Selbstgefühl: Eine historisch-systematische Erkundung*. STW 1611. Frankfurt: Suhrkamp, 2002.

Frei, Hans W. "Feuerbach and Theology." *JAAR* 35 (1967): 250–56.

Green, Garrett. *Theology, Hermeneutics, and Imagination: The Crisis of Interpretation at the End of Modernity*. Cambridge: Cambridge University Press, 2000.

Gruen, Erich S. *Heritage and Hellenism: The Reinvention of Jewish Tradition*. Hellenistic Culture and Society 30. Berkeley: University of California Press, 1998.

Harvey, Van A. *Feuerbach and the Interpretation of Religion*. Cambridge: Cambridge University Press, 1995.

Helmer, Christine. "Schleiermacher's Exegetical Theology and the New Testament." In *Cambridge Companion to Schleiermacher*. Edited by Jacqueline Mariña. Cambridge: Cambridge University Press, forthcoming.

Hill, Charles E. *The Johannine Corpus in the Early Church*. Oxford: Oxford University Press, 2004.

Hossfeld, Frank-Lothar, ed. *Wieviel Systematik erlaubt die Schrift? Auf der Suche nach einer gesamtbiblischen Theologie.* QD 185. Freiburg: Herder, 2001.

Janowski, Bernd. "Theologie des Alten Testaments: Plädoyer für eine integrative Perspektive." Pages 329–50 in vol. 3 of *Der Gott des Lebens: Beiträge zur Theologie des Alten Testaments.* Neukirchen-Vluyn: Neukirchener, 2003.

Janowski, Bernd, and Norbert Lohfink, eds. *Religionsgeschichte Israels oder Theologie des Alten Testaments?* Jahrbuch für biblische Theologie 10. Neukirchen-Vluyn: Neukirchener, 1995. 2nd ed., 2001.

Lenowitz, Harris. *The Jewish Messiahs from Galilee to Crown Heights.* Oxford: Oxford University Press, 1998.

Nagel, Titus. *Die Rezeption des Johannesevangeliums im 2. Jahrhundert: Studien zur vorirenäischen Aneignung und Auslegung des vierten Evangeliums in christlicher und christlich-gnostischer Literatur.* Arbeiten zur Bibel und ihrer Geschichte 2. Leipzig: Evangelische Verlagsanstalt, 2000.

Nautin, Pierre. *Origène.* Paris: Beauschesne, 1977.

Niehoff, Maren R. *Philo on Jewish Identity and Culture.* TSAJ 86. Tübingen: Mohr Siebeck, 2001.

Pagels, Elaine. *The Johannine Gospel in Gnostic Exegesis.* Philadelphia: Fortress, 1973.

Pearce, Sarah. "Belonging and Not Belonging: Local Perspectives in Philo of Alexandria." Pages 79–105 in *Jewish Local Patriotism and Self-Identification in the Graeco-Roman Period.* Edited by Sian Jones and Sarah Pearce. JSPSup 31. Sheffield: Sheffield Academic Press, 1998.

Pollard, T. E. *Johannine Christology and the Early Church.* SNTSMS 13. Cambridge: Cambridge University Press, 1970.

Rendtorff, Rolf. *Kanon und Theologie: Vorarbeiten zu einer Theologie des Alten Testaments.* Neukirchen-Vluyn: Neukirchener, 1991.

Scholem, Gershom. *Major Trends in Jewish Mysticism.* New York: Schocken, 1962.

———. *The Messianic Idea in Judaism, and Other Essays on Jewish Spirituality.* New York: Schocken, 1972.

Sorkin, David. *Moses Mendelssohn and the Religious Enlightenment.* Berkeley: University of California Press, 1996.

Stead, Christopher. *Philosophy in Christian Antiquity.* Cambridge: Cambridge University Press, 1994.

Stroumsa, Guy. "The Incorporeality of God: Context and Implications for Origen's Position." *Religion* 13 (1983): 345–58.

Sweeney, Marvin A. "The Emerging Field of Jewish Biblical Theology." Pages 83–105 in *Academic Approaches to the Teaching of Jewish Studies.* Edited by Zev Garber. Lanham, Md.: University Press of America, 2000.

Trigg, Joseph Wilson. *Origen: The Bible and Philosophy in the Third-Century Church.* Atlanta: John Knox, 1983.

Wiles, Maurice F. *The Spiritual Gospel: The Interpretation of the Fourth Gospel in the Early Church.* Cambridge: Cambridge University Press, 1960.

Wucherpfennig, Ansgar. *Heracleon Philologus: Gnostische Johannesexegese im zweiten Jahrhundert.* WUNT 142. Tübingen: Mohr Siebeck, 2002.

Index of Biblical Passages

Hebrew Bible

GENESIS
1:26   75, 81–82
3   12, 133–39
37:2   48
37:3   33 n. 1
39:8–9   40
39:12–15   33
40:23   33 n. 2
41:9–14   33 n. 2
41:14   33
41:38   33
41:40   42
41:42   33
41:46   43
42:6   53
42:7   53 n. 34
42:7–9   54
42:9   54
43:32 (LXX)   43 n. 26
45:3   54
45:28 (LXX)   36
49:43   47
50:19   46–47

EXODUS   79

DEUTERONOMY   79
4:24   79 n. 22, 80
23:18   41
26:17–19   25

ISAIAH   100
2:2–4   89
9:1–6   89
11:1–16   89

32:1–8   89
35   89
44:28   89
45:1   89
49–54   89
55   89
55:3   11, 89, 100–101
55:1–13   89
60–62   89
65–66   89
66:1   82
66:1–24   89

EZEKIEL
40–48   89

HOSEA
14:2–9   89

JOEL
3–4   89

ZEPHANIAH
3:14–20   89
12–14   89

HAGGAI
2:20–23   91 n. 10

PSALMS   82
34:10 (LXX)   79 n. 23
35:10   81
49:1   59
103:24   59

PROVERBS   79
8:22   59

JOB 5

ECCLESIASTES 5

Deuterocanonical Books

WISDOM
7:22–23   69 n. 33
7:22–27   66
10:14   42, 42 n. 24, 66

New Testament

MATTHEW
5:8   79 n. 22
11:27   79 n. 22

JOHN   10–11, 58, 61–62, 71, 79, 103–12, 130
1:1–3   151
1:1–18   11–12, 63, 68, 71–72, 141–54
1:1–13:33   57–58
1:1   65, 59
1:2   144
1:3   63–65, 79 n. 22
1:4   66
1:14   144
1:17   79 n. 22
1:18   63, 79 n. 22
1:28   63
3:20–21   70
4   62
4:12–15   68
4:15   68
4:19–20   68
4:20   79 n. 22
4:22   79 n. 22
4:23   79 n. 22
4:24   68–69 n. 33, 77, 79 n. 22, 80–81, 84
8   68–69
8:37   69
8:44   69
14:6   79 n. 22
14:23   79 n. 22

ACTS
17:24   121

ROMANS
2:29   58
9:11–14   58
11:12   125
11:25   125
11:36   118

1 CORINTHIANS
2:14–15   67
3:6   79 n. 22
3:12   79 n. 22
8:5–6   60
15:42   79 n. 22

2 CORINTHIANS
3:15   81
13:3   79 n. 22

EPHESIANS
2:6   82, 125 n. 60
2:12–16   118

PHILIPPIANS
2:5–11   143, 145, 153
3:20   82

COLOSSIANS
1:3–8   119
1:9–23   119
1:13   120
1:15–20   11–12, 113–31
1:15   59, 79 n. 22, 119, 126
1:15–16b   115–16, 130
1:16   20, 122–23
1:16a   121
1:17a   122
1:17b   121
1:18   122, 124, 126
1:18a   122
1:18b–20b   115–16, 124, 130
1:19–20   125
1:19   119, 124–25

1:20   120, 125
1:20b–c   124
1:21   120, 124–25

1 Thessalonians   58

1 Timothy   130

Hebrews
1:1   79 n. 22
1:1–2   26

5:8   79 n. 22
11:23   79 n. 22

1 John
1:5   80–81
5:5   79 n. 22

Revelation   58
7:2–5   58
19:14   58 n. 5

Index of Names

Abba Serapion, 75, 82
Adam (biblical), 133
Ahad Ha-'Am, 11, 91, 98–99, 101
Albertz, Rainer, 22 n. 19
Alexander the Great, 39
Ambrosius, 74 n. 7
Apollonius of Tyana, 83
Apuleius, 75
Aristotle, 67
Arius, 74 n. 6
Artapanus, 45, 48
Assmann, Jan, 29 n. 53
Athanasius of Alexandria, 74 n. 6
Attridge, Harold W., 10, 57–72, 75 n. 10
Augustus Caesar, 38–39, 40

Baal Shem Tov. *See* Israel ben Eliezer
Bakunin, Michael, 141
Barr, James, 18 n. 2, 87 n. 1
Barth, Karl, 155–57, 161
Basil of Caesarea, 74 n. 6
Bauer, Georg Lorenz, 21
Baur, Ferdinand Christian, 21, 106
Boyarin, Daniel, 34
Burckhardt, Jacob, 141

Cassian, John, 75 n. 8
Cazeaux, Jacques, 36
Celsus, 75
Childs, Brevard S., 24, 26, 32, 89 n. 7
Chrysostom, John, 115–16
Clarke, Elizabeth, 60 n. 9, 67 n. 28, 75 n. 9
Cleopatra, Queen, 38, 40, 42
Cölln, Daniel George Conrad von, 21
Cohn, Leopold, 37 n. 13
Colson, Francis H., 37 n. 13

Cyril of Alexandria, 74 n. 6
Cyrus of Persia, 89

Daniel-Nataf, Suzanne, 37 n. 13
Didymus, 74 n. 6
Dio, 38–39
Diogenes of Oneoanda, 83

Ebeling, Gerhard, 17 n. 1, 31
Eissfeldt, Otto, 89 n. 7
Elijah (prophet), 90
Engels, Friedrich, 141–42
Esau (biblical), 58
Eusebius of Caesarea, 45

Ferdinand, King, 92
Feuerbach, Ludwig, 9, 13, 155–63
Fichte, Johann Gottlieb, 3, 9, 11, 103–12, 147, 151, 154
Flavius Josephus, 9–10, 34–56
Fränkel, R. David, 95
Frank, Manfred, 7 n. 2, 117, 141 n. 1
Frei, Hans, 156
Freud, Sigmund, 160, 162
Friedrich Wilhelm IV, King, 142

Gabler, Johann Philipp, 19, 20 n. 11, 21, 32, 113 n. 1
Geiger, Abraham, 34, 96
Gese, Hartmut, 26
Ginzberg, Asher. *See* Ahad Ha-'Am
Goethe, Johann Wolfgang von, 109
Goshen-Gottstein, Moshe, 87 n. 2
Gräb, Wilhelm, 12, 141–54
Graetz, Heinrich, 91 n. 16
Grätzel, Stephan, 11, 103–12
Green, Garrett, 13, 155–63

Gregory of Nazianzen, 74 n. 6
Gregory of Nyssa, 74 n. 6
Gruen, Erich S., 36 n. 11, 44 n. 27
Gunkel, Hermann, 21 n. 16

Hardmeier, Christof, 27
Harvey, Van A., 157
Hegel, Georg Wilhelm Friedrich, 3–4,
   8–9, 12, 103-104, 107, 133–39, 141–
   42, 147, 150, 154
Heidegger, Martin, 2, 6, 107
Heinemann, Joseph, 34
Helmer, Christine, 11–12, 113–31, 113
   n. 1, 115 n. 3
Heracleon, 9–10, 57–72, 83
Herder, Johann Gottfried, 106
Herms, Eilert, 23 n. 22
Herodotus, 39
Herzl, Theodor, 98
Hill, Charles E., 57 n. 1
Hippolytus, 74 n. 7
Hirsch, Samson Raphael, 96
Hofius, Otfried, 118 n. 22
Holtzmann, Heinrich Julius, 21 n. 14
Homer, 61
Hossfeld, Frank-Lothar, 23 n. 21

Irenaeus of Lyons, 65 n. 24
Isabella, Queen, 92
Israel ben Eliezer, 90

Jacob (biblical), 40, 48–49, 50–51, 58
Janowski, Bernd, 9-10, 17–32, 22 n. 20,
   23 n. 21, 24 n. 24
Jeremias, Joachim, 23 n. 21
Jesus, 77
   doctrine of, 78
   as eternal word, 110
   as founder of Christian religion, 106
   as image of God, 161
   historical, 121, 143, 151
   historical appearance of, 104, 144
   life of, 62
   life of as reason, 107
   of Nazareth, 12, 91, 151
   passion of, 58 n. 5

   the Redeemer, 117
   Samaritan woman and, 62, 68–69, 84
John (Baptist), 58
John (Evangelist), 10, 57–72
John of Damascus, 77 n. 15
John of Gischala, 51, 53
Joseph (biblical), 10, 33–56
Joseph ben Mattitahu, 51, 56
Joseph ben Yaakov, 51, 56
Joseph's brothers (biblical), 45–46, 48,
   50–51, 53, 56
Justin Martyr, 74 n. 3

Kähler, Martin, 22 n. 17
Kant, Immanuel, 2-3, 6–7, 95, 103, 111,
   133, 138, 147
Kierkegaard, Søren, 141–42
King, Karen L., 65 n. 23
Kochba, Shimon bar, 91
Kuhn, Thomas S., 160

Leibniz, Gottfried Wilhelm Freiherr von, 6
Lenowitz, Harris, 88 n. 5
Levenson, Jon D., 25 n. 35, 87 n. 1
Lubavitcher Rebbe, 91
Lücke, Friedrich, 116
Luria, Isaac, 11, 91–93, 101

Maimonides, 95
Mark Antony, 38, 40, 42
Marx, Karl, 142, 155–56, 160, 162
Mayer, Gustav, 142
Mendel, 95
Mendelssohn, Moses, 9, 11, 91, 95, 101
Moses (biblical), 49, 74 n. 3, 99
Mowinckel, Sigmund, 88 n. 5

Nagel, Titus, 57 n. 1
Nautin, Pierre, 82 n. 33
Niehoff, Maren R., 9–10, 33–56, 35 n. 6,
   49 n. 32
Nietzsche, Friedrich, 6, 156, 160, 162
Numenius, 75

Oeming, Manfred, 23 n. 23
Origen of Alexandria, 9–11, 57–72, 73–84

Pagels, Elaine, 57 n. 2
Patsch, Hermann, 116
Paul (Apostle), 110, 116–17, 119–20, 123, 128, 131
Paulus, H. E. G., 141 n. 1
Pearce, Sarah, 37 n. 14
Pharaoh (biblical), 33
Philo of Alexandria, 9-10, 34–56, 59, 65–66
Philo the Epic Poet, 42
Photius, 75
Plato, 2, 74 n. 3
Pollard, T. E., 57 n. 1
Potiphar's wife (biblical), 33, 40, 46, 48, 55
Preuß, Horst Dietrich, 23

Rachel (biblical), 48
Rad, Gerhard von, 23–24, 25 n. 32
Ranke, Leopold von, 141
Reed, Esther, 116–17
Rendtorff, Rolf, 24
Reuben (biblical), 51
Reventlow, Henning Graf, 25 n. 35
Ricoeur, Paul, 160
Ringleben, Joachim, 12, 133–39
Rorty, Richard, 161
Rufinius, 77 n. 15

Saebø, Magne, 30 n. 57
Savigny, Friedrich Karl von, 141
Schelling, Friedrich Wilhelm Joseph von, 8–9, 12, 104, 141–54
Schleiermacher, Friedrich Daniel Ernst, 3–6, 9, 11–12, 113–31, 156, 161
Schlomo, Avineri, 97 n. 34
Schmid, Dirk, 116
Schneerson, Menahem, 91
Scholem, Gershom, 90 n. 8, 91, 92 n. 21, 94, 97
Seneca the Younger, 42
Shabbetai Zvi, 91–94
Shalit, Abraham, 48 n. 31
Shealtiel, Zerubbabel ben, 90–91

Shimon bar Kochba. *See* Kochba, Shimon bar
Shimon bar Kosiba. *See* Kochba, Shimon bar
Shukr Kuhayl I, 91
Shukr Kuhayl II, 91
Socrates, 95
Sorkin, David, 95 n. 27
Spener, Philipp Jakob, 19 n. 7
Stead, Christopher, 74 n. 3
Strauss, David Friedrich, 106
Stroumsa, Guy, 76, 82
Stuhlmacher, Peter, 18 n. 3, 26
Sweeney, Marvin A., 8, 11, 87–102, 87 n. 1, 88 n. 3, 89 n. 6, 89 n. 7, 91 n. 10, 92 n. 21

Thackeray, Henry St. J., 48 n. 31
Theodoret, 116
Theophilus, 75, 84
Torjesen, Karen Jo, 9–11, 59 n. 6, 73–84
Trigg, Joseph Wilson, 59 n. 6
Tsevat, Mattitiyahu, 87 n. 2

Valentinus, 60, 71
Vespasian, 51

Welker, Michael, 18 n. 5, 23 n. 22, 30 n. 59
Wendland, Paul, 37 n. 13
Westermann, Claus, 23
Wette, Wilhelm Martin Leberecht de, 21
Whitaker, G. H., 37 n. 13
Wiesel, Elie, 90 n. 9
Wiles, Maurice, 57 n. 1
Wittgenstein, Ludwig, 6
Wrede, William, 21
Wucherpfennig, Ansgar, 57 n. 2

Zenger, Erich, 26 n. 39, 29 n. 53
Zerubbabel ben Shealtiel. *See* Shealtiel, Zerubbabel ben
Zimmerli, Walther, 24, 25 n. 35

Index of Subjects

Absolute Idealists, 4–5, 111
Academics, 75
Actium, 38
Alexandria, 39, 46, 58, 74, 84
allegory, 78
anthropology
    Heracleon's, 70, 72
    Valentinian, 70
anthropomorphism, 75, 82
    biblical, 76
    criticism of, 83
apologetics, for Joseph, 54
appearance (*Erscheinung*), 123, 127
atheism, 105, 155
authorship, 118

Bar Kochba Revolt, 99
being, 3
    and consciousness, 107–108
    and existence, 110–12
Berlin, 95
Bethabara, 63
Bethania, 63
Bible, 143, 145, 154, 156, 159, 162
    Christian, 26
    Hebrew, prophets of, 98
    and philosophy, 5, 9
blessedness, doctrine of, 111–12

Caesarea, 58, 68
canon, 27, 30
    coherence of, 29
    closure of, 29
canonical approach, 23–24, 32
    unity and revelation, 26

Christ
    consummation in, 126
    in creation, 116, 120–21, 131
    dignity of, 115, 119
    person of, 120
    preexistent, 120
    priestly office of, 25 n. 63
    in redemption, 116, 120, 131
    as revelation of God, 144, 153
    as second person of the Trinity, 120
    simultaneous contemporaneity of, 128
    whole, 120, 126, 131
    work of, 120
Christianity, 151
    essence of, 157
    as religion of revelation, 143
Christological bias, 116
Christology, 63, 66, 120, 128, 144
concept
    formation, 127, 131
    and predicate, 127
    of transhistorical reality, 130
consciousness, and being, 107–8
Constantinople, 75
consummation, 122
conversion, 119
corporeality, 110
cosmos, 63
cosmology
    Gnostic, 65
    Platonist, 76
creation, 64–65, 77, 90, 93, 108, 112, 121, 130
    Christ in, 116, 120–21, 131
    of evil, 65

ex nihilo, 121
   in relation to "establish," 122
   through the word, 105
Creator, 64, 77
   /creature, 66
   inferior, 64
criticism, 71
   literary, 61
   text, 61
culture
   Greek, 44, 56
      and Jewish customs, 44
   Jewish and Egyptian, 36, 39, 40,
Cynics, 75

Davidic
   covenant, 89, 100–101
   figure, 89
death, 111
Demiurge, 62, 64
Dessau, 95
Deuteronomistic History, 27
dialogue, Jewish-Christian, 30–31
Diaspora, 96, 99
dreams, of Joseph, 49–50, 52, 56

earth. *See* heaven, and earth
Easter Festal Letter, 75
Egypt, 37, 39, 42, 56, 92
   assimilation to ways of, 45–46, 47
   countryside and Alexandria, 39
   Jewish life in, 40
   Roman ruling class in, 42
Egyptian
   esteem for Joseph, 43
   and Jewish relation, 40, 45–46
   Jews, Joseph as representative, 46
   morality, 41
   vices, 45
enkrateia, 41
Enlightenment, 95
   Jewish, 92
Epicureans, 75
epistemology, 6
essence, 68. *See also* nature
ethics, and justice, 98–99

evil, 93, 133, 135–39
   and freedom, 138
   and good. *See* good, and evil
exegesis, allegorical, 35, 71, 84
   Fichte's principle of, 106
experience, 146–47
   explication of transcendence, 28

fact, historical, 104, 144
faith, 150
Fall, 134, 139
freedom, 144, 153
   and evil. *See* evil, and freedom
   genesis of human, 133
   history of human, 138
   incarnation as principle of, 145
   and sin. *See* sin, and freedom

Galilee, 51, 53
Gentiles. *See* Jews, and Gentiles
Gnosticism, 61, 76, 106
G-d
   character of, 93
   kingdom of, 90
   as righteous king, 100
God, 50, 52, 59, 67
   angry, jealous, vengeful, 92
   attributes of, 155
   as being, 107
   and Christ, 119
   corporeality of, 75
   doctrine of, 78
   the Father, 66–67, 153
   image of, 81, 83
   incorporeality of, 73–84
   and inferior creator, 64
   and knowledge, 151
   knowledge of, 161
   as light, 80
   as moral lawgiver, 105
   as object, 105
   the Son 153
   as Spirit, 80
   transcendence of, 76
   unity, simplicity of, 76, 80
   and world, 66

good, and evil, 135–36
Goshen, 48
gospel, 58
Great Revolt (against the Romans), 51
ground, 146
    of being, 150
    transcendental, 148

HaBaD, 93, 97
Hasidic movement, eighteenth century, 90
Hasidic teaching, 90
Hasidism, 93
    and Kabbalah, 92
Haskalah, 92, 97–98
heaven, and earth, 123–24
Hegelians, left-wing, 142
Heliopolis, 48
hermeneutics, 5
    of suspicion, 160
history, and nature. *See* nature, and history
Holy Spirit, 66
    doctrine of, 78
Hovevei Zion movement, 98

idealism, transcendental, 147
ideas, Platonic, 59, 65
identity
    Jewish, 40
    theory of, 107
imagination, 155–63
    and error, 158
    and illusion, 157, 159, 162
    and reality, 160
imperative (*Sollen*), 108, 112
incarnation, 109–10, 144
    as principle of freedom, 145
innocence, 134, 139
interpretation, grammatical, 118, 130
    existential, 141–54
    literal, 158
interrelations, of forms, 30
intertextuality, 80
invisible/visible, 123
Israel, 95, 98–99

Jerusalem, 53, 92

Temple, destruction of, 99
Jewry, Spanish, 92
Jewish
    acculturation to Egyptian ways, 47
    Enlightenment, 92, 97
    life in Russia, 98
    mind/spirit, 97
    modern thought, 87–101
    mysticism, 91–92, 94, 100
    national spirit, 98–99
    values in contrast with Egypt, 40
    Wisdom and Greek philosophy, 66
Jews
    in Egypt, 37, 40
    and Gentiles, 125
    in Heracleon's interpretation of John, 69
    role in sanctifying world, 95
Judaism
    and Christianity, 151
    Conservative, 99
    modern Orthodox, 94–96
    modern Reform, 92, 94–96
    as rational religion, 96
    Reconstructionist, 99–100
justice, and ethics, 98–99

Kabbalah, Lurianic, 93, 101
kingdom
    of heaven, 123
    of the Son, 119
knowledge
    and being, 108
    of contingent origin, 146
    fact as source of, 109
    and God, 151
    of God, 161
    of self, 104
    sensible, 107
    spiritual, 81

language, scriptural, 78–80, 83–84
Law
    Mosaic, 99
    Noachide, 100
Letters, of Paul, 58, 79

life of Jesus research, 106
light, 70
    God as, 79–80
    as spiritual power, 81
Logos, 59, 64–67, 72, 153
    as mediator of creation, 144
    as reason, 144–45
Lord's Supper, 110, 112, 159
love, 104, 111

Messianism, 87
metaphysics, 2–3, 113–31
    potency-act, 2
    potentiality-actuality, 67, 72
morality, and religion, 105
mysticism, Jewish, 91–92, 94, 100
myth, 133–34
mythology, 149

nature, 68–69, 71–72
    children by, 70
    and history, 149
negativity, positive, 137, 139
New Testament, 143

Odessa, 98
Old Testament, 25, 26–28, 82, 147

parallel, literary, 115–16
perspective, individual, 7
Philologus (Heracleon), 61, 70
philosophy
    and Bible, 5, 9
    and Christian theology, 83
    critical, 103
    enscripturation of, 73–84
    Greek and Jewish Wisdom, 66
    and preaching, 81–82
    rational, 101
    and religion, 4, 147
    of religion, 150–51
    and scripture, 73
physical. *See* spiritual, and physical
Platonizing, of biblical texts, 67
pneuma, Stoic notion of, 77
power (*Kraft*), 123, 127

preaching, 81–82
projection theory, 157, 162
Psychics, 70

reason, 103–112, 153–54
    a priori, 103
    genesis of, 104, 111
    historical and speculative, 116
    in history, 103
    as logos, 144–45
    as principle of reality, 148
    transcendental ideas of, 3
reconciliation, 124
    in Absolute, 138–39
    as absolute unity, 136
    of all things, 111, 131
    soteriological goal of, 125
    universalistic, 126
redaction, 28–29
redemption, 119, 130
    Christ in, 116, 120, 131
reflection, 107
religion, 104, 149, 151
    of ancient Christianity, 23
    essence of, 156–57, 162
    of Israel, 23
    Judaism as rational, 96
    and morality, 105
    of mythology, 147
    and philosophy, 4
    rational, 95
    of revelation, 143, 147, 151
    study of, 3
religions, history of, 21–22
revelation, 112, 157, 162
    and canon, 26
    Christianity as religion of, 143
    of God, 151
    historical fact of, 145
    and history, 23
    as recognition of reason, 105–106
    religion of. *See* religion, of revelation
    and sensation, 107, 109
Roman
    intellectuals in Egypt, 44
    ruling class in Egypt, 42

sacraments, 159
Safed, 92
scripture, 161
    center (*Mitte*), 25–26, 32
    hidden meanings of, 77
    liturgical reading of, 82
Second Temple period, 52
self/world/God, 3
Sephirot, 92–93
Shabbatean movement, 97
Shechem, 51
Shoah, 88
simplicity, of God, 80
sin
    as contradiction in spirit, 137
    and freedom, 133–39
    original, 109, 136, 138
Sinai, Mount, 95–96
soteriology, 63, 80
    Origen's, 76
speech, God's, 28
spirit, 77, 134
    God as, 79–80
    Jewish, 97
spiritual
    and meaning, 67, 84
    and physical, 123
Stoics, 75
story, historical, 133
subjectivity
    contradiction in, 135
    genesis of, 134
symposium, two kinds of, 44

Tall Brothers, 75
Tanakh, 27
text, 6
    and context, 115–17

theology, 80
    biblical, 8, 17–32
    dogmatic, 20
    and exegetical, 117
    as historical, 18–20
    and history, 7
    Jewish, 87–88, 100
    as normative, 32
    of New Testament, 21
    of Old Testament, 21
    of Paul, 118
Therapeutae, 44
Tiberias, 53
Tikkun Olam, 93–94, 99, 100–101
Torah, 95
Torah im Derekh Eretz, 96
transcendence, of self, 148, 154
truth, 107

Ukraine, 98
unity
    of canon, 32
    of Christian Bible, 31–32
    contrastive, 26, 30, 32
    of God, 80
    theological, 24

visible/invisible. *See* invisible/visible

will, of God, 107
Wisdom, 65
women, in Greco-Roman Egypt, 41
Word. *See* Logos

Zionism, 101
    cultural, 98
    modern, 97
zoolatry, Egyptian, 38

www.ingramcontent.com/pod-product-compliance
Lightning Source LLC
Chambersburg PA
CBHW031313150426
43191CB00005B/211